ALL ABOUT WELLER

A History and
Collector's Guide to
Weller Pottery,
Zanesville, Ohio

ANN GILBERT McDONALD, Ph. D.

Photography by
Glen Leach
David Richardson
Deana Tullius

All rights reserved. No part of this book may be reproduced or used in any form or by any means, electronic or mechanical, including photocopying and recording, or by any information storage or retrieval system, without permission in writing from the publisher. Inquiries should be addressed to: Antique Publications, P.O. Box 553, Marietta, Ohio 45750.

©Copyright 1989
Antique Publications
P.O. Box 553
Marietta, Ohio 45750

ISBN #0-915410-60-5

Table of Contents

Acknowledgments		v
Introduction		vii
Chapter I.	Weller Pottery 1872-1948	1
Chapter II.	Samuel A. Weller	12
Chapter III.	William Long and Lonhuda Pottery	21
Chapter IV.	From Louwelsa to Perfecto	26
Chapter V.	Sgraffito Work at Weller and the Dickensware Lines	33
Chapter VI.	Weller at the World's Fair	43
Chapter VII.	Lamps and Lighting Devices	48
Chapter VIII.	Early Weller Lines 1897-1910	52
Chapter IX.	The French Connection: Art Nouveau, Matt Green, Sicard	60
Chapter X.	New Weller Lines 1906-1910	68
Chapter XI.	Weller Hudson and the Cream Colored Wares	76
Chapter XII.	From Baldin to Woodcraft	86
Chapter XIII.	The Twenties at Weller	95
Chapter XIV.	The Twenties: Art Deco and Weller	127
Chapter XV.	The Thirties at Weller: 1930-1934	139
Chapter XVI.	The Thirties at Weller: 1934-1940	148
Chapter XVII.	Garden Ware, Planters, Wallpockets, and Cookware	157
Chapter XVIII.	The Weller Artists	164
Chapter XIX.	Artists of Distinction: Laughead, Lorber, Rhead, and Upjohn	174
Chapter XX.	Conclusion	181
Appendix A.	Chronology of Weller Pottery	184
Appendix B.	Officers of Weller Pottery	186
Appendix C.	Signatures of the Weller Artists	187
Appendix D.	Artists at Weller Pottery before 1904	195
Appendix E.	Marks on Weller Pottery	196
Resource Centers		200
Bibliography		201
Biography		206

Dedicated
with gratitude and admiration
to
Norris F. Schneider

Acknowledgments

With admirable clairvoyance Norris F. Schneider researched the Zanesville potteries long before collectors discovered them. He interviewed artists, plant managers, and salesmen of the Owens, the Roseville, and the Weller Potteries. In a series of books from *Zanesville Art Pottery in Color* to *Weller Art Pottery in Color*, Louise and Evan Purviance and Norris Schneider told the history of each pottery.

Mr. Schneider's acquaintance with Weller Pottery began in 1922, when he visited the Pottery to buy a vase for his mother's birthday. After the Weller Pottery closed in 1948, Mr. Schneider rescued from oblivion the catalogs of the company, photographs of the plant, price lists, plant operation memos, and correspondence. As the years progressed, he interviewed surviving Weller artists, wrote to descendants of deceased artists, and filled black notebooks with a veritable history of the Pottery. These notebooks he generously shared with me. I am deeply grateful to Norris Schneider for his help and encouragement, and with joy, I dedicate this book to him.

Weller collectors responded magnanimously to my call in the late 1970s for photographs of their Weller pieces. Often, at their own expense they sent photographs; sometimes, they mailed their pottery to me to photograph. William and Dora Betts provided detailed descriptions and photos of their fine Weller collection. The Betts were towers of strength and support, as were Sheila Amdur, Bob and Kathy Bettinger, Lee Dietrich and Barbara Dietrich Watson, D. L. and Ozella Hill, Robert Miller, Dick and Nancy Sigafoose, Glen Vogt, and Allan Wunsch. They patiently and most generously contributed hours of consultation, correspondence, and dozens of photographs to further my book.

I am grateful to everyone who sent photos or helped in the preparation of this book: Betty Adams, Byron and Barbara Baldwin, Bill and Madeleine Beck, Rosalie Berberian, Edward Blas, Virginia Buxton, Donald Calkins, Diane and Mike Cole, Duke and Lin Coleman, Robin Crawford, Jean and Richard Danielson, Ben Davis, Kelly and Cheryl Devlin, H. M. Dietrich, Bill Dobbins, Paul and Rosemary Enoch, James Fanale, Bob Flanders, Ed Gisel, Norman Haas, Foster and Gladys Hall, Gerald Harrington, Elaine and Wesley Hart, Sally Hautmann, Martha Horman, Russ Jones, Gaylord Larson, Phyllis Larson, Seymour Lazerowitz, Dr. Amos Loveday, Ohio Historical Society, the W. E. Lyons, James Martin, Cort and Chris Michener, William Micheli, the James Morgans, Esther and Martin Myers, Tom O'Connor, Robert Newton, Harold Nichols, Nick Pedotto, Kathryn Powell, Dave Rago, Lee Reid, Lillian Saxe, Carl and Amy Schaefer, Carol Sessions, Larry and Teena Seyler, Tommy and Norma Smith, Gary Struncius, Larry and Mary Swaney, Arthur and Rita Townley, Don Treadway, Bill and Alice Truszkowski, Ron Van Lieu, Sheila M. Waters, Jim Watson, Edward Wilson, and Ken Word.

In Zanesville, Ohio, in 1985, 1986, and 1988, I photographed pottery belonging to George and Judy Alig, Betty Blair, Lewis and Alice Bettinger, Lewis and Susan Bettinger, Jr., Archie and Dorothy Browning, Bill Clarke, Elvin R. Culp, Richard Harmer, and Si Lambert.

With the able assistance of Dr. Charles Dietz, Director of the Zanesville Art Center, his secretary Mrs. Joseph Howell, and Mose Mesre, Dave Richardson, Deana Tullius and I photographed Weller pottery from the Art Center, from the National Road-Zane Grey Museum, and from the collections of Dick Downey and Mose Mesre, on July 12, 1988. Dr. Dietz and Mose Mesre assisted me with photos and with research throughout the 1980s.

Dorothy Daniel, who helped edit the book, let me borrow dozens of Weller vases from her copious collection to study and to photograph. I want to thank her and Howard, and all the other Weller collectors for their kindness.

Decorators Ruth Axline and Dorothy Laughead told me about their work at Weller Pottery, Ruth by correspondence during 1980, and Dorothy in an interview in November 1978. They described the production of Bonito, Cactus, Chengtu, and Hudson. They discussed their jobs, their co-workers, and the daily operation of the plant. Their accounts provided a lively picture of Weller Pottery in the twenties and thirties.

Blaine Andrus, Bernard Bumpus, and Paul Evans suggested sources of information on the artists and on the operation of the Pottery. Norma P. H. Jenkins and Virginia Wright of the Corning Museum of Glass Library made copies of Weller data from the trade journals for me. The Weller family, William Curphey, Jr., Frederic Grant, Richard S. Weller, Robert J. Weller, and Margaret Weller, provided genealogical and personal information about the family.

Glen Leach took the majority of the photographs for this book. I am indebted to him for his fine work not only on this book, but also on my earlier book *Evolution of the Night Lamp*. Lauren May prepared the manuscript beautifully for publication, while Ronda Ludwig executed the layout superbly.

Begun in 1976, this book was a labor of love. I wrote hundreds of letters, made dozens of phone calls, traveled thousands of miles, read hundreds of trade journals in the Library of Congress, the Ohio State University Library, and the Corning Museum of Glass Library. In my twelve year odyssey, like Ulysses, I wondered if I would ever reach home port. Highpoints of the journey included the publication of chapters from the book in *Hobbies* and in *Spinning Wheel*.

In conclusion, I wish to thank my family, especially my mother Claire Gilbert, who spent hours editing the manuscript, my father Dr. Perry Gilbert, a model of scholarship, and my husband Bradley, who gave me the encouragement and the stamina to continue toward the goal.

Introduction

Although the Weller Pottery failed to keep a detailed record of its operations from 1872 to 1948, I was able to discover and to document an inexhaustible supply of data on the Pottery itself, and on the remarkable man who gave it life, sustenance, and success. I have relied heavily on the contributions of Norris F. Schneider, both the records he salvaged from the company, and his fine articles about Weller in *The Times Recorder* of Zanesville, Ohio.

Because they were contemporaneous with the Pottery, the trade journals were also a rich source of material with their Weller advertisements and their descriptions of each new line as it appeared. From the promotional material and the ads, I gleaned a fairly detailed history of the Pottery, which allowed me to date and to describe lines from Alvin to Zona. I learned such recondite facts as these: the flower embossed on Sydonia was a marsh mallow, and the Coppertone frog sprinkler threw out a stream of water within a radius of 16 feet.

In preparing this book I had to examine what had happened before and during the period of production, not only in Weller Pottery, but also in other potteries at home and abroad. For example, it was impossible to discuss Jacques Sicard, creator of Weller Sicard, without mentioning Clement Massier. I found it was essential to investigate decorative influences such as Art Nouveau and Art Deco to see to what degree they had influenced the Weller potters.

My biggest dilemma was always how to distinguish among the various lines. As any serious collector knows, the Pottery used one mold for several lines. For example, Neiska and Seneca shared the same molds, as did Woodcraft and Voile. Initially my rule was: the glaze determines the line. With my perceptions heightened, I modified this to: the glaze, the decoration, and the coloring determine the line. In the catalog, for example, one page stipulated, "Malta Plain, Brighton Decorated." This meant that Brighton birds and figurines were decorated with glossy, naturalistic colors, while the Malta figurines were given monochromatic, plain white, or pastel backgrounds.

The lines were named capriciously and were often a mass of contradictions. One might find a Glendale shape with a matt green finish, or a Pumila candleholder with a Coppertone glaze. In its haste to turn out pots, the factory often mislabeled them, putting a Dickensware stamp on the bottom of a molded ware. Certain items fit no classification whatsoever. As every family tree has its bastards, so did Weller Pottery. Considering the large volume of production, however, it was remarkable how many lines conformed to a defined glaze, shape, and color. For example, Wood Rose always resembled a brown oaken bucket.

I have tried to keep the names of the lines as accurate as possible, based on the Weller catalogs and the documentation from the trade journals. On rare occasions, I have given a name to a line such as Etched Floral in Chapter V. For the most part, however, I have tried to avoid this. When one line had several offshoots or variations, I embellished its name, for example,

Decorated Burntwood in Chapter X, or Raceme Glossy in Chapter XVI.

To simplify the copious and extensive documentation, I have eliminated footnotes and incorporated the references into the text itself. Abbreviations were used for the trade journals, which have long and cumbersome titles. The Key to the Abbreviations of the Trade Journals follows.

Key to Abbreviations of the Trade Journals

C & G	*Crockery and Glass Journal*
CGL	*China, Glass and Lamps*
P & G	*Pottery and Glass*
PGB	*Pottery, Glass and Brass*
PGBS	*Pottery, Glass and Brass Salesman*
PCN	*Pottery Collectors Newsletter*
HF	*House Furnisher*
GPW	*Glass and Pottery World*

Chapter I

Weller Pottery 1872-1948

Fig. 1: Samuel A. Weller, founder of Weller Pottery. Courtesy of Norris Schneider.

Samuel Augustus Weller founded the Weller Pottery Company in Fultonham, Ohio in 1872. It began as a one man plant lodged in a simple log cabin. From local clay beds, Sam Weller dug up the clay, then ground and mixed it, and made by hand the numerous flower pots which he sold in nearby Zanesville. His horse Whitey hauled the crude clay from the clay beds to the cabin, where he pulled a twenty foot boom attached to the grinding mill, to break up the clay. Since clay and firewood were abundant on the farm, Weller found that he could easily fill the numerous orders for milk pans, crocks, flower pots, vases, and cuspidors.

As the demand grew, Weller and his assistant Sumner Fauley realized that they could not do all the work alone. Therefore, in 1882, Weller leased a frame building on South Second Street in Zanesville to use as a warehouse. Six years later he left his log cabin for a factory in a frame building at the foot of Pierce Street in Zanesville. By 1890 he had bought the old show grounds in Putnam and erected a plant between Pierce Street and Cemetery Drive. Here he began to manufacture the most popular items of the day: jardinieres and pedestals, umbrella stands, hanging baskets, and vases. Business grew so rapidly that Weller had to build an addition to his Pierce Street plant in 1892 and another in 1894.

In later years, critics claimed that Weller was primarily a businessman, but unquestionably, he was a potter first (Fig. 1). He himself handled the clay and threw the first pots. In Zanesville he experimented with glazes and colors, using salt glaze, then Albany slip, and finally colored glaze. He knew all the aspects of pottery-making and often rose in the middle of the night to draw a design for a new vase.

When Weller saw Lonhuda ware at the Chicago World's Fair in 1893, he was so entranced that he bought Lonhuda Pottery from William Long and asked him to come to Zanesville to supervise its production. Long agreed. A new addition, filled with modern machinery, was constructed in the Putnam plant to house the Lonhuda operations. Then on May 10, 1895, the gold kiln at the plant overheated, and the timbers above it caught fire. Although it took only thirty minutes for the firemen to arrive after the night watchman called them, flames engulfed the south end of the building where the offices, the Lonhuda Department, and the power plant were. Bystanders rescued valuable books, papers, and even a large safe, but much of the building was ruined. It measured 300 feet by 90 feet, one part of it erected in 1892, the other in 1894 at a cost of $30,000. Weller quickly rebuilt the plant, and soon standard glaze ware issued in abundance from the factory.

After Long's resignation from the company in 1896, Sam Weller introduced Louwelsa Weller, the standard glaze brown ware derived from Long's formula for Lonhuda. Weller hired artists to decorate Louwelsa with sprightly flowers, fruits, dogs, cavaliers, and Indians (Fig. 2). For the first time Rookwood Pottery had a real competitor for its Standard Glaze line.

Weller generously paid his best artists. He spent $50,000 in salaries and materials for Jacques Sicard and Henri Gellée. Less skilled artists took home meager wages. As an apprentice, at age 16 in 1904, Charles Chilcote worked his first year at the factory for nothing but transportation and art lessons. In the 1930s, Ruth Axline earned only $10.50 a week. Weller often took young men and women, trained them to paint flowers, scenery, or portraits on pottery, and paid them low wages. The daily wage for pottery workers in Zanesville in 1910 was $1.75, or $10.50 for a six day week, exactly what Ruth earned twenty years later! Some workers at Weller in 1910 received more than $10.50 a week, but others, especially women, received less.

Weller hired Charles Upjohn in 1895 to head the decorating department. A few years later, Second Line Dickensware appeared. With characters from Charles Dickens' *Bleak House*, *David Copperfield*, and *Dombey and Son* as inspiration, Upjohn employed the sgraffito technique of incised

Fig. 2: *Impressed Louwelsa Weller:* Pitcher 12¼″ high, decorated with raspberries, artist signed V.A., and handled vase 13″ high, decorated with pansies, artist signed H.P. Photo by Leach.

Fig. 4: *Impressed Dickensware Weller:* Dragon vase 15″ high. Collection: Ed Gisel.

JARDINIERE AND PEDESTAL. BY S. A. WELLER, ZANESVILLE O. NEW YORK OFFICE, 57 PARK PLACE.

Fig. 5: Weller jardiniere and pedestal, pictured in *House Furnisher: China, Glass and Pottery Review,* July 1901.

decoration to produce marvelous vases with scenes from Dickens, and with Indians, monks, mermaids, knights, and dragons (Figs. 3, 4).

By 1897 Weller was making Dickensware I, Louwelsa, Turada, and mammoth jardinieres and pedestals. In 1900 C. H. Taylor, Weller's New York sales representative, received from the factory an inverted dolphin pedestal, the dolphin holding a jardiniere on its tail. Another pedestal featured a griffin. These large pieces were decorated in plain and mottled glazes, with knights on horseback, cherubs, and sea creatures (Fig. 5). Throughout 1897 Weller's ads proclaimed him the largest jardiniere manufacturer in the world.

In 1899 Weller purchased the old American Encaustic Tiling Company plant on Marietta Street for $25,000. Here the company produced cooking utensils, flower pots, and toilet articles. The plant had four jigger wheels and three kilns. Weller expanded operations to include twelve kilns by 1902. At Putnam in 1901, he added a third floor decorating studio, where artists designed and decorated pottery. Louwelsa was then the most popular line in production, and necessitated the expansion to the third floor. Made in 500 shapes and sizes, from vases to clocks, ashtrays, and umbrella stands, it sold voluminously from 1896 to 1920. When Jacques Sicard arrived from France in 1902 to make the beautiful iridescent Sicard pottery for the company, Weller had achieved a near monopoly of the mass produced, art pottery market.

The Clay Worker reported on "The Potteries of Zanesville, Ohio," in June 1902, after sending a reporter to visit the Weller factory. The reporter noted that the clay was ground in ball mills, that the wares, instead of coming from presses or machines, were all molded by hand in molds made in the plant. He saw fifteen kilns at Putnam, each 16½ feet in diameter. In three kilns the factory used coal for fuel, and in the other twelve, gas. The wares were burned in saggers, protective casings of previously fired clay. The reporter could not enter the decorating department, which was walled off to prevent competitors' access to new designs and glaze formulas. Weller foreman D. C. Applegate, however, showed him fine examples of Dickensware and Louwelsa. The reporter watched as the pottery was packed in crates with straw for shipment.

Fig. 3: *Impressed Dickensware Weller:* Dombey and Son mug 5½″ high; pitcher 7″ high, with elk, and pillow vase 5½″ high, with birds. Collection: Robert Miller and Glen Vogt.

Until 1900 Weller jars and pedestals, umbrella stands, oil lamps, and large vases sold very well. These commodious pieces adorned lawns, porches, hotel lobbies, cemeteries, parks, automobile showrooms, private homes. It was de rigueur for every stylish hallway to have a jardiniere and pedestal, commonly called a jar and ped, with a fern, and an umbrella stand. After 1900, smaller items became popular: ashtrays, hair receivers, puff boxes, powder jars, pitchers, bowls, jugs, cuspidors, and vases. The company continued, however, to make jars, peds, and umbrella stands well into the twenties.

Around 1905, Weller put out a small color catalog to enumerate the various lines offered: Art Nouveau, Aurelian, Dickensware, Eocean, Floretta, Golbrogreen, Hunter, Jap Birdimal, Louwelsa, Monochrome, Oriental, Perfecto, Pictorial, and Sicardo. Called simply *Weller Pottery*, the catalog bragged: "Our factory has increased in size, until today it stands the largest pottery in the world, covering over 300,000 feet of floor space, employing hundreds of skilled hands, and thoroughly equipped with all the latest, improved machinery for the manufacture of fine Art Pottery." It claimed, too, that students from the leading art schools and skilled artists from England, France, Germany, Hungary-Austria, Italy, and Japan were employed as decorators. The catalog had color photos of Art Nouveau, Aurelian, Eocean, Jap Birdimal, and Louwelsa vases.

Contemporary critics praised Weller Pottery. In *Glass and Pottery World*, March 1907, Marcus Benjamin wrote an encomium to Weller. He listed and described the making of several wares, with a special bow to Sicard: "The most interesting of Mr. Weller's products is the remarkable metallic luster which he has succeeded in obtaining, and to which the name Sicardo is given in honor of the French ceramic chemist and artist, J. Sicard." He concluded, "The ceramic art wares of Mr. Weller are of high character and deserve commendation."

"This is the most famous pottery in Zanesville, and has had a remarkable development," wrote *Clay Worker* in September 1903. "Not many years ago Mr. Weller used to peddle his wares about the country with a one-horse wagon, now his pottery covers twelve acres and he is one of the wealthiest men in Southeastern Ohio."

Weller's pride in his company was reflected in his mammoth display at the St. Louis Exposition in 1904. In response to the promotion of the Pottery at the Exposition, customers in stores asked for Weller pottery, and by Christmas 1904, the factory shipped out and sold thousands of pots.

During 1904 the Weller decorating studio was alive with activity. Levi J. Burgess decorated Louwelsa vases with Indian portraits, while Albert Haubrich painted monks and cavaliers on pitchers and steins. Female artists ornamented vases and jars with flowers and fruit. Frederick H. Rhead developed Jap Birdimal. Hugo Herb modeled the shapes or forms of each pot. The studio was a pleasant place to work with draperies at the windows, paintings and plaques by Weller artists on the walls, and fresh flowers near the workbenches. Charles Upjohn headed the decorating department until 1904, when the renowned artist Karl Kappes replaced him. Kappes had trained some decorators before he joined Weller Pottery.

Charles Chilcote learned pottery decorating from him and from Upjohn. Chilcote began by decorating Louwelsa, graduated to Eocean, and finally to Dickensware. Upjohn made all the original drawings of the characters from Dickens, which Chilcote and the other artists copied on to the vases.

Between 1899 and 1905, plaster of Paris molds replaced the use of the potter's wheel at the factory. When a potter threw a vase or a jar by hand on the potter's wheel, he could never reduplicate it. With the use of molds and the jiggering process, the potter could make hundreds of identical pieces. The casts or molds had two sections fastened by hoops of iron. The potter inserted moist clay into the mold, placed on a jigger wheel, a standard rotated by foot or steam power. With a wooden forcer, he pressed the clay firmly into place against the sides and the bottom of the cast. Then he let the piece dry before the first firing, placing it in a drying room to "set." Beneath the slatlike platform on which the raw vase or jardiniere sat, steam heated pipes hastened the process of drying.

After it had dried, the vase or jar was removed from the cast and taken to the cleaning department, where workers removed seams and blemishes, then added handles. Next, they placed the item in the damp room to await the blender, who gave the ware a blending or body to assist it to retain the colors and prevent their spread during the firing process. After the blending, an artist painted the piece with flowers or fruit. Finally, the workers put the piece in the sagger and fired it in the kiln. Firing required about forty-six hours of heat, gradually applied, ranging from 1000 to 2400 degrees Fahrenheit. Emerging from the kiln, the ware was in the "biscuit," and ready for the glazing preparation (Fig. 6). Workers applied the matt or gloss glaze in fluid form by either dipping or spraying the piece. After the second firing, the piece was finished and ready for market.

Fig. 6: Workers carrying the "biscuit" ware on their heads, prior to glazing, at the Weller Pottery factory, Zanesville, Ohio. Courtesy of Norris Schneider.

A booklet published by Weller Pottery, called "A Definition of Art Pottery," discussed the differences between hand turned pieces and molded wares:

> The word "hand turned" or "hand thrown" when applied to a piece of pottery means that the clay used is placed on the "potter's wheel" which throws it out of the center by means of centrifugal force while the potter uses his hands to shape the piece. A "molded piece" is one made up by the modeler in clay and then cast in plaster of Paris or other materials to form a die after which any number of molds may be made. From these molds, duplicates of the original modeled pieces are taken and they may be plain in surface, embossed or carved.

The booklet described the process of molding: "In the cast piece that has been made in a mold, the clay with the consistency of paint is poured in the mold and allowed to stand for a predetermined time and then poured out leaving the reproduction of the modeled piece. The mouth of such vessels or vases may be made quite small and the shape unusual whereas in the jiggered or 'hand thrown' piece, we must have the openings large to permit the use of one's hands. 'Hand-turned' or 'hand-thrown' and 'jiggered pieces' are necessarily rounded shapes." After 1900, jiggering and molding replaced hand turning at the factory. Foreman Aloysius J. Schwerber directed the work in the mold room and created many of the shapes in the Weller Shape Book.

The modeler and the artist each had a specific job to do. The modeler devised the clay shape or form of each pot. From this shape, the mold maker produced a mold to duplicate the ware innumerable times. When the piece was ready for decoration, the blender applied the background colors in slip with an atomizer. "Slip containing glaze or color or both in refined clay is blown on vessels and art objects, with beautiful effects by means of the air brush, an American invention," the booklet noted. Finally, the artist painted on the decoration of flowers or fruit, using brushes of various sizes. Then the piece was fired.

Sometimes, problems occurred with the finished product. In a section labeled "Defects in Pottery," the booklet admitted that some vessels leaked, while others were subject to crazing. "Many of these highest priced art pieces will craze." Crazing, a network of tiny cracks in the glaze, occurred on some of the glossy wares such as Aurelian or Louwelsa. "A Definition of Art Pottery" provided a candid and comprehensive look at Weller Pottery.

Before and after 1905, Weller had several competitors, notably J. B. Owens, Rookwood, and Roseville Potteries (Fig. 7). Seeking higher wages, artists migrated back and forth between these companies and took with them the secrets of new glazes, lines, and decorations. William Long brought the standard glaze formula from Weller to J.B. Owens, where it became Owens Utopian. At Roseville, it was called Rozane, or Rozane Royal. When Rookwood displayed Iris Glaze vases with flying storks at the St. Louis Exposition in 1904, the other potteries created imitations. Weller made Eocean stork vases, while Owens made Lotus wares. The success of Roseville's Donatello inspired Weller modelers to create Fairfield. The

Japanese artist Gazo Fudji developed Roseville's Woodland and Fujiyama, and Weller's Fudzi line. Weller and Owens duplicated each other's wares: Dickensware II vs. Henri Deux, Souevo vs. Aborigine, and Turada vs. Cyrano.

Founded in 1890 in Roseville, Ohio, Roseville Pottery was Weller's biggest competitor. In 1898 the company moved some operations to Linden Avenue in Zanesville and began to create art wares. Weller lost three superb artists to Roseville: Frank Ferrell, John J. Herold, and Frederick H. Rhead. Herold created the famous Mara line, an imitation of Weller Sicard. Rhead brought Aztec, Della Robbia, and Olympic to the company. As art director of Roseville from 1904 to 1908, he transferred his skill at tube lining from Jap Birdimal and Rhead Faience to Roseville's Aztec. Frank Ferrell developed the famous Pine Cone line at Roseville, after Sam Weller rejected it at Weller Pottery. Several artists worked for both Roseville and Weller: Virginia Adams, Anthony Dunlavy, Madge Hurst, Josephine Imlay, Claude Leffler, Lillie Mitchell, Hester Pillsbury, Tot Steele, and Mae and Sarah Timberlake. The loss of Ferrell, Herold, and Rhead, the decrease of profits due to competition with the other Ohio potteries, all had an adverse impact on Weller in later years.

Critics described Weller Pottery in 1905 as a mammoth enterprise, covering several acres with 500-600 employees making twenty-two different lines. Decorators were often sent abroad to study in the famous potteries of Europe and to visit museums and art centers. The factory shipped three railroad carloads of goods to market each day in 1905.

Business continued to grow from 1906 to 1908. In 1907 Weller set an export record with large shipments to England, Germany, and Russia, this in addition to a large domestic trade. In 1908 the company had forty men on the road promoting and selling the pottery. At the Pittsburgh Glass and Pottery Exhibition of 1908, Weller showed the Souevo line with its Indian and Aztec shapes and decorations, as well as Cerise, Dresden, Greenaways, and Matt Green.

In 1908 Weller gave serious thought to setting up a factory in Colorado, according to *Clay Record*, November 16, 1908. He went to Colorado Springs

Fig. 7: The Weller Competition: McCoy Sylvan vase 6" high; Owens Lotus vase 4" high; Roseville Pastel Rozane vase 4" high, and Rookwood Standard Glaze ewer 7" high, artist signed F.V. Collection: Dorothy Daniel. Photo by Leach.

to look at clay formations and claimed that if he found suitable clay, he would build a factory there equal in size to one of his eastern factories. Worried about high shipping rates to the West, he hoped to use Denver to transport pottery through by rail to California and to the western states. He could then sell pottery on the West Coast for the same prices it brought in the East. Accompanied by Thomas Applegate, a geologist and clay expert, Weller considered sites in Boulder, Colorado Springs, Denver, and Pueblo. Eventually, Weller rejected all these locations and did not build in Colorado.

Japanese competition in pottery began to cut into the Weller market by 1910. Japan brought out several near perfect imitations of Weller wares at half the cost. Weller pottery continued to sell, however, with increased demand from florists, who gave away pottery vases with their floral bouquets. Large amounts of pottery for florists and for gardens issued from the factory, particularly in the 1920s and 1930s with catalogs, *Garden Decorations by Weller* and *Pottery for the Florist*, to merchandise the wares.

Weller Pottery was always a family business. Mrs. Weller's brother Edwin L. Pickens headed the art department around 1909. In 1915 Sam's nephews Harry and Frank had charge of the cookware and the fancy goods departments. That same year Weller ads boasted that the Pottery was the largest one in the United States.

In 1920 Weller purchased the Zanesville Art Pottery, previously operated by David Schmid from 1900 to 1920, and called it the Ceramic Avenue plant (Fig. 8). On July 1, 1922, to insure the perpetuation of the company after his death, Sam Weller incorporated Weller Pottery as S.A. Weller, Inc., with a capital of $750,000 fully paid. The three plants in operation included: #1 the Putnam plant for high grade artistic wares, #2 the Marietta Street plant for brown and white cookware and yellow bowls, and #3 the Ceramic Avenue plant for glazed jardinieres and umbrella stands.

After Sam Weller's death on October 4, 1925, his nephew Harry Weller became president of Weller Pottery. With the help of his brother Frank, who mixed the glazes, Harry ran the company from 1925 until his tragic death in an auto accident in 1932. He modernized the plant with continuous kiln operation, in which the pottery moves within the kiln, from the coolest section to the hottest, and then on to gradual lowered temperatures, until it is cool enough to leave the kiln. He introduced attractive half page ads in *House and Garden* and *Better Homes and Gardens* in 1928 and 1929, and consolidated three plants into one plant at Ceramic Avenue.

On July 29, 1927, the night watchman discovered a fire in the Ceramic Avenue plant of Weller Pottery. Although the plant was made of brick, the flames devoured the wooden floors and supports, resulting in a $500,000 loss. The Ceramic Avenue plant was less than ten years old and was quickly rebuilt.

The factory produced a fine assortment of pottery in the late twenties, with some of the new lines devised by modeler Rudolph Lorber. The 1928 Price List included: Alvin, Ardsley, Flemish, Florenzo, Forest, Glendale, Graystone, Hobart, Hudson, Ivory, Lavonia, Malta, Marvo, Muskota, Pumila

Fig. 8: The Ceramic Avenue plant of the Weller Pottery Company, Zanesville, Ohio. Courtesy of Norris Schneider.

Fig. 9: The Weller decorators painting Blue Ware jardinieres at the Weller factory in Zanesville. Courtesy of Norris Schneider.

Roma, Velvetone, Voile, Wayne Ware, Woodcraft, Zona, as well as utility ware, decorated teapots, and cookware. Japanese imports, however, continued to compete with Weller ware. In January 1934, over twelve million pieces of pottery flooded the U.S. from Japan. Hard work and low wages enabled the Japanese companies to undersell the American potteries.

The Depression caused a big reduction in profits at Weller. Hence, in 1931 all the plants, #1, 2, 3, were consolidated into one plant, #3 Ceramic Avenue. The factory curtailed freehand artist decoration. In 1932 Frederic Grant, Weller's son-in-law, became president of the Pottery for one year. Following his divorce from Ethel Weller, Grant asked for and received the right to reproduce Zona dinnerware, as part of his divorce settlement. He took this line to Gladding, McBean and Company of California, where it became the famous Franciscan dinnerware.

During the Depression, the Pottery made cookware, beer mugs, garden ware, and vases in plain and simple shapes. Some decorators became modelers, devising molds to mass produce most of the pottery. Designs were embossed on the surface of the pottery, and decorators painted the embossing (Fig. 9). This new method was faster and cheaper than hand decorating. Rudolph Lorber headed the decorating department in 1933 and introduced Neiska, Seneca, and Ting.

Irvin Smith, another Weller son-in-law, became president of the company in 1933. The final president Walter Hughes succeeded him in 1937. Hughes had worked for American Encaustic Tiling Company and had a degree in Ceramic Engineering. He joined Weller Pottery in 1933, quickly worked his way up to vice president, then president. In the 1950s he provided valuable information to Norris F. Schneider.

In a series of letters and interviews with Mr. Schneider in 1956 and 1957, Hughes discussed the operation of the Pottery. He remarked that in the thirties and forties, increased competition from abroad, higher wages, and more expensive materials caused Weller to make cheaper products and to curtail hand decoration. After Sam Weller died in 1925, Harry Weller substituted continuous kiln operation for periodic kiln operation, to increase control and to economize. Hughes also noted that in the thirties the factory devoted half its production to cookware, garden and utility wares. During World War II, wages climbed even higher. The factory compensated by making lines, like Bouquet and Cameo, which were cheap and easy to manufacture. Hughes remarked that the Pottery sold all that it could produce. With labor and materials limited and many of its employees at war, the company prospered, nonetheless, and paid its top executives handsomely.

William Curphey, Sr., the vice president of the company from 1939 to 1948, claimed that Weller had its largest profits during World War I and II. After World War II, however, foreign competition from Europe and Japan increased dramatically and eventually brought about the demise of the Pottery. In the last decade of its existence, the company faced inexorable competition from the Japanese, who duplicated each new Weller line and undersold it in the United States.

In 1945 Essex Wire Corporation of Detroit leased space in the Weller plant. In 1947 they bought the controlling stock in the company and continued to operate the plant. When sales of pottery dropped, Essex Wire closed the factory in 1948, and Weller Pottery ceased to exist.

From 1872 to 1948, Weller Pottery provided Americans with cookware, dinnerware, teapots, jardinieres, vases, umbrella stands, and figurines to beautify their homes, porches, patios, and gardens. It was a uniquely American pottery, responding to successive waves of fashion, from Art Nouveau to Art Deco, from the pre World War I lavish decoration and huge glazed pieces to the World War II simple cookware and molded vases. Utilizing the brightest immigrant and native talent, the Pottery left behind a treasury of ceramic art.

To understand the success of Weller Pottery, one must examine the life and times of its founder, Sam Weller. In the days before the income tax, it was possible for a man to rise from poverty to great wealth, to overcome lack of education through hard work, acumen, and self discipline, as Sam Weller did. Chapter II follows Weller from his modest farm in Fultonham to his mansion in Zanesville.

Chapter II

Samuel A. Weller

With his Pottery well established, Samuel A. Weller emerged as a successful, conservative citizen of Zanesville, dedicated to his business and to his community. He built the Weller Theater, served as a delegate to the Republican National Convention, and purchased the Zanesville newspaper, *The Times Recorder*. He was an active member of the Elk's Club, the Zane Club, and the Grace Methodist Episcopal Church. With his wife and two daughters he lived in a large mansion at Sixth and Market Streets in Zanesville.

Sam Weller's background may explain his dedication to his work and his community. Weller family genealogist Richard S. Weller researched the family tree and discovered that around 1711, George Weller of Berlin, Germany and his wife emigrated to America, settled in the East, and raised a large family. From this line came Eli Weller, Sam's great grandfather, born in Wellersburg, Pennsylvania around 1765. Eli's son Henry Weller, Sam's grandfather, moved his family to Ohio in 1814, after serving in the War of 1812. He began to farm in Morgan County near Deavertown. On March 25, 1815, Henry Weller had a son Adam, who became the father of Sam Weller. Adam Weller was born near McConnelsville in Morgan County, Ohio. He was a farmer, a member of the school board, and held various offices in the town. On February 15, 1836, he married Sarah Longstreath. They had ten children: Anna, Rachel, William, Sarah, Lydia, Martha, Samuel, Franklin, Almeda, and Amy. Sam Weller was born April 12, 1851. When he was 15, his mother died, on September 29, 1866. Richard Weller believes that Sam left home "at an early age," perhaps after the death of his mother. By 1872 he had established the Pottery in the log cabin at Fultonham and was on his way to fame and fortune.

When he was 36, Sam Weller married Hermine Pickens in 1887. They had two daughters, Louise, born July 23, 1896, and Ethel, born July 26, 1898 (Fig. 10). In 1892 the Wellers moved into a large house on Market Street in Zanesville, built in 1865 by Fred Blandy of the Blandy Foundry. The three story house had cast iron exterior window arches, sills, door grills, and twenty-two spacious rooms with high ceilings, each with interior window and door frames made of oak. Plaster of Paris ceilings and cornices ornamented the rooms. A long porch, added by Weller and designed by Charles B. Upjohn, surrounded two sides of the house, facing Sixth and Market Streets (Fig. 11).

Although the front of the house faced Sixth Street, the family used the Market Street entrance. The formal entry from Sixth Street brought the visitor into a large hallway which extended the length of the house. To the

Fig. 10: Samuel A. Weller and his daughter Louise, circa 1898. Courtesy of Norris Schneider.

Fig. 11: The Weller house at Sixth and Market Streets in Zanesville. It was torn down in 1955 and replaced by a motel. Photo courtesy of Norris Schneider.

Fig. 12: Samuel Weller's desk facing the windows overlooking Market Street. A Sicard bowl sits on the desk, in the den. Courtesy of Norris Schneider.

left of the hall was a stairway to the second floor; to the right was the commodious Gold Room, and behind it the music room with a grand piano. To the left of the hall and staircase was the parlor and the den (Fig. 12). Behind the den was another hallway, then the dining room. The breakfast room and large kitchen adjoined the laundry and the powder room, all at the back of the house.

Sam Weller filled the house with the finest furniture and accessories from Europe and the United States. The Gold Room epitomized the affluence and elegance of the newly prosperous Weller family (Figs. 13-17). They

Fig. 17: A Rosemont II vase, a Sicard lamp, and a Hudson Pictorial vase stand on a table in the Weller home. Courtesy of Norris Schneider.

Fig. 14: The west end of the Gold Room with a Louis Quinze sofa, chairs, and vitrine. Courtesy of Norris Schneider.

Fig. 13: The Gold Room with its gilt furniture, chandelier, and Sicard jardinieres. Courtesy of Norris Schneider.

Fig. 15: The elaborate carved mirror on the second mantel in the Gold Room, with a Hudson vase, a Louwelsa lamp, and on the adjacent table, a Ting lamp. Courtesy of Norris Schneider.

Fig. 16: The wood and marble mantel surmounted by a carved mirror, porcelain vases and figurines. Two Sicard jardinieres are on the floor below. Courtesy of Norris Schneider.

furnished it with Louis Quinze chairs, sofas, vitrines, embellished with gilt or gold leaf, elaborate fireplaces, mirrors, and the best pieces from the Pottery. Two carved wood and marble fireplaces, surmounted by ornately carved mirrors, enhanced the room. On the mantels stood European porcelain vases and figurines, a Hudson Pictorial vase, and a Louwelsa oil lamp. Sicard vases and jardinieres predominated in the Gold Room, which was a veritable showcase of Weller pottery.

The formal dining room had a long table which seated twenty persons (Fig. 18). For festive occasions the servants set the table with damask and lace tablecloths, gold bordered Haviland china with silver underplates, sterling silver, crystal goblets, and a centerpiece with cut glass vases and a bowl filled with roses. A pair of cut glass candlesticks stood at each end of the table. Here Thanksgiving and Christmas dinners, which went on for hours, brought together the large, extended family: children, grandchildren, aunts, uncles, brothers, sisters.

The Weller grandsons, William Curphey, Jr. and Frederic Grant, recalled the traditional Christmas dinner with several courses served to the family on silver platters in the dining room by a retinue of servants. Mr. Curphey remembered the crystal goblets, in many sizes, and a profusion of food from juices and appetizers to meats and desserts. He also recalled

Fig. 18: The formal dining room in the Weller home, with cut glass goblets, candlesticks, and vases filled with roses. Courtesy of Norris Schneider.

seeing new lines of vases and jars from the Pottery each time he visited the house.

As his wealth increased, Sam traveled abroad frequently, invested his money in Zanesville, and shared it with those who supported him in his lean years. Several family members worked for him: his brother Bill Weller, his nephews Harry and Frank, his brother-in-law Ed Pickens, and his two sons-in-law Frederic Grant and Irvin Smith. His nephew Harry became vice president of the company and then president in 1925 after Sam died.

The building of the Weller Theater on North Third Street epitomized Sam Weller's importance in the community (Fig. 19). Norris Schneider in *The Times Recorder,* January 19, 1964, recounted the genesis of the Theater. It began with a game of checkers between Sam Weller and Bill Adams in 1902. Sam told Bill, "I'm going to build a theater." Bill replied, "I'd like to build it for you." Sam agreed. A year later, when the Theater was completed, the two men were again playing checkers. "How much do I owe you?" Sam inquired. Bill quoted a price, and Sam wrote him a check. However apocryphal it sounds, both families corroborate the truth of this story.

In those days, a theater was a status symbol for the rich. Flush from the sales of his product, Star Soap, Robert Schultz erected the Schultz Theater on North Fifth Street in Zanesville. Weller also sought status. Like Schultz, he built a theater and named it after himself. Zanesville didn't need two theaters. So, on the day the Weller Theater was to open, Sam leased the Schultz Theater and closed it down for two years to eliminate the competition.

On opening night, April 27, 1903, Sam, his family, and guests sat in a box at the Weller Theater and watched the comic opera, "When Johnny Comes Marching Home." The Theater was resplendent that evening. Three large Sicard vases, measuring from two to three feet high, graced the lobby. Hugo Herb, the Weller modeler, had designed and executed the stucco work on the walls, the mural decorations, and the sculptures of Adagio, Allegro, Comedy, and Tragedy above the boxes, and of War and Peace above the stage. Patrons received small Dickensware souvenirs, marked "Weller's Theatre." Every seat was occupied, all 1700 of them on the first, second, and third floors, as well as those in the side boxes. The stage measured 42 by 70 feet with a height of 69 feet. The Weller Theater was a magnificent monument to a self-made man, a product of the Gilded Age.

The Theater's vaudeville productions featured: George M. Cohan, John Drew, Al Fields, the minstrel, Victor Herbert, and Ignace Paderewski. James England manged the Theater with verve. In 1914 he produced "The Garden of Allah," on a set filled with sand, live camels, donkeys, and goats. The audience was greatly annoyed when the sand from the stage blew all over them. From opera to vaudeville to movies and finally to empty houses, the Theater had a slow decline. It was torn down in 1963.

On February 14, 1903, *Clay Record* announced that Sam Weller had purchased *The Times Recorder* of Zanesville for $47,000. In 1903, he owned the Weller Theater, the Weller Pottery, and *The Times Recorder*. He was also active in politics. In 1908 Sam and Zane Burley of Crooksville

Fig. 19: The Weller Theater on North Third Street in Zanesville. It was built in 1902-1903 and was torn down in 1963. A vacant lot stands in its place today. Photo by Mose Mesre.

were delegates to the Republican National Convention, according to *GPW*, June 1908. At this convention the Republicans nominated William Howard Taft as Theodore Roosevelt's handpicked successor. Taft later won the election and was president from 1909 to 1913.

World War I did not affect the prosperity of Weller Pottery nor the optimism of Sam Weller. Near the end of the war, Weller was in Pittsburgh and commented on post war economic development to *Brick and Clay Record,* March 12, 1918:

> If all the business people of the United States would look upon the inevitable postbellum period of readjustment with the same optimism as I find in Pittsburgh, there would be no retrenching

> after the war, but a general improvement in our economics, and a resultant prosperity, the scope of which we now little dream . . . . I have talked with many representative businessmen lately, and the consensus of opinion among them is that our domestic affairs will expand in a way that will be unprecedented in the history of the United States. We need the same fighting spirit in business and finance as those boys of ours in France are now showing. We need business enthusiasm, enthusiasm invulnerable to the whims and plaints of the ever ready pessimist. With that, America is bound to be the most prosperous country on earth.

Sam Weller was conservative yet bold in his vision, seeing the expansion of business and capital like a magnificent rainbow arching over America.

To Dorothy Laughead and the Weller employees, Sam Weller was primarily a businessman. True to his era, he paid the male decorators considerably more than he paid the female decorators. Some of the men considered Weller a generous employer. Lawton Gonder reported that when his parents, who worked for Weller at the Putnam plant, were married, Sam Weller gave them a party, hired a band, served refreshments, and presented them with gifts.

Sam Weller died of a stroke on October 4, 1925, at the age of 74. He became ill on a business trip to Washington, D.C., and died there three weeks later in a private sanitorium. The obituaries in the trade journals eulogized him. *PGBS* wrote October 8, 1925: "Throughout his fifty-three years in the pottery industry, Mr. Weller had always been the dominating figure in his business. He was thoroughly familiar with it in all its ramifications, and no important step was taken in any department without his personal sanction . . . . Save for brief periods when he was out of town or ill, Mr. Weller was at the pottery every day and all day." The obituary continued, "Mr. Weller was always a keen, aggressive businessman; a veritable human dynamo. Even when well past seventy he did not show his age, but looked a man fully ten years younger. His greatest recreation was billiards, at which he was an expert, and after business hours he could invariably be found in the billiard room of the Elk's Club in Zanesville, whose magnificent clubhouse he took the initiative in building."

The *PGBS* obituary revealed that Weller had suffered from intestinal indigestion for years, and that several times death had seemed imminent, but he always recovered rapidly and returned to work at the Pottery. Weller was survived by his wife Hermine, or Minnie, two married daughters Louise and Ethel, two grandchildren, two nephews Harry and Frank, the sons of his late brother Bill, and by his sister Mrs. Noah Tanner of Zanesville. The family buried him in the Woodlawn Cemetery in Zanesville in a large mausoleum which stands today on the rise of the hill near the Putnam plant, where Weller artists decorated Aurelian, Dickensware, and Louwelsa eighty or ninety years ago.

After her husband's death, Minnie Weller lived on in their home for twenty-nine more years, a total of sixty-two years in all. For many years she was an invalid and came downstairs rarely. After her death on May 3, 1954, at age 92, the contents of the house were put up for auction. Mirrors, pictures, china, pottery, three large crystal chandeliers, the furniture from the famous Gold Room, all came under the gavel and were sold on June 24, 1954. The beautiful Weller home at Sixth and Market Streets was torn down in 1955 and replaced by a motel.

Today in Zanesville, Sam Weller lives on in the anecdotes of workers from the Pottery, in the fine Dickensware, Hudson, Louwelsa, and Sicard vases on display at the Zanesville Art Center, and in the minds and hearts of friends, family, and pottery collectors. The story of Weller Pottery did not begin and end with Sam Weller alone. The decision to make fine quality American Art pottery depended upon the acquisition of the Lonhuda formula from William A. Long. The history of Lonhuda Pottery and William Long comprises the next chapter, Chapter III.

Chapter III

William Long and Lonhuda Pottery

William A. Long was born July 18, 1844, but he was nearly 50 years old before the pottery world knew his name (Fig. 20). On August 6, 1862, when he was only 18, he enlisted in Company I, the 98th Regiment, Carrollton, Ohio, during the height of the Civil War. For three years he served as a musician in the army, and on June 26, 1865, he was discharged for illness, according to Norris Schneider, who obtained his discharge papers and war record.

Years before he actually became a potter, Long was a student of pottery. At the National Museum in Washington, D.C., he examined carefully all the pre-Columbian vases and bowls on display and memorized their shapes. Around 1880 Long moved to Steubenville, Ohio, and became a pharmacist. He set up a kiln four feet in diameter in the backyard of the pharmacy where, over a twelve year period, he experimented with glazes. He often watched his pots disintegrate in the great heat he thought was needed to temper the white ware. When in 1892 he produced the perfect glaze, a fine blended coloring, similar to Rookwood's Standard Glaze, Lonhuda Pottery was born!

Fig. 20: William A. Long at work in his studio at the Clifton Art Pottery in 1906. Photo from Paul Evans and *Crockery and Glass Journal*, December 20, 1906.

With W. H. Hunter and Alfred Day, who became his partners, Long formed a corporation. Taking the "Lon" from Long, the "Hu" from Hunter, and the "Da" from Day, he christened his pottery with the acronymic title "Lonhuda." Each piece was signed Lonhuda with either the monogram L.P. Co. or an Indian head in profile.

"The Lonhuda pottery is this autumn offered to the public for the first time, and clearly proves that there is abundance of material for more than one enterprising firm . . . . It closely resembles Rookwood in general effect . . . . Like its rival it is somewhat costly and beyond the reach of many who may admire its worth, but good things are never cheap, and the Lonhuda is surely deserving of a rank among the best," wrote *PGBS* on December 15, 1892.

An announcement in *China, Glass and Lamps*, December 20, 1893, traced the genesis of Lonhuda and stressed its unique American character:

> All the shapes are prehistoric American, from the Cherique, made of American clays and decorated by American artists . . . . It is distinctively American and is made nowhere else in the United States or Europe. The beauty of the ware depends on the form and brilliancy of the glaze colors, which are so harmoniously blended that it is quite difficult to tell where one color begins and the other leaves off. The depth, the translucency of these colors—browns, reds, greens, yellows, etc. are marvelous in their richness.

Professor W. H. Holmes of the Smithsonian Institution, repository of ancient pottery, noted that Lonhuda duplicated the shapes of the pre-Columbian pottery of the Cherique province. From its inception, Lonhuda served as a prototype for American potters who wished to develop a unique American pottery, one which did not imitate European pottery. Displayed at the 1893 Chicago World's Fair, Lonhuda pottery won great admiration.

By December 1893 the company had expanded its output to 150 different shapes, with prices ranging from 50¢ to $50. The beauty of the underglaze decoration won notice not only in Chicago, but also throughout the country. Sam Weller was one of the many who came to the Liberal Arts Building in Chicago to see and to admire Lonhuda.

From 1892 to 1894, with Long at the helm, Lonhuda Pottery moved forward, expanded, and promoted itself. *China, Glass and Lamps* wrote about Lonhuda on February 14, 1894: "The Lonhuda Pottery Company continue to add new things to their line. The latest are a teaset, tete a tete, beer mug, etc., all in beautiful decorations. Lonhuda seems to be getting a foothold and pleases the people, recent shipments going to New England, New York and the Pacific Coast." In March 1894, *CGL* remarked that the company had won favorable comment from art critics in the U.S. and Europe and "has come to stay."

William Long was also a painter of fruits, flowers, and other still life subjects. His artistry was evident in Lonhuda pottery, in the decorations and the lead glazes, many of which defy crazing and are perfect even today, nearly 100 years later.

Lonhuda attracted noteworthy artists: Laura A. Fry, Helen Harper, Sarah R. McLaughlin, and Jessie R. Spaulding. Laura Fry brought with her

Fig. 21: Lonhuda portrait vase 5″ high, made at Weller Pottery and marked with the impressed Lonhuda Faience shield mark. Collection: Dora Betts.

from Rookwood the spray gun technique and shared it with Long. She claimed that the atomizer technique of applying and shading the underglaze backgrounds on standard glaze ware was her own invention and specialty. But Maria Longworth Nichols of Rookwood Pottery said she had discovered it: "It seems strange that any one can talk of 'originality' in a process which, technically is as old as Egypt. Neither was the mixing nor the use of the colors any secret whatever, and it was simply an artistic decoration of colored slip on clay." Nichols continued to defend her position in the *Bulletin of the American Ceramic Society,* May 1932: "What is peculiar and distinctive in 'Rookwood' pottery is its glazing . . . . The rich glow is given solely by the special glazing which belongs to Rookwood pottery alone. This warm effect of color through glaze I discovered in 1883, when attempting to give a rich tone to red clay under the glaze."

Laura Fry and William Long sued Rookwood. When Judge William Howard Taft ruled for Rookwood against Fry and Long, Long was irate and bitter, according to his grandson Daniel Long, who wrote about the suit to Norris Schneider. As a result of the trial, dozens of potteries were free to adopt the atomizer technique.

By late 1894 Lonhuda Pottery was losing money. William Long decided he had to accept Sam Weller's offer to move to Zanesville, to make Lonhuda for Weller Pottery. On November 7, 1894, *CGL* announced that Lonhuda had been sold to the S. A. Weller Clay Novelty Works of Zanesville, and that Weller would build an additional kiln to manufacture Lonhuda. Furthermore, the journal said that Mr. Long would go to Zanesville himself to give the new Lonhuda ware all his attention. The new company was christened "Lonhuda Faience," the ware signed "LF" with the letters intertwined in a shield, and the word "Lonhuda" impressed above the mark (Figs. 21-23).

Fig. 22: Lonhuda vase 5⅜″ high, made at Weller Pottery and marked with the impressed Lonhuda Faience shield mark. Artist signed A.W. Collection: Bill Dobbins.

Fig. 23: Lonhuda bowl 9½″ long, made at Weller Pottery and marked with the impressed Lonhuda Faience shield mark. Artist signed by Elizabeth Ayers. Collection: Dick and Nancy Sigafoose.

The Lonhuda Department had been in operation at the Putnam plant only three months, when on May 10, 1895, a fire destroyed it. Six months later, on November 6, 1895, *CGL* reported in an interview with William Long in New York City, that the company was working to restore order in the Lonhuda Department. Long said that the company had seventy-five different shapes ready to go and a number of decorators at work on them. He expected to hire twenty more decorators in the near future.

Brick reported in March 1897 that shortly after the fire in 1895, even though Lonhuda was a commercial success, Long wished to leave Weller to go to Chicago or some other large city. Long was an artist, a creator. He needed the business acumen of Sam Weller who produced, marketed, and promoted Lonhuda. Weller needed Long to compete with Rookwood and its monopoly of standard glaze ware. It was a marriage of convenience, which brought fame to both men.

The trade journals indicated no bitterness or acrimony between Long and Weller when they separated. But Daniel Long, grandson of William, wrote Norris Schneider on September 16, 1963, that his grandfather was angry that Weller had taken his formula for standard glaze, and he decided to leave the Pottery. In 1899 Long became art director at J. B. Owens Pottery, where he introduced Owens Utopian in standard glaze. He remained there until 1900. In 1901 Long established the Denver China and Pottery Company in Denver, where he continued to make Lonhuda until 1905, signing it with the shield mark and the word Denver above it (Figs. 24-25).

Long established the Clifton Art Pottery in Newark, New Jersey in 1905. Here he produced Crystal Patina, with a crystalline glaze, and Clifton Indian Ware. Based on forms and designs from American Indian pottery, Clifton Indian Ware used red clay and a glossy jet black interior glaze. *Glass and Pottery World* heralded the new line in February 1906: "The Crystal Patina ware is brought out in a china body covered with crystalline

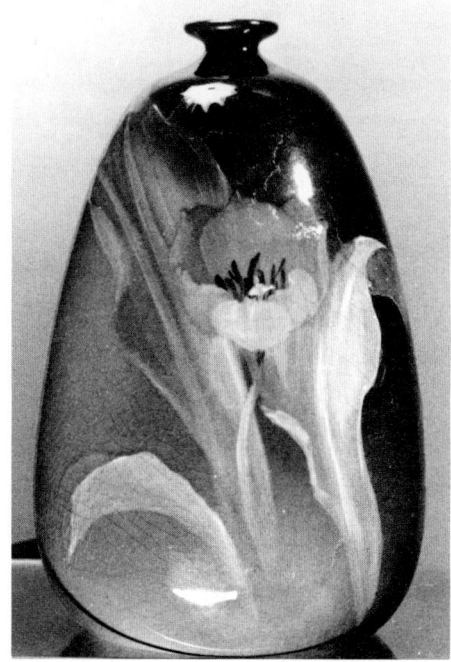

Fig. 25: Denver Lonhuda vase 8½" high, made at the Denver China and Pottery Company, and marked with the impressed shield mark with Denver above it. Collection: Dora Betts.

Fig. 24: Lonhuda handled vase 6" high, made at the Denver China and Pottery Company, and marked with the impressed shield mark with Denver above it. Artist signed E.R. Collection: Dora Betts.

glazes, chiefly of a rich cream shade, somewhat flecked with tan and light green markings." The journal praised Long and his new wares: "The shapes run somewhat to old Chinese and Indian designs, but the lines are brought out differently through the characteristic genius of Mr. W. A. Long . . . the originator of the famous Lonhuda ware." Both Weller and J. B. Owens imitated Clifton Indian Ware. Weller developed Souevo with a red clay body and a glossy, water resistant black interior.

William Long returned to Zanesville in 1909 to work for Weller. After a dozen years, he was back at Weller Pottery to introduce a new ware with a porcelain-like body and a decoration of fire effects, according to *GPW*, March 20, 1909.

By 1912 the Zanesville City Directory listed Long as an employee of Roseville. In 1914 he worked for the American Encaustic Tiling Company. He died of pneumonia October 14, 1918, at a Cincinnati sanitorium. Renowned for his pottery, especially the superb Lonhuda ware, Long also left behind some beautiful still life oil paintings and portraits.

Pottery scholars cannot minimize Long's contribution. Indeed, he is revered as a leader, a true artist, an indefatigable worker who labored over a decade to perfect the shapes and glazes on Lonhuda pottery. Without Long there would be no Louwelsa, and Sam Weller might have made only clay pots in Zanesville. Long gave an artist's impetus to Weller Pottery. In hiring Long, Weller established a tradition of seeking out the best contemporary artists and potters.

Chapter IV

From Louwelsa to Perfecto

After William Long left Weller Pottery, Sam Weller continued to produce Lonhuda, renaming it Louwelsa Weller. Louwelsa was an acronym like Lonhuda, named for Weller's daughter Louise, using the first three letters of her name, Lou, the first three letters of their surname, Wel, and Samuel Weller's initials, S.A. Like Lonhuda, Louwelsa had a dark shaded background sprayed on with an atomizer and an underglaze slip decoration. It came in more than 500 shapes. From 1896 to 1920, Louwelsa was one of the company's best sellers.

Some of the finest Weller artists decorated Louwelsa vases, jars, umbrella stands, oil and electric lamps, clocks, tobacco jars, and ashtrays. Lizabeth Blake painted dogs like the soulful Irish setter, pictured here (Fig. 26). Frank Ferrell, Albert Haubrich, Josephine Imlay, and Hester Pillsbury drew a variety of flowers such as crocuses, daffodils, nasturtiums, pansies, and fruits, from apples to raspberries. Cats and horses graced Louwelsa vases and jars. Fish and birds, from goldfish to swallows, also appeared as did human subjects, from Dutch cavaliers to American Indians. Levi Burgess painted dozens of handsome Indian chiefs on Louwelsa vases. He also did the splendid portraits of the smiling Dutch cavalier and the painter Jean François Millet (Fig. 27). Burgess was famous for his portraits which are zealously collected today.

Rarest of all the Louwelsa pieces were those decorated with silver overlay. Artists wrapped thin sculptured pieces of silver around the deep brown Louwelsa vases, allowing the slip decorated daffodils or roses to peer out, like gems in a silver setting (Fig. 28). *GPW* described the Louwelsa silver overlay vases in May 1908.

In a letter to Norris Schneider, decorator Josephine Imlay, who worked on Louwelsa for Weller around 1899 to 1905, described the decorating process: "We used clay colored paints such as black, white, yellow, brown, red, green. We used glass palettes, mixing the paint with a spatula... The background was put on with atomizers with compressed air. The ware was kept in a damp room after it was blended." She described how the artists put each vase on a one inch thick plaster of Paris bat and avoided touching it with their hands. They applied the decoration with brushes of varying sizes. The vase was left to dry, then fired once, glazed, and fired a second time (Figs. 29, 30).

Perhaps the best tribute to Louwelsa appeared in *Pottery Collectors Newsletter* in June 1977. Author James Fanale diligently collected Louwelsa for a number of years. He wrote: "Just as the shapes are varied, so is the decoration. Florals range from a simple violet or crocus to elaborate

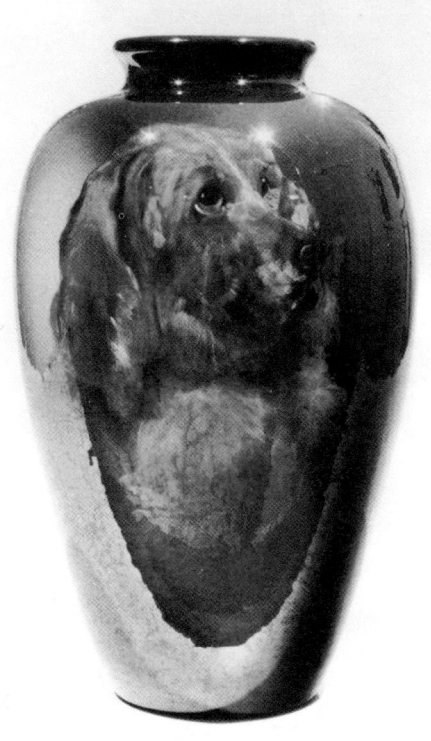

Fig. 26: *Impressed* Louwelsa Weller vase 11" high, with a portrait of an Irish setter. Artist signed L. Blake in slip. Photo by Leach.

Fig. 27: *Impressed* Louwelsa Weller vase 14" high, with a portrait of artist Jean François Millet. Artist signed L.J. Burgess in slip. Photo by Leach.

Fig. 28: *Impressed* Louwelsa Weller silver overlay vase 6″ high, decorated with pansies. Photo courtesy of the Zanesville Art Center.

bouquets of roses or poppies. There are colorful arrangements of fall leaves, and a gourmet's selection of fruits, nuts, and berries." He continued, "Artistic merit can be a rather subjective judgement, but my own favorites are the often lush florals of Mae Timberlake and the graceful, delicate work of Josephine Imlay. Frank Ferrell's forte was fruit! While these pieces decorated with florals and fruit remain the least expensive and the most plentiful, their quality shouldn't be underestimated . . ." Speaking of Louwelsa portraits, he said, "While the Indians are the most rare and marketable today, I have found the cavaliers to be a splendid cast of fellows. From the stiff and sober gentlemen with frilled, starched collars to the jovial, disheveled 'Falstaff' type, they make fine friends on the shelf. Levi Burgess remains my favorite artist for the human subjects."

Fig. 29: *Impressed* Louwelsa Weller: Vase 5″ high, with pansies, artist signed M.P.; handled vase 6″ high, with roses, artist signed T.S., and jug 4½″ high, with cherries, artist signed J. Photo by Leach.

Fig. 30: *Impressed* Louwelsa Weller: Vase 6½″ high, with a daffodil; ewer 6¼″ high, with sweet peas, and vase 6½″ high, with a carnation. Photo by Leach.

Clay Record heralded the arrival of Louwelsa on September 28, 1896, noting that Weller had introduced a new art ware, an improvement of Lonhuda. It resembled Rookwood but was less expensive to produce. Since Louwelsa utilized domestic clays with a little English ball clay in the mix, it was cheaper to make than Rookwood's Standard Glaze, which used more expensive clay. "The decorations will be built on in slip, while the ware is in the biscuit, and the colors will be thrown on," wrote Clay Record.

By October 12, 1899, Weller boasted in an ad in C & G: "Never before has our line been so large and attractive. Louwelsa the highest perfection of art pottery in underglaze blends and decorations. Consists of Vases, Tankards, Mugs, Clocks, Lamps and Jardinieres." (Figs. 31, 32). It was made in all shapes and sizes from tiny ashtrays to giant five foot high vases. In New York City, C. H. Taylor managed a show room where Weller ware was displayed. Here stood a magnificent five foot high Louwelsa vase which was over three feet in circumference.

Louwelsa portrait pottery was introduced around 1905, with pictures of dogs, cats, Indians, and famous men under the glaze. Dutch cavaliers, Moroccans, Russians, and Turks adorned the vases. Some of the cavaliers and jesting peasants recalled the subjects of the seventeenth century Dutch realist painters, Frans Hals, Nicholas Maes, Jan Steen, and Jan Vermeer. The decorators may have copied paintings by these artists.

With the vast success of the Louwelsa line, the Pottery was encouraged to experiment, to invent derivatives. Employing the same mark on the base, the Louwelsa impressed circle mark, and the same molds, the potters created high glaze green, red, and blue Louwelsa, and also a matt finish ware that collectors call Matt Louwelsa (Fig. 33). Made in 1905, it differed from its high glaze twin, with its dull, matt finish and the heavy overglaze slip decoration of fruit or flowers. Muted pastel background colors, such as blue, gray, green, orange, or beige, enhanced the crisp slip decorations.

Fig. 31: *Impressed* Louwelsa Weller clock 8¾" high, with an Aladdin lamp case. Collection: Sheila Amdur.

Fig. 33: *Impressed* Louwelsa Weller: Blue Louwelsa vase 11" high, with berries; Matt Louwelsa pitcher 12" high, and Blue Louwelsa vase 11" high, with roses. Courtesy of James Fanale. Photo by Leach.

Fig. 32: *Impressed* Louwelsa Weller jardiniere and pedestal 33" high, with storks, artist signed A. Haubrich in slip. Collection: Tommy and Norma Smith. Photo by Sigafoose.

To the touch, Matt Louwelsa vases often felt rough and sandy. Picturing a tall, grape-decorated Matt Louwelsa vase, Weller advertised the ware in *GPW* on September 20, 1905.

Perfecto was a beautiful line. With delicate shades of salmon, pink, and green, it evoked the glow of early summer, embodied in a full blown pink rose. Some extant vases have the Perfecto impressed circle mark. One is a tall pink vase decorated with currants, another, a pillow vase with a horse portrait (Figs. 34, 35). The portrait vase shades from light green at the rim to tan in the middle and light green at the base. The artist Hester Pillsbury drew the horse with a platinum mane and a light brown coat. Touches of pink appeared at the mouth of the horse, which was bridled and ready to ride.

The trade journals documented the Perfecto line. *C & G* announced it August 13, 1903: "It has been named 'Louwelsa Perfecto.' The ware is in light color, a sea green predominating, but this is shaded with delicate pinks and salmon. The artistic shapes which have characterized the Louwelsa are maintained, and the paintings are of even a higher order of merit."

China, Glass and Pottery Review heralded Perfecto in September 1903: "These goods are made with a matt finish and decorated in floral and figured designs, as well as character heads and heads of a number of prominent actors. There are also monks, cats, dogs, frogs and other animals. The predominating colors of this ware are sea green, blending into a delicate pink. For decorative purposes they are certainly most ornamental. About forty different shapes, all beautifully modeled, and measuring in size from seven to fifteen inches, which are listed at from $8. to $30. a

Fig. 34: *Impressed* Perfecto Weller vase 12" high, with currants, artist signed L.J.B. Collection: Lewis and Alice Bettinger.

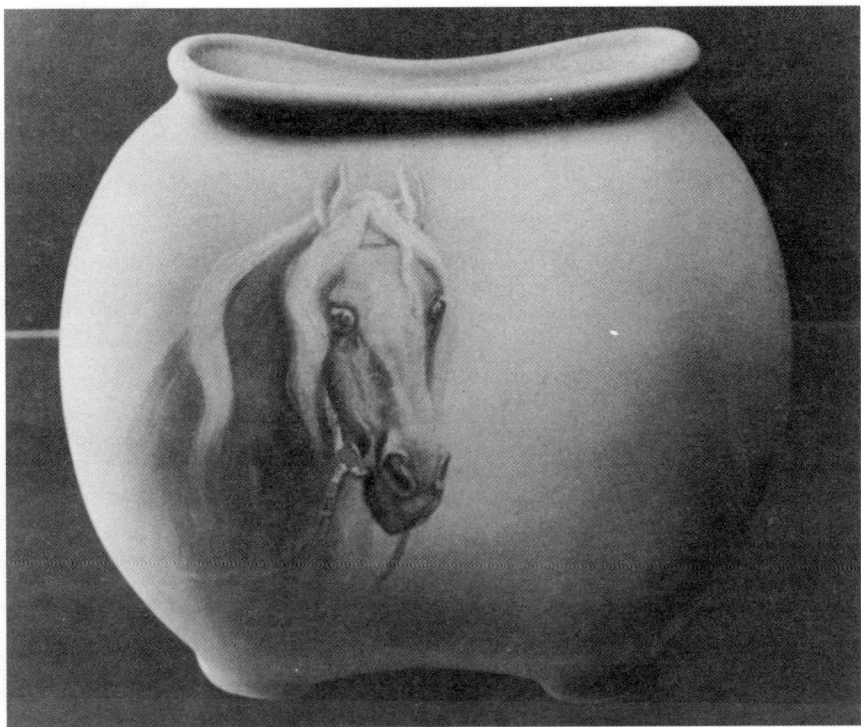

Fig. 35: *Impressed* Perfecto Weller pillow vase 10½" high, with a portrait of a horse, artist signed by Hester Pillsbury. Photo courtesy of Bill and Alice Truszkowski.

piece." This account astonished me. First, the cost of Perfecto, $8.00 to $30.00 per vase, was very high for 1903. Secondly, I wondered what happened to all the Perfecto portraits, in particular the portrait "heads of a number of prominent actors?" Few marked pieces of Perfecto exist today.

Crockery and Glass referred to Perfecto again on June 30, 1904: "Delicacy of coloring is the dominating trait of the Perfecto ware from S. A. Weller's factory. The groundwork is executed in pale tints of green, ivory and gray. Over this have been applied well-selected floral, fruit and animal studies in tones somewhat deeper than ground, but not heavy enough to sacrifice the daintiness of the decoration. The pieces are unglazed, and this serves to more clearly bring out the tints. Vases, tankards and large jardinieres are in the assortment."

The trade journals agreed on several points about Perfecto: 1. that it had a matt or an unglazed finish, 2. that it shaded from green to pink, or came in shades of green, 3. that it was decorated with fruits, flowers, or portraits, done in pale pastels, 4. that Louwelsa molds were used for Perfecto, which was first called Louwelsa Perfecto. References to the line occurred in three trade journals from 1903 to 1904, when it was discontinued.

Named by collectors, Blue Louwelsa was a high gloss line shading from medium blue to cobalt blue, with underglaze slip decorations of raspberries, roses, daffodils, or lilies of the valley. Sometimes, portraits appeared, for example, the house portrait by Gordon Mull, or the dog portrait by Albert Wilson, both exhibited in the last decade at the Zanesville Art Center. Weller artists decorated Blue Louwelsa in harmonious shades of white, cobalt, and light blue slip. Since few pieces were made, they are rare and sought after today.

The Weller catalogs depicted a mysterious line called Delta, shown here with twenty-four vases and one mug, all slip decorated (Fig. 36). Researchers have had great difficulty identifying Delta. Based on an examination of the catalog page, they inferred that Delta had a dark blue slip decoration on a matt blue background.

Pictured in the color section is a Delta vase, discovered just recently (C-9). It replicates the vase from the Delta catalog on the top row, far right in Figure 36. It has the same impressed shape number, 95, and is marked on the base Louwelsa Weller, although it is not Louwelsa. The vase shades from blue green at the top rim to deep lavender blue at the base. A lavender blue flower peers out from a mass of leaves. With its superb art work, its blue on blue decoration, and its early pinched neck shape, the vase is a rarity and a perfect example of the transition from Louwelsa to Hudson. Unlike the rough finish on Matt Louwelsa, the Delta vase has a semi-smooth, matt finish.

Appearing before 1910, Delta resembled Blue Louwelsa in shape and decoration. The same molds, 512, 602, 525, X314J, and X501, were used on five Delta and Blue Louwelsa vases. The trade journals offered no clues to when Delta was made or to how it looked. There may be a vase marked Delta Weller, but so far none has appeared. The Weller Delta catalog page provided the most solid evidence of its existence.

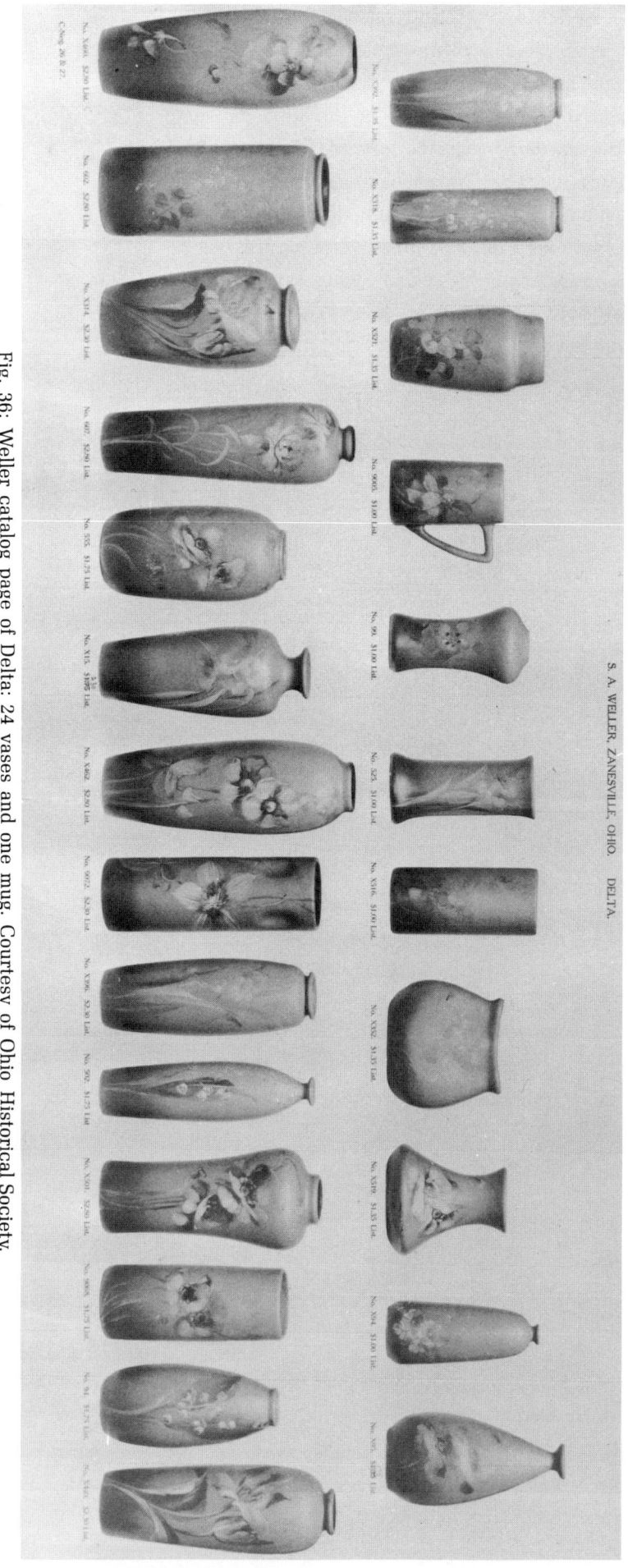

Fig. 36: Weller catalog page of Delta: 24 vases and one mug. Courtesy of Ohio Historical Society.

With Louwelsa, Sam Weller found a popular, marketable ware. Its dark background, shading from deep chocolate brown to mahogany, or from mahogany to avocado green, harmonized well with the velvets, heavy damasks, and ornately carved walnut furniture of the Victorian era. Louwelsa vases and jardinieres were cherished as wedding gifts and displayed in hallways and conservatories. The small vases adorned mantels and curio cabinets. The gentleman of the house could store his tobacco in a Louwelsa humidor and empty his pipe into a Louwelsa ashtray, as he read by a Louwelsa oil lamp. In all shapes, sizes, and decorations, Louwelsa was appealing and modestly priced. Compared to Rookwood Standard Glaze, Roseville Rozane, and Owens Utopian, it glowed with energy and spirit.

Chapter V
Sgraffito Work at Weller and the Dickensware Lines

In 1895 Sam Weller hired Charles B. Upjohn as head designer of Weller Pottery. Upjohn lacked previous experience as a potter, but he had studied art. Born in 1866, he came to Weller at age 29, after studying in New York under the Viennese sculptor Karl Bitter and after traveling several months in Europe. He stayed with Weller until 1904 and developed some of the finest sgraffito pottery ever made in the United States, calling it Weller Dickensware. Collectors call it Second Line Dickensware or Dickensware II. From it evolved three other lines of sgraffito pottery, Etched Matt, Etched Floral, and Hunter.

Sgraffito pottery had existed for centuries. It was made in Syria and Persia until the thirteenth century. Artifacts of Mesopotamian pottery with incised decoration dating back to 5000 B.C. were found in Iraq and Syria. The art of sgraffito, which means scratched in Italian, reached its peak in the Sung Dynasty in China, when delicate flowers were incised on pottery.

When he arrived at Weller Pottery in 1895, Upjohn had a rich background of travel, study, and experience. Visions of English cities, Italian circuses, and naturalistic paintings must have passed before his eyes as he created Dickensware. The line was named after Charles Dickens and some of the scenes on the vases were taken directly from Dickens' novels: *Bleak House*, *David Copperfield*, *Great Expectations*, and *The Pickwick Papers*.

To begin the process of making Dickensware II, Upjohn would draw pictures of Dickens' characters. Then, women employees at Weller would trace them several times and cut them out with scissors, punching pin holes for the inside lines. These patterns were set on wet clay vases and pounced with a bag of charcoal dust so that the pinholes would appear. At the blending box the vases were sprayed with background colors. When the glaze was dry, the paper patterns were removed and the decorators marked the lines in India ink with a fine pointed brush and filled in the color decorations. Finally, the decorators made a thin wire loop out of the eye end of a darning needle. With this they followed the lines and excised thin threads of clay, leaving the fine etched in lines unique to Dickensware. Afterwards, the vases were fired in the kiln.

Various subjects appeared on Dickensware II: Indian chiefs, tiny Indian and Dutch girls, soldiers of the Revolutionary War, Robin Hood in Sherwood Forest, Jesus and the woman at the well, scenes from *The Canterbury Tales* and the contemporary Italian circus, male and female golfers swinging their clubs, hunting scenes by Sir Edwin Landseer, and a bevy of imaginative creatures: cats, dogs, elk, dragons, ducks, fish, seagulls, mermaids. Franciscan monks were depicted in a variety of poses: drinking beer, praying, playing the mandolin, even shaving!

In myriad vases, mugs, and pitchers, Dickensware had rich background colors in matt, semi-gloss, and high gloss glazes. One of the most effective was the shaded, tan matt finish which allowed the design to confront the viewer with full force. Other background colors included a semi-gloss royal blue, green shading to blue or to brown, and the rare pink or white. The gladiator vase illustrated here shades from pink to blue gray and depicts a gladiator with sword and shield in the arena (Fig. 37).

With his rich imagination, Charles Upjohn added to the diversity of Weller pottery. Collectors treasure pieces signed by Upjohn. He designed large scenic pieces, such as the incomparable Italian Circus Vase, and vases with monks, birds, deer, fish, mermaids, and dragons. He incised his signature on Dickensware with a U entwined with a J, which was often incorporated into the design, so that it looked like part of the decoration.

It was Charles Upjohn who created the Dickensware tobacco jars: the Admiral, the Chinaman, the Irishman, and the Turk (Fig. 38). These unique jars resembled sculpted heads and were incised and colored by hand. Upjohn gave the Chinaman a long, brown braided pigtail which began at the crown of his head and wound down around his neck. A combination of graceful molding and incising characterized the heads, which had a certain fierceness, particularly the Turk and the Admiral. The Admiral wore his hat with the brim low, almost over his eyebrows, while the Turk sported a turban and an upturned moustache. The Irishman had the deeply-lined facial features typical of Upjohn's work, with detailed smile lines around

Fig. 37: *Impressed* Dickensware Weller, Second Line: Mug with Indian Chief 5½" high; handled monk vase 10¼" high, artist signed by Anthony Dunlavy, and pink gladiator vase 7" high. Photo by Leach.

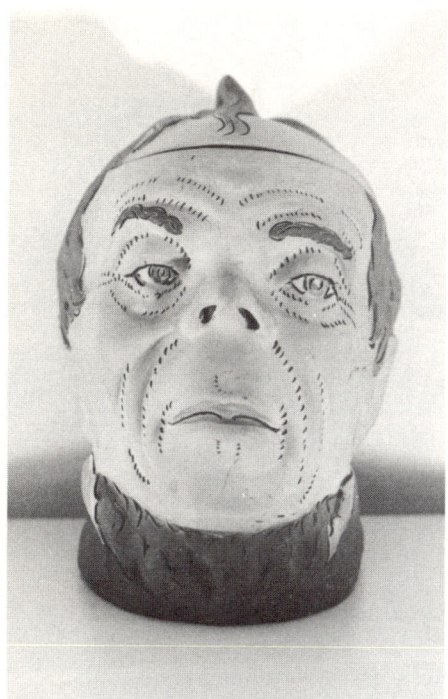

Fig. 39: Weller Dickensware Irishman Tobacco Jar 6½" high. Photo courtesy of the Zanesville Art Center.

the mouth and query marks on the brow (Fig. 39). A fifth tobacco jar, the Skull, which was molded, not incised, resembled a human skull. The tobacco jars had a matt finish and were marked Dickens Weller under the lid.

The trade journals acknowledged the advent of Dickensware II with enthusiasm. Remarking that the scenes from Dickens and from Scripture were done in a striking manner, C & G noted its appearance October 18, 1900. GPW praised Dickensware in November 1902: "The new ware is called Dickens Ware, the name being suggested by the fact that Samuel Weller is the name given by Dickens to one of the characters in the Pickwick Papers." Samuel Weller returned the compliment, naming his new pottery line for Charles Dickens. GPW also noted that some of the subjects on Dickensware were taken from the French, and from posters which were then very popular.

Weller decorators copied illustrations, sketched by Upjohn, from Charles Dickens' novels on to the Dickensware II and III vases. Upjohn preferred to duplicate the work of illustrators Frederick Barnard and Hablot Knight Browne. Examining the works of Dickens, I have discovered several original etchings which the decorators reproduced on Dickensware vases. "Captain Cuttle Gives Them 'The Lovely Peg'" was an engraving from *Dombey and Son* by Frederick Barnard, appearing in *The Household Edition of Dickens* in 1877 (Fig. 40). Note the vase illustrated here with the cheerful figure of Captain Cuttle, singing his favorite song "The Lovely Peg," in the midst of his friends who are sharing some Madeira (Fig. 41).

The Weller decorators used another illustration by Barnard from *Dombey and Son* and titled it "Dombey and Son," (Fig. 42). It showed little Paul Dombey sitting by the fire next to his father. Charles Dickens described the scene as follows:

Fig. 38: Weller Dickensware Tobacco Jars: The Admiral 7" high, The Turk 7" high, and The Chinaman 6" high, all designed by Charles Upjohn. Photo by Mose Mesre.

Fig. 40: Frederick Barnard's illustration of Captain Cuttle Gives Them "The Lovely Peg," from *Dombey and Son* by Charles Dickens.

Fig. 41: *Impressed* Dickensware Weller: Second Line Captain Cuttle vase and Glazed Dickensware Captain Cuttle vase, both 10″ high. Incised on the back of each vase are the words: "Captain Cuttle Gives Them 'The Lovely Peg.' *Dombey and Son*."

Fig. 43: A close up view of the Second Line Dickensware vase 13″ high, marked Dickensware Weller, with the title incised on the back of the vase: "Mr. Micawber impressing the names of the streets upon me that I might find my way back again early in the morning. *David Copperfield*." Artist signed H.S.

Fig. 42: Dickensware Weller Second Line vase 10½″ high, titled "Dombey and Son." Collection: Dora Betts.

> [Little Paul] had a strange, old fashioned, thoughtful way . . . of sitting brooding in his miniature arm-chair, when he looked (and talked) like one of those terrible little beings in the fairy tales, who, at a hundred and fifty or two hundred years of age, fantastically represent the children for whom they have been substituted . . . But at no time did he fall into it so surely as when, his little chair being carried down into his father's room, he sat there with him after dinner, by the fire. They were the strangest pair at such a time that ever firelight shone upon. Mr. Dombey, so erect and solemn, gazing at the blaze; his little image, with an old, old face, peering into the red perspective with the fixed and rapt attention of a sage. (*Dombey and Son*, Chapter VIII).

The Dickensware vase depicted this solemn scene, copied from Barnard's illustration. Barnard created both "Dombey and Son" and "Captain Cuttle" for *The Household Edition of Dickens*, 1877.

Weller artist Helen Smith drew Mr. Micawber and David Copperfield on a large 13 inch high Dickensware II vase (Fig. 43). David holds Mr. Micawber's hand as they pass through the London throng: ladies in bonnets, bobbies in tall hats, ragged children. Mr. Micawber looks jaunty as ever, swinging his walking stick as he guides David home to Windsor Terrace.

Charles Dickens provided the background to the design on the vase in *David Copperfield*, Chapter XI. David had just found a job working for Murdstone and Grinby's counting house, where he washed bottles. The nearly impoverished Mr. Micawber came by the firm and offered David lodging. After work, Mr. Micawber called for David to lead him through the streets to his new home at Windsor Terrace. Dickens described the scene, speaking through David: "At the appointed time in the evening Mr. Micawber reappeared. I washed my hands and face, to do the greater honor to his gentility, and we walked to our house, as I suppose I must now call it, together; Mr. Micawber impressing the names of the streets, and the shapes of the corner houses upon me, as we went along, that I might find my way back easily, in the morning." Decorator Helen Smith copied this illustration from one by Frederick Barnard, done for *The Household Edition of Dickens* of 1873, and incised the title on the back of the vase: "Mr. Micawber impressing the names of streets upon me that I might find my way back early in the morning."

Knowledge of the two Dickens' illustrators, Frederick Barnard and Hablot Knight Browne, enhances our appreciation of their efforts and successes. Frederick Barnard executed the majority of illustrations for *The Household Edition of Dickens*, 1873 and 1877, published simultaneously in London by Chapman and Hall and in New York by Harper and Brothers. He made 450 drawings, transmitting them into wood engravings, which were copied by photogravure and reproduced as illustrations in the novels.

Called the "Illustrator of Dickens," Hablot Knight Browne was a close friend and a traveling companion of the novelist. Nicknamed Phiz, Browne drew characters for ten of the fourteen principal novels and worked with Dickens for twenty-three years. He illustrated *Bleak House, David Copperfield, Dombey and Son,* and *The Pickwick Papers*. With engraver Robert

Young who "bit" in the plates, Browne did the original drawings or watercolors and worked with Young to etch them on steel plates.

Weller artists duplicated at least two of Hablot Knight Browne's illustrations on Dickensware vases. "God Bless Me! What's the Matter?", a Dickensware II vase, showed Mr. Pickwick down on his knees examining a small broken stone which he thinks is a rare archeological treasure (Fig. 44 and C-3). He dusts it off with his handkerchief and examines its inscription rendered fully on the vase: "Bilst Um Pshi S. M. Ark." With great enthusiasm, Pickwick buys the stone from the laborer who stands, scratching his head in puzzlement, in front of his thatched roof cottage. The original illustration was in *The Pickwick Papers, The Household Edition of Dickens,* 1874.

Browne also drew "David Copperfield at the Public House," which appeared on a glossy gray Dickensware III carafe with cup, measuring 14½ inches high (Figs. 45, 46). Here the young David Copperfield tries to order a glass of ale from a bartender. "What is your very best — the VERY best — ale, a glass?" he asks boldly. The landlord replies that the best ale is Genuine Stunning, and David orders some. The landlord smiles at David and calls his wife over. The gentle humor was captured well on this Dickensware carafe, as the landlord and his wife, behind the counter, confront the young David Copperfield, leaning nonchalantly on the bar. I discovered this humorous illustration by Browne in the Frederick Kitton edition of Dickens, *David Copperfield,* Volume IV.

Upjohn may have found these illustrations in American editions of Dickens' novels, or on posters. My search for the original illustrations, copied by the Weller artists, was exciting and lengthy. Not only did they borrow the illustration, but they also took the caption. Usually, Dickensware

Fig. 44: Impressed Dickensware Weller: Second Line vase 10″ high, with the title incised on the back of the vase: "God Bless Me! What's the Matter? *Pickwick Papers.*" Collection: Bill Clarke.

Fig. 45: Marked Weller: Dickensware Third Line Carafe with Cup 14½″ high: "David Copperfield at the Public House." Courtesy of Elaine and Wesley Hart.

Fig. 46: The back side of the Dickensware Third Line Carafe with Cup 14½″ high, showing a disc with the bust of Charles Dickens and a tube lined disc with the title of the novel, *David Copperfield.* Courtesy of Elaine and Wesley Hart.

Fig. 47: Doulton Ware vase 10″ high, artist signed by Hannah Barlow, dated 1897, with incised cows and horses. Photo by Leach.

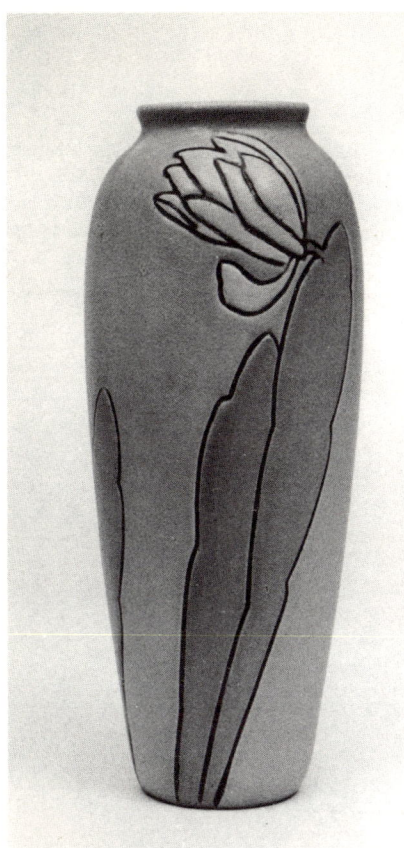

Fig. 48: *Incised* Weller: Etched Floral vase 12¼" high, artist signed Ferrell on the side of the vase. Photo by Leach.

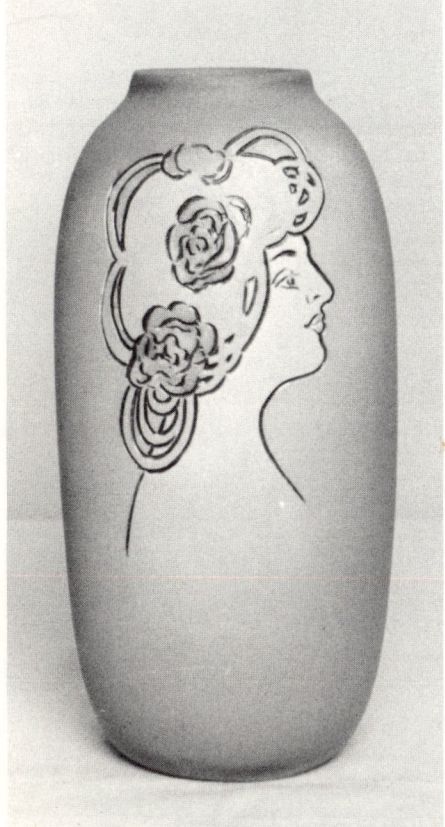

Fig. 49: *Incised* Weller: Etched Matt vase 8½" high. Collection: Dora Betts.

came complete with a scene on the front and a quotation on the back of the piece.

It is possible that Upjohn found his inspiration for Dickensware II during his tour and his studies in England, where he may have seen the pottery of Hannah B. Barlow or the Martin brothers. Hannah Barlow used sgraffito to draw animals on salt-glaze Doulton Ware. She signed and dated each vase she decorated. Each piece was unique. Sheep, storks, cats, cows, horses, donkeys, and pigs comprised her gallery of incised birds and animals. She drew storks with their long legs brushing against submerged water grasses, and cows reclining while horses graze in the meadow, as illustrated here (Fig. 47).

Like Hannah Barlow, the Martin brothers also incised decorations on stoneware. Their productions began in 1873 in Fulham, England. They invented grotesque fish, bird, and animal designs. Edwin Martin decorated vases with flying ducks, gigantic fish, weird demons, and flowers. Edwin and R. W. Martin had a predilection for flying ducks, a favorite motif of Charles Upjohn, who often incised flying ducks on Dickensware mugs and pitchers. Upjohn's love of the grotesque paralleled the Martin brothers'. I have seen one Dickensware mug he decorated with a duck which has two heads, one on each end of the body! In general, Weller Dickensware was simpler, less formal, less highly decorated than the work of the British sgraffito artists.

The sgraffito technique proved to be popular again at Weller in 1905-1906. A line with flowers or berries etched out and then outlined in black appeared in 1905, according to *C & G*, November 23, 1905. "Flowers are the inspiration in each instance and they possess uncommon effectiveness because of the almost solid toned surfaces of green, red, blue, ivory and salmon which they surmount. The character of the paintings is further improved by reason of the fact that each is etched out. The process is applied after the design has been finished, so that the latter bears the appearance of having been inlaid. It is a striking and decidedly original idea." Since Weller gave no name to this line, I will call it Etched Floral.

Usually, the decoration on Etched Floral extended from the top to the bottom of the vase, as illustrated here on the tulip vase (Fig. 48). The background was green, orange, yellow, beige, or pink. The artist incised the long stemmed tulips or roses and then outlined them in black. Frank Ferrell decorated some Etched Floral vases like the one shown here in matt green with a tall yellow tulip. The vase was signed Ferrell on the side and incised Weller on the base with the mark outlined in black like the floral decoration. The line was rarely artist signed. Etched Floral differed from Dickensware II, in that the incisions on Etched Floral were deeper, wider, bolder, and blacker than those on Dickensware. The etched lines on Dickensware, which were done with a finer, less blunt tool, had a subtlety totally lacking in Etched Floral.

Etched Matt resembled Dickensware II. Most Etched Matt vases or plaques had the bust of a woman, usually with blond hair, either bound in a wreath of roses or loose in the wind (Fig. 49). The decorators incised and hand colored each piece on a pale green or a tan background. Ed Pickens decorated a magnificent Etched Matt plaque with a woman with golden hair blowing out in front of her. These pieces all possessed a dramatic Art Nouveau quality. Both Etched Floral and Etched Matt continued the sgraffito technique initiated by Charles Upjohn.

The gloss glaze differentiated Glazed Dickensware from Second Line Dickensware. Otherwise, the two were identical in subject matter, monks, scenes from Dickens, and the sgraffito technique (Fig. 50). Instead of the plain matt, shaded background, Glazed Dickensware usually had a shaded blue or a brown background covered with a gloss glaze. The Captain Cuttle vase came both in matt and in high glaze with the scene from the novel on the front of the vase and the inscription carved on the back, as in Figure 41. Dutch cavaliers, monks, Indians, knights, all appeared on Glazed Dickensware, a striking variation of Dickensware II.

Popularly called Matt Floretta, some Floretta employed the sgraffito technique. Pitchers and mugs, in a shaded matt green or brown finish with etched apples or pears on tree branches, typified this line which resembled Dickensware II. Note the Matt Floretta pitcher in the color section (C-3).

There were three Dickensware lines: First, Second, and Third Line. First Line Dickensware emerged in 1897, three years before Second Line Dickensware appeared. Third Line Dickensware came out last, in 1905. Each of the three lines had distinct characteristics, reflecting adaptation to a changing pottery market.

Weller introduced Dickensware I at the Monongahela House Glass and Pottery Exhibition in Pittsburgh in 1897. Jardinieres, pedestals, and umbrella stands were on display, with glazes as fine as Rookwood's, according to *CGL*, February 10, 1897. The Pottery hired some Rookwood artists to decorate Dickensware I and Louwelsa. The background on Dickensware I was usually a solid color, either honey brown, dark brown, green, blue, or black. Vases, jars, mugs, pitchers, and oil lamps appeared in this line, with flowers, sometimes in high relief, under the glaze. Witness the chrysanthemums on the honey brown Dickensware I jardiniere pictured here, with thickly applied slip decoration and tangible petals like a real flower (Fig. 51). Occasionally, portraits of animals or men graced Dickensware I vases or jars.

Dickensware II was so expensive to make that it was soon succeeded by Dickensware III, marketed in 1905. Third Line Dickensware resembled Etna, with a dark gray background shading to light gray, a high gloss glaze, and a raised decoration. *American Pottery Gazette* pictured some Dickensware III on August 5, 1905, with the caption: "A selection from a most noteworthy assortment of new Dickens ware, made by S. A. Weller... The picture of Mr. Micawber will be readily recognized in this group as being a facsimile of the famous drawings of the well-known illustrator of Dickens' works, Fred Barnard. The illustration on the center piece is Krook in 'Bleak House,' and that on the right is Carker in 'Dombey and Son.' The figures are in bas relief and are beautifully colored." As the caption noted, characters from Dickens' novels appeared on Dickensware III, taken from the illustrations of Frederick Barnard.

Weller artist Gordon Mull attributed the invention of Dickensware III

Fig. 50: *Impressed* Dickensware Weller: Glazed Dickensware turquoise monk vase 15″ high, artist signed by Helen Smith. Collection: Dora Betts.

Fig. 51: *Impressed* Dickensware Weller: First Line jardiniere 6″ high, with yellow chrysanthemums. Photo by Leach.

to Frederick H. Rhead. Bernard Bumpus, Rhead expert in London, concurred, pointing out that on the discs on the back of most Dickensware III pieces, the names of the characters and the novels were tube lined, a technique which Rhead employed on Jap Birdimal and Rhead Faience. Bumpus also confirmed that Rhead knew Frederick Barnard the illustrator. Besides the work of Barnard, the Weller artists also copied the work of Hablot Knight Browne, as noted earlier with the Dickensware III carafe and cup, "David Copperfield at the Public House." Characters from *Bleak House, David Copperfield, Dombey and Son,* and *The Pickwick Papers* came to life on Dickensware III vases, teapots, creamers, pitchers, and mugs.

The Hunter line appeared sometime before 1910, with its shaded, glossy brown glaze and incised colored decorations of birds, animals, or butterflies. The company made small pillow vases, mugs, and ewers. Shown here is a signed Hunter mug with an incised seagull flying over the ocean (Fig. 52). The background on the mug shaded from dark green and yellow to deep brown at the base. Hunter resembled Glazed Dickensware in technique, if not subject matter. The subjects were usually naturalistic: shore birds on a beach, deer, or seagulls. The artists used the sgraffito technique and a gloss glaze for both Hunter and Glazed Dickensware. What distinguished one from the other was not only the subject matter, but also the coloration, since Hunter usually employed dark earth tones.

When Karl Kappes took Upjohn's place as head of the art department at Weller in 1904, the production of Dickensware II continued, but the decoration changed. Indians, golfers, animals, and tavern scenes replaced

Fig. 52: *Incised* Hunter: Mug 6″ high, with a seagull. Collection: Paul and Rosemary Enoch. Photo by Ralph Crowell Associates.

scenes from Dickens' novels as the subject matter (Fig. 53). The Upjohn years at Weller were years of high artistic achievement. From this period came some of the best work Weller produced, the magnificent Dickensware Circus Vase, discussed in Chapter XIX, and *The Canterbury Tales* vase on display at the Zanesville Art Center. With the work of Upjohn on Dickensware II and Rhead on Dickensware III, the years from 1895 to 1904 were halcyon years at Weller Pottery.

Fig. 53: *Impressed* Dickensware Weller, Second Line: Sleeping monk vase 9″ high; Weller Theater 1903 souvenir vase 8″ high; lady golfer vase 12″ high, artist signed H.S., and dragon vase 12″ high, artist signed E. Roberts '03. Collection: Robert Miller and Glen Vogt.

Chapter VI

Weller at the World's Fair

Samuel Weller believed in publicity. He enjoyed promoting his products, the pottery vases, lamps, jardinieres, pedestals, and umbrella stands. Most of all, he liked a big show. At the St. Louis Exposition in 1904, Weller put on a very big show. He built a working pottery, 150 feet by 200 feet, with one kiln, at a cost of $30,000, so that visitors to the Fair could see how pottery was made.

American Encaustic Tiling, Arc-En-Ciel, Brouwer, Newcomb, Peters and Reed, Rookwood, and Roseville Potteries, all had displays at the World's Fair, but only Weller had a complete pottery plant. *House Furnisher* wrote in October 1904: "One of the greatest attractions and most interesting features of the World's Fair is S. A. Weller's model art pottery factory in operation. Situated in a most convenient part of the grounds, opposite the Michigan State Building and close to the Government and Fisheries Buildings, it is attracting thousands of visitors daily."

The purpose of the St. Louis Expo was to commemorate the purchase of the Louisiana Territory from Napoleon in 1803 for $15,000,000, and to mark the progress of the world from 1803 to 1903. The Louisiana Purchase doubled the area of the United States, providing territories for expansion and development. The country was in its golden age in 1903-1904. It was the age of Tiffany, of the robber barons, of the Vanderbilts and the Rockefellers. Life was luxurious.

The Exposition opened April 30, 1904, and closed the following December. It covered 1,240 acres and encompassed fifteen large buildings, twelve arranged in fan shape, holding exhibits from Argentina, Austria, Belgium, Brazil, Britain, China, Cuba, France, Germany, Italy, Japan, Mexico, Morocco, Siam, Sweden, and the United States. France presented a replica of the Trianon with views of the gardens of Versailles; Britain duplicated the Orangery at South Kensington.

An area called the Cascades highlighted massive waterfalls, lagoons, gardens, and water displays (Fig. 54). The Cascades were a naturalistic wonder, utilizing 90,000 gallons of water per minute. The central cascade was 290 feet long with a total fall of 80 feet in twelve leaps. The side cascades were 300 feet long with a total fall of 65 feet. Two miles of lagoons began and ended in the Cascades. Gardens and sculpted mythological creatures completed the impressive display. Crowning the vista of the Cascades was the Festival Hall, a circular building 192 feet in diameter with a dome equal to that of St. Peter's in Rome. Several million people visited the Fair at St. Louis. It was larger than any previous Expo, twice as

Fig. 54: A postcard view of the Festival Hall and the Cascades at the St. Louis World's Fair in 1904.

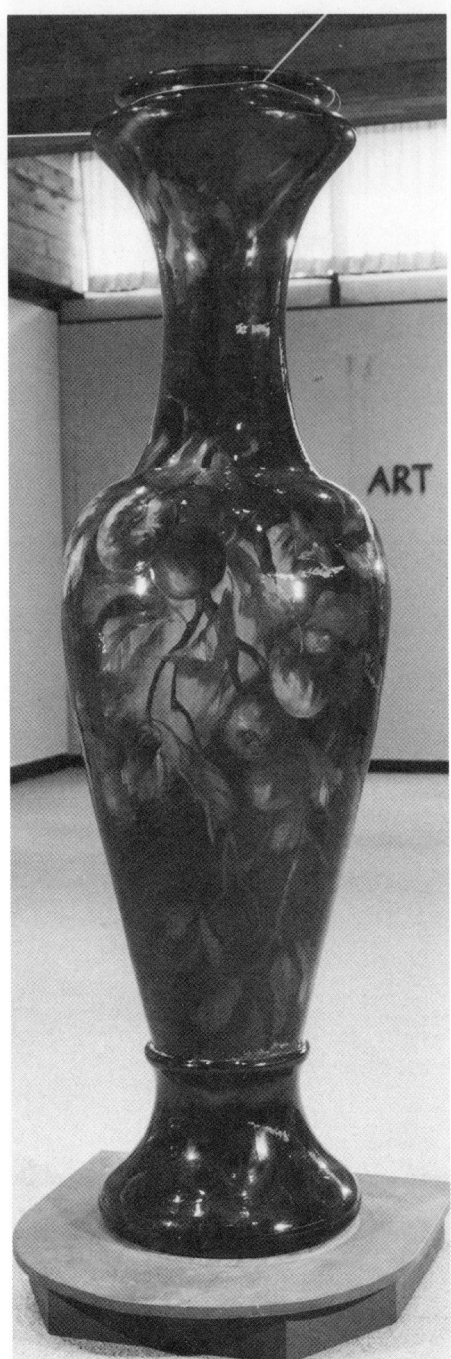

Fig. 55: Weller Aurelian vase 7 feet high, dated 1897, decorated with apples and artist signed by Frank Ferrell. This vase won a Gold Medal at the St. Louis World's Fair. Collection: Harold Nichols.

large as Chicago in 1893, and grander than the Pan American Expo in Buffalo in 1901.

Sculpture predominated at the St. Louis Fair, with $500,000 allocated for the work. The sculptures represented various occupants of the Louisiana territory in chronological order, the wild animals, the Indians, the trappers, the pioneers, the explorers, and lastly, the French and the Spanish. The most impressive sculpture at the Fair was the Statue of Liberty which crowned the Festival Hall. Designed by Evelyn B. Longman, the statue depicted a young man with both arms raised and in his left hand the laurels of victory. He symbolized the strength and the vitality of America.

The fairgoer of 1904 entered the St. Louis Expo through one of eleven gates. From the Lindell Gate, he viewed the Louisiana Purchase monument, the great basin of the Cascades, the Terrace of the States, the Fine Arts Building, and the forest in the background. He traveled from building to building on a railway which encircled the whole Exposition and had seventeen stops. At night he enjoyed the illumination of the fairgrounds. Most striking was the Palace of Electricity glowing in the dark with a diamond-like intensity. The peaks and parapets of each building were illuminated. It was a spectacular tribute to the infant god of electricity. Extending from one end of the Fair to the other, from the Lindell Gate to the Palace of Transportation, a distance of one mile, was the Pike or the main street of the Fair.

The displays of the pottery companies had an excellent location, the Palace of Mines and Metallurgy, to the left of the Lindell Gate. Here the potters worked in an area of 20,000 square feet. The Mines Building was a monument of Art Nouveau architecture, created by Theodore C. Link. It covered nine acres and cost $498,000 to construct. This building housed potteries such as Rookwood, Roseville, and Weller, tableware producers, and representatives of the clayworkers' magazines. Roseville Pottery had a large display in section ten on the north aisle. Here G. W. Parker turned jugs and vases on a small potter's wheel. Roseville exhibited Rozane and

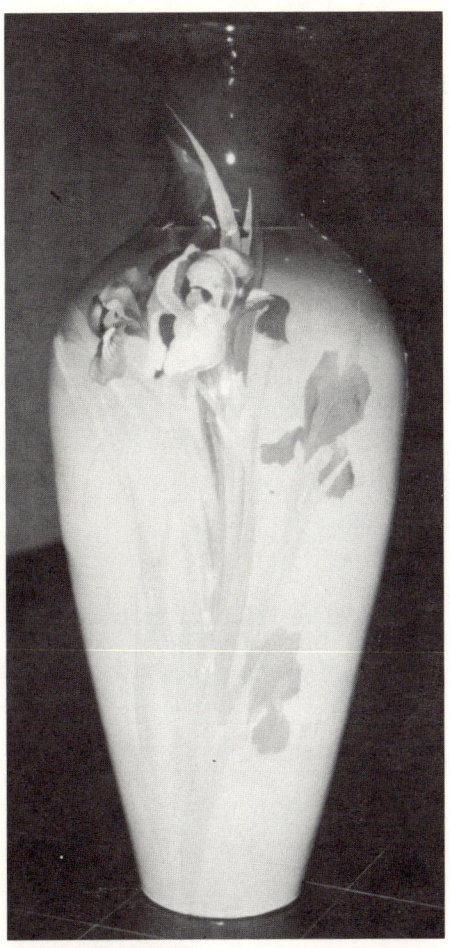

Fig. 56: Weller Eocean vase 51½" high, decorated with irises and artist signed by Frank Ferrell, exhibited at the St. Louis World's Fair. Collection: United Technologies. Photo courtesy of Rosalie Berberian.

Fig. 57: Weller Aurelian vase 39½" high, decorated with grapes and leaves, and exhibited at the St. Louis World's Fair. Collection: United Technologies. Photo courtesy of Rosalie Berberian.

Mongol, blood red vases created by John J. Herold, which won first prize at the Exposition.

Rookwood Pottery displayed a large Gothic window, a replica of one created for a New York cathedral. They also showed specimens of tile for the New York subway and a beautiful tile decorated mantel. H. A. Wheeler supervised Rookwood's exhibition. Weller Pottery had three displays, one in the Mines Building between Ohio Clay Products and the *Brick* exhibit, and two in the Jerusalem concession.

Of the thirty-two potteries which vied for the honor of building a model pottery, Weller Pottery was chosen. The model pottery was located in the Gulch near the Palace of Mines. Arthur Rose, in *House Furnisher*, October 1904, described it: "Starting with the various component parts, you are conducted through the different processes of grinding and pugging, throwing and turning, modeling, painting and decorating; in fact, everything but the firing and drawing of the kiln, these latter processes not being permitted by the officials for the general safety of the surrounding buildings." Rose described the process of turning. After he threw the pot on the wheel, the potter turned it on a lathe and removed the uneven thicknesses and the rough edges left by the throwing. When the pot was ready for decoration, the potter delivered it to the female decorators for slip painting.

The model pottery was quite an achievement. The fairgoer watched the clay transform from a crude mass of earth to a finished product, either a vase or a plaque. Clay bins at one end of the pottery held flint, spar, ball, and china clay. Viewers watched the clay mixed, sifted in the sifter, and agitated. They saw the clay go through a filter press where excess water was removed, then through a pugmill where it was tempered and shaped for use. They watched the jigger man jigger the clay, or throw it on the wheel. A kiln waited to receive the finished product.

The model pottery was quite complete, with the kiln and the clay bins on one end of the building, and a sales room on the other end. The Pottery had on display for sale: Dickensware, Lonhuda, Louwelsa, and Sicard, the latter much admired. People left St. Louis praising Weller Pottery. Sales increased dramatically after the Fair.

Sam Weller's investment of $30,000 at St. Louis, however, was a loss leader in terms of actual profits at the Fair. Pottery sales were good at the Expo, but they did not equal capital outlay. Promotion was the aim, and the promotion was a resounding success.

A large seven foot high Weller Aurelian vase, dated 1897, won the Gold Medal at the Fair (Fig. 55). Decorated with huge ripe red apples by artist Frank Ferrell, the vase measured four feet in diameter and weighed over 400 pounds. With its bright gold highlights, glossy brown glaze, and superb decoration, the vase truly deserved its Gold Medal in the Arts Category.

In addition to the seven foot high Aurelian vase, Frank Ferrell also decorated with purple irises a huge Eocean vase, 51½ inches high, exhibited at St. Louis (Fig. 56). This was one of four large vases: the second an Eocean vase about 52 inches high, and two Aurelian vases, one 39½ inches high, decorated with grapes and leaves, and another Aurelian vase over five feet high (Fig. 57). Author and pottery scholar Rosalie Berberian recently discovered these magnificent vases at the Corporate Headquarters of United Technologies in Hartford, Connecticut. Hidden away since 1904-1905, these four vases were found in an inventory of the Essex Wire Company. Essex Wire took over Weller Pottery in 1947 and acquired four large crates, marked with exhibition labels from the St. Louis Fair. When United Technologies bought Essex Wire in 1974, they discovered the four vases in the Zanesville plant and had them shipped to corporate headquarters in Hartford, Connecticut, where they reside now in the corridor outside the executive offices. Unfortunately, they are not on display to the general public.

The five large vases Weller exhibited at St. Louis competed for medals with the other potteries. As noted above, the seven foot Aurelian vase won the Gold Medal. For the general public, Weller provided plaques and red clay vases as souvenirs of the Fair. The workers made these simply and quickly and left them unglazed. They decorated some vases in slip with figures of children. They slip painted one tiny vase with a boy in a dunce's cap. Some vases sported handsome Indian chieftains, signed and dated "LPE St. Louis 04" (Fig. 58). Most of these red clay jugs, pitchers, and vases were unmarked.

The Pottery made plaques of white clay, pressed in molds, sometimes stained in pastel pink or green colors and signed on the reverse in tiny block letters, WELLER. Workers molded several presidential plaques, notably busts of Grant, Jackson, Lincoln, McKinley, Roosevelt, and Washington (Figs. 59-61). Sicard also made plaques with busts of famous men like President McKinley. President McKinley was assassinated in 1901 at the Pan American Exposition in Buffalo, the Fair that preceded St. Louis. His vice president Theodore Roosevelt became president after his death and was president during the St. Louis Expo.

Weller produced several map plaques of the United States with the Louisiana Purchase outlined, signed LPE, and dated 1803. Shown here is one in red clay marked "World's Fair St. Louis 1904" above the map and the name of the pottery, "Weller Pottery, Zanesville, Ohio," below it (Fig.

Fig. 58: Weller World's Fair souvenir mug 5¼" high, incised with an Indian chief and marked LPE '04 St. Louis. Collection: Dora Betts.

Fig. 59: *Marked Weller*: World's Fair presidential plaque of William McKinley, 4⅝" diameter.

Fig. 60: Three *marked Weller* World's Fair presidential plaques: George Washington, Andrew Jackson, Ulysses Grant. Each is 4⅝" diameter. Collection: Dick and Nancy Sigafoose.

Fig. 61: *Marked Weller*: World's Fair presidential plaque of Abraham Lincoln, 4⅝" diameter.

Fig. 63: Weller World's Fair souvenir vase in red clay 3½" high, with a small girl holding a banner which says: St. Louis 1904.

62). The plaque on the right, Fig. 62, shows the 1904 Democratic presidential candidate Alton B. Parker. Modeler Hugo Herb created the circular plaques with the presidential heads and the maps.

Other souvenir items Weller produced at the Fair included: a small round red clay vase with a little girl holding a banner proclaiming "St. Louis 1904" (Fig. 63); a white clay mug with the Louisiana Purchase map; coasters with the Purchase map embossed and colored red, white, and blue; tiny tableware favors, with the name of the Pottery etched out, handpainted with red flowers, red clay vases with white decorations signed Jerusalem. Weller had two displays in the Jerusalem concession, which may explain the Jerusalem signature.

Sam Weller won acclaim at St. Louis and his Pottery became famous and respected. Arthur Rose wrote in *House Furnisher*, October, 1904: "Mr. Weller is to be congratulated on his enterprise as a public benefactor and educator, for he gives the opportunity to hundreds of thousands of people to become conversant with the various methods of the art of potting."

Fig. 62: Three *marked* Weller World's Fair plaques: Theodore Roosevelt, Map plaque of the United States with the Louisiana Purchase outlined, and Alton B. Parker. Each is 4⅝" diameter. Collection: Dora Betts.

Chapter VII
Lamps and Lighting Devices

"I am ready to show samples of my new lines. Pottery lamps will be a feature," Weller announced on January 13, 1898, in *C & G*. From 1898 until well after 1920, the Pottery offered an impressive array of lighting devices: oil lamps, boudoir lamps, candelabras, chandeliers, and floor lamps.

"C. H. Taylor, representing S. A. Weller, has some beauties in pottery base lamps. The signed pieces are works of art, and the Louwelsa is fast taking a front rank in the potteries of the world. The Dickens line, for a cheaper grade, is also good," wrote *C & G*, April 7, 1898. The company boasted in the same journal, June 9, 1898: "Our lamps, of 'Louwelsa' and 'Dickens Ware' Pottery, are becoming equally popular with our line of Jardinieres. We are now painting special globes, thereby enabling us to show a lamp complete and more desirable than ever." Typical of the attractive lamps offered by the company was the Louwelsa oil lamp pictured here which stands 26 inches high (Fig. 64). Artist Frank Ferrell painted bright red and yellow roses on it. The pottery base was fitted with a large brass oil canister made by the Success Company.

Weller developed pottery lamp bases in many lines: Aurelian, Dickensware I, Louwelsa, Matt Green, Turada, and Woodcraft. Note the three feet high Aurelian oil banquet lamp pictured in Chapter XX. The company fitted the lamps with cylindrical brass oil canisters made by Success or the Edward Miller Company. Weller shipped pottery bases to C. H. Taylor in New York, where they were combined with oil canisters, burners, chimneys, and shades. The Pottery made several Dickensware I lamps. J. W. Brooks, Jr., whose name was impressed inside the lamp bases: "Designed by J. W. Brooks, Jr.," created some of them.

As noted above, for a brief period in 1898, Weller decorators hand painted not only the pottery bases, but also the glass ball shades to match each other. It is a joy to find a complete Weller oil lamp with the brass fixtures, burner, chimney, and matching shade all intact.

The golden years for Weller lamps, from 1898 to 1920, were a splendid testimony to the competence, the originality, and the artistry of the decorators. Their hand painted designs and unusual shapes delighted the consumer. On April 20, 1899, *C & G* described an odd lamp: the pedestal base sprouted dolphin-like arms which held a vase containing an oil font. Aladdin-shaped Louwelsa oil lamps appeared in this same period. On April 26, 1900, *C & G* announced that C. H. Taylor had received Louwelsa and Aurelian lamps, including one Louwelsa lamp molded like a Roman urn, with a full blown white rose as decoration.

Fig. 64: *Impressed* Louwelsa Weller oil lamp 26" high, artist signed by Frank Ferrell. Photo by Leach.

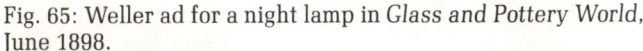

Fig. 65: Weller ad for a night lamp in *Glass and Pottery World*, June 1898.

Fig. 67: Roma chandelier, 22" diameter, marked with the ink stamp Weller Ware mark, and signed Rush Brothers, Pd. June 21, 1912. Collection: Robert Miller and Glen Vogt.

Fig. 66: *Impressed Louwelsa* Weller electric lamp, with a 13" high base, artist signed L.M. Collection: Dick and Nancy Sigafoose.

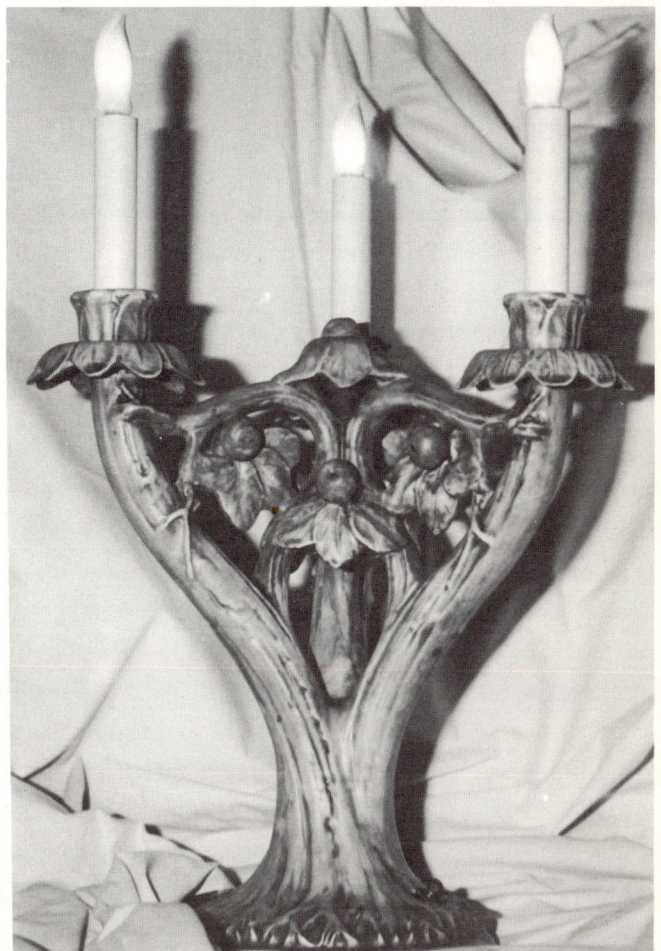

Fig. 68: *Marked Weller:* Woodcraft candelabra lamp 13½" high. Collection: Esther and Martin Myers.

In 1900 Weller continued to produce Aurelian, Dickensware I, Louwelsa, and Turada lamps. The Dickensware I lamps came in glossy dark blue, brown, or black, illumined by a burst of color from the rose or daffodil underglaze decoration. The company also made a night lamp advertised in *GPW*, June 1898 (Fig. 65). Notable for its molded shells and seaweed, its handpainted shade, and its petite size, the lamp was a rarity. The Pottery offered graceful, footed Turada oil lamps with lace-like decoration typical to the line. The bases alone were about eight inches high. On November 27, 1902, *C & G* announced that Weller would discontinue the production of Louwelsa oil lamps. By 1908 Louwelsa electric lamps had supplanted them. Note the one pictured here, decorated with a rose by artist Lillie B. Mitchell (Fig. 66).

In 1907 and 1908 matt finished lamps appeared: Matt Green and Matt Ware lamps with blue and reddish brown backgrounds. Molded figures emerged in relief on the lamp bases: a nude male, an embossed eagle in flight, and a bird perched on a tree branch, according to *C & G*, April 11, 1907. In May 1908, *GPW* praised the Matt Green table lamps with colored glass shades, priced from $6.00 to $10.00. These Mission style, Grueby imitation lamps caught the public fancy. There was "a good call for lamps," *C & G* declared, October 22, 1908, since Weller had improved the shades and fittings.

Weller displayed electroliers or electric lamp supports at the Pittsburgh show in January 1908. On February 27, 1908, *C & G* noted the good reception given to Weller's new line of portable gas and electric lamps. The new lamps could take either oil or electricity, since they had the regulation five inch openings.

In 1914, Weller began to sell boudoir lamps. "The S. A. Weller Co. have just sent to C. H. Taylor . . . a line of small vases for lamp mounts for the new Princess lamps. They are in the concern's well-known Copra ware—a combination of rich coloring with a matt finish," announced *C & G*, October 8, 1914. Since this was the only description in the trade journals of Copra ware, it is impossible to identify the line. The Princess lamps were probably small bedside or table lamps.

The company introduced massive Roma lighting fixtures and chandeliers between 1912 and 1914. They usually measured about 18 to 22 inches in diameter and some weighed nearly twenty pounds. The chandelier pictured here has green leaf sprays and pink roses against its matt cream background (Fig. 67). The chandeliers often had the block impressed or the ink stamp Weller mark inside the fixture.

In 1918 Weller developed wall lamps resembling sconces with two light bulbs. Made in the Woodcraft finish, these wall lamps had molded birds in nests surrounded by flowers and framed by two tree branches. Each branch held a light bulb. The workers painted the birds, tree limbs, and fruit in naturalistic colors. The Weller catalogs pictured these sconces and a candelabra lamp to match them. The lamp had three branches, each one holding a candle lamp with a silk shade (Fig. 68). The company also made Woodcraft lamps with full size bluebirds and woodpeckers perched on tree stumps. These lamps were popular until 1920.

Fig. 69: A close up view of the Brighton parakeets on a floor lamp. Collection: Robert Miller and Glen Vogt.

Fig. 70: Brighton parakeet floor lamp 5½ feet high. Collection: Robert Miller and Glen Vogt.

Weller Brighton birds decorated floor lamps produced at another company. Note the floor lamp here and its colorful Brighton parakeets with red heads, blue bodies, and yellow breasts (Figs. 69, 70). The birds stand right below the lamp shade. The Pottery probably sold the Brighton parakeets to a lamp company, to be used as decorative accessories.

After 1920 Weller Pottery continued to display, to advertise, and to sell electric lamps. They came in the new lines: Blo Red, Blue Ware, Bo Marblo, Bronze Ware, Frosted Matt, Hudson, LaSa, Selma, and Voile (Fig. 71). From the early Louwelsa oil lamps to the electrified Roma chandeliers and Woodcraft sconces, the company presented a dramatic collection of lighting devices.

Fig. 71: Weller electric lamp bases: Blue Ware, Louwelsa, and Hudson. Collection: H.M. Dietrich.

Chapter VIII
Early Weller Lines 1897-1910

Edwin AtLee Barber in *Marks of American Potters,* 1904, mentioned seven lines of Weller Pottery: Aurelian, Auroro, Dickensware, Eocean, Louwelsa, Sicardo, and Turada. These lines all appeared before 1904. From Barber and from the trade journals came accounts of the new lines, approximate dates they appeared, and descriptions of them. The period from 1897 to 1910 was innovative and productive for Weller. Lines grew out of other lines like buds shooting forth from leafy foliage. From Eocean grew Etna and Cameo Jewel. From Louwelsa came Aurelian.

Weller Pottery proclaimed itself "the largest Jardiniere Manufacturer in the World," in *C & G* on March 4, 1897. The journal pictured several jars and pedestals with intricate raised decorations: cherubs, Greek figures, men and mermaids riding dolphins, seahorses, shells, and snails. Overly ornate, verging on rococo, these large jars, peds, and vases decorated many a Victorian porch or conservatory. Note here the matt blue vase, possibly designed by Albert Radford, with graceful mermaids riding conch shells drawn by seahorses, and boys riding dolphins, in white clay relief designs (Fig. 72). These wares were made from about 1897 to 1901. *C & G* pictured a jardiniere with a boy riding a dolphin on April 4, 1901. On the rim of the jar were seahorses, snails, and ribbons, while the pedestal had raised leaves, flowers, and fish heads. There was an exuberance to these early jars, molded and designed so intricately. The modelers seemed to believe that more was better and to let imaginations soar.

Fig. 72: Weller matt blue vase 10" high, decorated with mermaids riding conch shells drawn by seahorses. Collection: Allan Wunsch.

Designed by Henry Schmidt, Turada was offered as early as 1897, noted in *CGL* on September 22, 1897 (Fig. 73). The renowned scholar and potter William P. Jervis, in his *Encyclopedia of Ceramics,* described it: "Turada ware, an invention of Mr. Weller, consists of pieces in vari-colored clays, sombre browns, orange and cream, with applied ornaments of pierced work judiciously and artistically introduced. The color schemes are admirable, and the general effect pleasing in the extreme . . ." The 1897 selection in the New York show room presented glossy blue, green, jet black, olive, and claret brown Turada ware. These pieces were festooned with raised, tube lined decorations and were impressed Turada Weller on the base. In 1898 J. B. Owens Pottery offered a similar ware called Cyrano, which was often unmarked and confused with Weller Turada. Both Cyrano and Turada had "applied ornaments" on a high gloss, dark background. Most Turada, however, was signed.

In 1898, Aurelian made its appearance (Figs. 74, 75). C. H. Taylor received a shipment of Aurelian and Eocean in July 1898. Very similar to

Fig. 73: *Impressed* Turada Weller mug 6" high. Collection: Lee Dietrich.

Fig. 74: *Incised* Aurelian: Umbrella stand 23½" high, artist signed C.L.L. Collection: Paul and Rosemary Enoch. Photo by Ralph Crowell Associates.

Louwelsa in its standard brown glaze, Aurelian differed in the method of application of background colors. Marcus Benjamin explained the technique in *GPW*, in March 1907: the background colors were applied with a brush instead of with an atomizer. As noted in Chapter IV, Louwelsa background colors were applied with an atomizer. Anyone who examines an Aurelian vase can see the brush strokes verging sharply into one another, especially in the golden sunburst of light around the decoration. The decorators usually chose fruit and flowers as subjects. John J. Herold, however, did a fine portrait in Aurelian of a mother duck and her ducklings, (C-7). The world's tallest vase was an Aurelian vase, measuring seven feet high, displayed at the St. Louis World's Fair.

Weller made several gigantic Aurelian vases, described in *CGL*, August 3, 1899, and discussed in Chapter VI. The vases stood five feet high and weighed 160 pounds each. They were hand decorated with roses or with grape clusters. The workers put seven five feet high vases in the kiln at one time, and all came out intact! The company displayed one vase at a street fair, and two at the St. Louis Exposition.

Fig. 75: Two *incised* Aurelian jardinieres and pedestals, 37½" high, the one on the left decorated with grapes and artist signed J., the one on the right decorated with roses, artist signed H.M. Collection: Paul and Rosemary Enoch. Photo by Ralph Crowell Associates.

Fig. 78: *Marked Weller:* Late Eocean vases 6″ high and 7″ high, decorated with violets. Collection: Dorothy Daniel. Photo by Leach.

Fig. 77: *Incised* Eocean Weller: Stork vase 8″ high, artist signed S. Collection: Dick and Nancy Sigafoose.

Fig. 76: *Incised* Eocean Weller: Vase 14″ high, artist signed by L.J. Burgess. Photo by Leach.

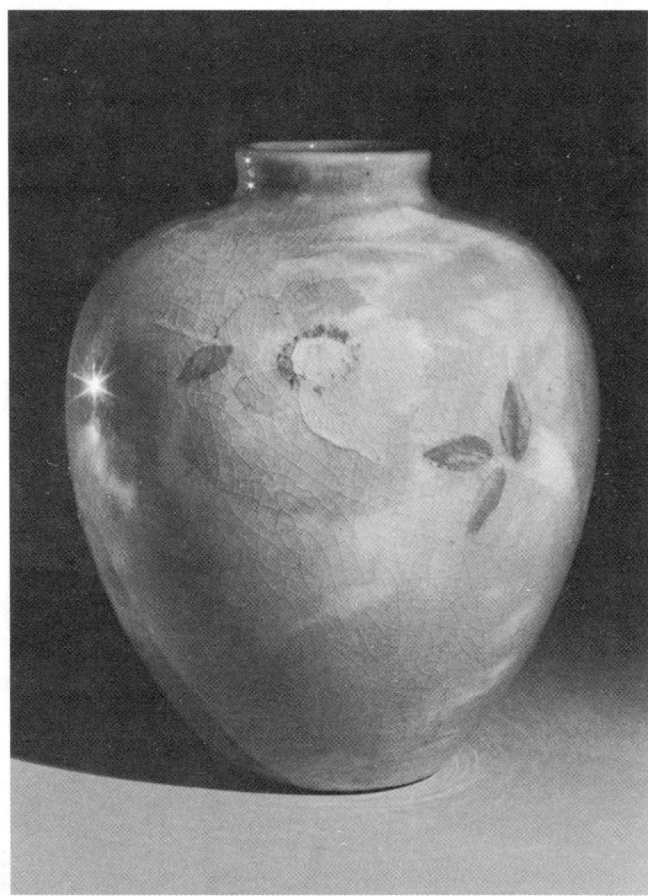

Fig. 79: *Marked Weller:* Auroro blue vase 6″ high. Photo by Leach.

Eocean was heralded as the best Weller ware ever in C & G, July 14, 1898. The early Eocean vases had a subtle romantic quality. On one vase a shadowy nude woman floated through space in shades of sea green and coral pink, while on another, bulrushes emerged from a sea green background. Light grays, pinks, pale blues, and greens predominated. Decorators sprayed on the background colors with an atomizer and painted flowers, fruit, and figures on Eocean. The name derived from ocean and suggested the ware was of the ocean, with sea colors and tones. Early Eocean was usually artist signed and developed no crazing. Frequently, the flowers had long stems as on the tall, daisy vase by Levi Burgess (Fig. 76). The line was popular, offered for a number of years, and mentioned frequently in the trade journals from 1898 to 1923. It came in all shapes and sizes from jars to vases to mugs. Animals and birds, especially storks, often embellished the vases.

Eocean passed through three stages of background coloring and decoration. The first stage, epitomized by the Levi Burgess vase, featured the pale grays, pinks, blues, and greens with graceful, artistically drawn flowers or fruit. The second stage was bolder with dark gray at the rim shading to light gray at the base and with decorations such as the stork (Fig. 77). The third stage or Late Eocean differed dramatically from the first two. The background colors again shaded from dark to light gray, but splashes of pink or green enlivened the backdrop and highlighted the heavy slip decoration of fruit or flowers, impressionistically and sometimes hastily applied at the top of each piece. Late Eocean was called Rochelle by collectors for years. The Weller catalogs pictured both lines and distinguished between them. Late Eocean came in vases, bowls, and a series of candlesticks ranging from six to ten inches high. Often, pink and purple violets adorned the vases (Fig. 78). The Late Eocean pieces were simple and visually pleasing.

CGL mentioned Late Eocean on February 26, 1923: "The Eocean line . . . is hand decorated, underglazed, with a type of decoration that is also very summery. Many flowers have been exploited. Here we find the delicate rose, side by side with the hardy daisy; the forget-me-not next to the carnation, etc. This line, too, embraces all shapes of candlesticks, bowls, jardinieres, baskets and also produces a new novelty in the form of handled bowls, nested." Workers signed Eocean on the base of each piece with the script incised Eocean or Eosian mark, and on occasion, Eocean Rose. All three signatures denoted the same line. At times, Eocean Rose had a rose decoration under the glaze.

When the Weller decorators decided to vary the background colors on Louwelsa from the deep browns to lighter colors, probably in response to Rookwood's success with the Iris Glaze and the Aerial Blue lines, they created a pastel rainbow of colors from the pale grays of Eocean and Etna to the sky blues of Auroro. Auroro had a high gloss glaze. The decoration was often the variegated background itself, with one or more flowers or fish in contrasting shades. On the Auroro vase shown here, the artist either brushed or sponged on the background colors of blue, cream, white, yellow, and peach, then painted a bright peach colored flower with a yellow pistil and stamen (Fig. 79). While some vases were marked Auroro or Auroral, this one was signed Weller on the base. The Auroro line usually had a mottled pink and blue, or blue and white background and an underglaze slip decoration of flowers or fish. Auroro embodied the lovely impressionistic quality of a Monet painting of field flowers. The company offered the line before 1904.

Appearing in 1906, Etna and Cameo Jewel resembled Eocean. Eocean, however, was artist decorated with an underglaze slip painting, while Etna had the decoration molded in relief, then hand colored (Fig. 80). Both were glossy gray wares. Etna usually sported embossed fruit or flowers, though occasionally, a molded salamander or a snake emerged. The Pottery offered Etna until 1917 or later.

Cameo Jewel resembled Etna. The earliest pieces comprised cameo decorated jars and peds, with jewels inlaid around the rims or the bases. The jewels were clay raised in relief and painted bright red, green, purple, black, or blue. Famous characters such as Beethoven or Pope Leo XIII appeared on raised white cameo discs. The background colors were glossy or matt gray, lavender, or green, or shades of all three. The raised discs recalled Dickensware III. The Weller catalogs pictured Cameo Jewel in jars, peds, low bowls, and umbrella stands. Some jars and peds featured cameo profiles of ladies. Peacock feathers with inlaid jewels decorated vases and umbrella stands (Fig. 81).

One Cameo Jewel vase highlighted Pope Leo XIII. Since the Pope died in 1903, the company may have made it as a commemorative piece. A rosary was draped over the front and the back side of the vase, while

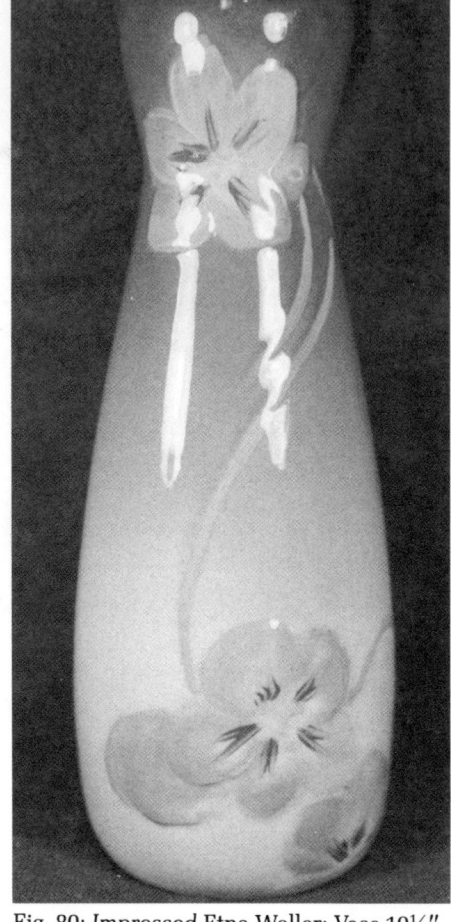

Fig. 80: *Impressed* Etna Weller: Vase 10½" high, decorated with pansies. Collection: Dick and Nancy Sigafoose.

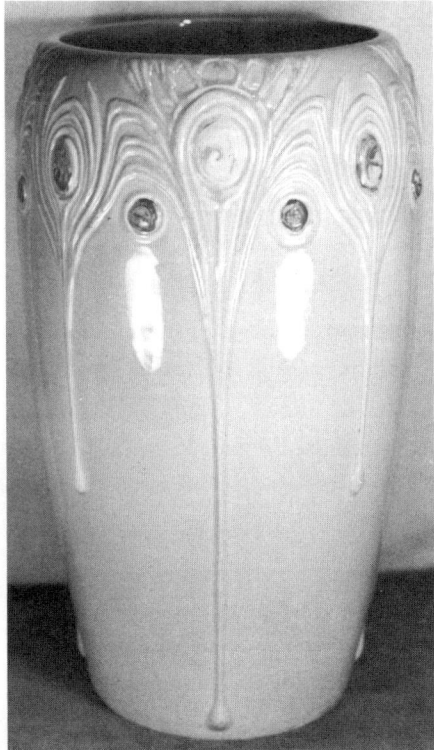

Fig. 81: *Marked Weller:* Cameo Jewel umbrella stand 20" high, decorated with peacock feathers. Collection: Dick and Nancy Sigafoose.

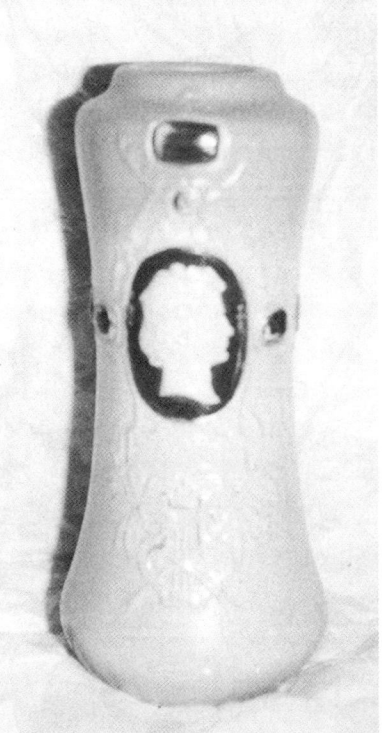

Fig. 82: *Marked Weller:* Cameo Jewel vase 14" high, with the bust of Beethoven. Collection: Arthur and Rita Townley.

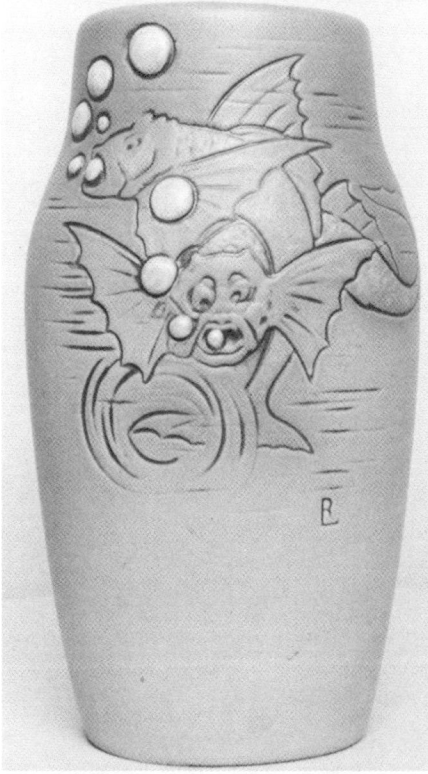

Fig. 83: *Marked Weller:* Cameo Jewel vase 11½" high, artist signed by Rudolph Lorber. Collection: Dora Betts.

on the front was a jeweled pectoral cross with the cameo portrait of Leo in its center. Decorators outlined the jewels and the cameo in gold and painted the background glossy gray. Another tall Cameo Jewel portrait vase had a cameo bust of Beethoven with an embossed harp below it (Fig. 82). Red, green, and blue jewels surrounded the portrait. Shown here is a Rudolph Lorber vase with fish blowing "jewel" bubbles against a matt blue and gray background (Fig. 83). In November 1907, *GPW* pictured a Cameo Jewel vase with an albatross at the top and a fish at the base.

By 1906 the Weller inventory included these lines: Art Nouveau, Aurelian, Dickensware, Eocean, Etna, Floretta, Jap Birdimal, Louwelsa, Matt Ware, and Sicardo. Floretta resembled Etna with its high gloss, and with its decoration of fruit or flowers, raised and hand painted under the gray or brown glaze (Fig. 84). The prettiest pieces of Floretta were glossy gray with purple grapes or pink daisies. *House Furnisher* described Brown Floretta in August-September 1904: "This is in the well known Louwelsa colors, and is decorated in bas relief with grapes, cherries and fruits in general. The beautiful shadings, from a dark to a light golden brown, and

Fig. 84: Three *impressed* Floretta Weller wares: Brown glaze vase 7" high; brown glaze ewer 4¾" high, and large gray Floretta vase 14" high. Collection: Sigafoose and Smith. Photo by Sigafoose.

the faithful reproductions of the natural colors of the fruit, give this ware especial artistic merit."

Jap Birdimal was a line with Japanese decoration, indicated by the title Jap, with animals and birds as subjects, implied by the word Birdimal, according to *C & G*, November 10, 1904. Jap Birdimal and Rhead Faience were the same line. Created by Frederick H. Rhead, the line had hand applied decoration put on with a squeeze bag, in a technique called tube lining or raised line decoration. Rhead described this technique in "Pottery Class," in *Keramic Studio,* October 1909: "Decorations can be done entirely in outline. Good effects are obtained by allowing the largest surface to be covered with a mat glaze; small medallions or details can be tubed and filled in with bright glazes." Rhead drew the original designs for Jap Birdimal and gave them to the artists to execute. He taught them how to tube line vases, jars, pitchers, and mugs. He decorated some pieces himself with raised line decoration on a glossy blue or a brown background.

"Birdimal Ware is another underglaze line which will command considerable attention. The decorations here are birds, animals, Japanese and conventional designs, upon a ground color of blue, sea green or rich brown," wrote *House Furnisher* in August-September 1904. Geese, swans, rabbits, fish, and peacock feathers ornamented Jap Birdimal. Note the fish vase pictured here (Fig. 85). Four fish, colored green and blue, tube lined in black, swim through a foamy surf, tube lined in white slip on a Wedgwood blue ground. Japanese characters also appeared on Jap Birdimal. Men and women in kimonas, geisha girls with umbrellas adorned mugs, vases, and umbrella stands.

Fig. 85: Jap Birdimal vase 7″ high, with fish, artist signed F. Photo by Leach.

The Pottery marked some Jap Birdimal pieces, Rhead or Weller Rhead Faience. Note the three footed, green vase shown here with the incised mark on the base: Weller Rhead Faience (Fig. 86). Rhead himself may have signed the three piece tea set, in blue slip under the glaze on the base: Rhead. Deep blue, tube lined scenes of Dutch windmills, houses, rambling fences, and trees graced the teapot, sugar bowl, and creamer (Fig. 87). Tube lined hearts, a characteristic of Rhead's work in England, festooned the lids on the teapot and the sugar bowl. Jap Birdimal reflected the youthful zest and creativity of Frederick H. Rhead, at age 24.

By 1906 landscapes decorated Jap Birdimal. Six sizes of jardinieres appeared in *C & G*, June 14, 1906, with the trees painted deep blue and occasionally tube lined in white slip on a pale blue background. Some jars had dark blue houses with white moons posed above them; others had forests and cottages, or even villages nestled among the trees. The leaves on the trees looked like an effusion of blue bubbles, a characteristic of Rhead's art work.

On July 17, 1902, *C & G* announced Rubina, a line like Louwelsa but without decoration. Made in jars, peds, and umbrella stands, the line had a glossy glaze which combined reds, browns, and greens. On July 23, 1903, *C & G* described Rubina: "The blended glazes also show a newness in the harmonization of colors—rich reds, browns and greens being exquisitely intermingled. One design has four panels on both the jar and pedestal. Each panel is separated by an embossed effect that takes the form of a

Fig. 86: *Incised* Weller Rhead Faience: Vase 4½″ high, decorated with six geese, artist signed C.M.M. Collection: Dora Betts.

lion's head at the top and its paws at the bottom. The subject is finely executed in natural colors."

As noted in Chapter I, the tiny catalog *Weller Pottery* enumerated the lines offered by the Pottery before 1910: "The lines we manufacture are the Louwelsa, Aurelian, Jap Birdimal, Golbrogreen, Eocean, Sicardo, Oriental, Monochrome, Pictoral, Hunter and Floretta in glazed, the L'Art Nouveau, Dickens and Perfecto in unglazed." Three of the lines mentioned in this catalog were impossible to document: Golbrogreen, Monochrome, and Oriental. The catalog also boasted about the Weller artists and their underglaze decoration. "Almost every flower known to Botanical science is employed in some form or other on softly blended grounds; new and exquisite decorations are produced; and each piece is regarded a complete and worthy work, the results of these craftsmen." From Auroro to Turada, the Weller lines introduced from 1897 to 1910 were artistic and imaginative.

Fig. 87: Weller Rhead Faience tea set, signed Rhead, with a creamer 4¼" high, a covered sugar bowl 3⅞" high, and a teapot 7" high. Collection: Sheila Amdur.

Chapter IX
The French Connection: Art Nouveau, Matt Green, Sicard

The Art Nouveau movement began in Paris in 1895 with the opening of a shop called L'Art Nouveau, specializing in modern design. By 1900 the name of the shop and its contents had instigated a whole decorative art style called Art Nouveau. French artists such as Emile Gallé, Louis Majorelle, and Alphonse Mucha developed and enhanced the style, creating asymmetrical, naturalistic works of art in glass, furniture, and posters. The Art Nouveau style incorporated these elements: the curved or asymmetrical line; the nude figure represented by the female with flowing golden hair; flowers on elongated stems such as the lily or the columbine; peacocks, butterflies, mermaids, fish, all in motion. The artists preferred pastel colors: pale gray, light green, blue, lavender, salmon, and pink.

Like the glassmakers and artists, French potters responded to the new style. They created flambé glazes, derived from Chinese and Japanese designs, and incorporated plant forms into their vases. Ernest Chaplet adopted flambé glazes, while his pupil Auguste Delaherche created new shapes and designs on pottery, using the colored glaze as ornament. Clement Massier perfected the iridescent glaze, and his pupil Jacques Sicard brought it to Weller in America. Edmund Lachenal made vases in flower forms. Many of these potters displayed their new wares at the Paris Exposition of 1893, where American potters could see and study them. They returned to America to imitate the new designs and to create an Art Nouveau movement in American pottery.

Always ready to respond to popular fashion, Sam Weller incorporated the Art Nouveau style in a line which he called Art Nouveau. With its soft matt finish in sea green, salmon, and white, the line included shell shaped vases, flower forms, vases with raised designs of grapes or poppies, and ewers or vases with ladies in flowing white garments surrounded by flowers (Fig. 88). Note here the Art Nouveau vase with the blonde lady in profile, the back of the vase decorated with a graceful, whorled shell design interspersed with pink blossoms (Fig. 89). Weller's lady resembled those of French artist George de Feure, who made a series of drawings of ladies in profile, with long wispy hair, aquiline noses, yearning eyes, and faces surrounded by lilies, roses, or hydrangeas. Weller's Art Nouveau lady appeared on a pale green background, her face accented by long stemmed poppies, her hair wispy and flowing, and her eyes pensive.

Fig. 88: *Marked Weller*: Art Nouveau vase 15" high, with two ladies. Collection: Robert Miller and Glen Vogt.

Fig. 90: *Impressed* Art Nouveau Weller jardiniere 9" high, with pheasants. Collection: Robert Miller and Glen Vogt.

Crockery and Glass Journal announced the Art Nouveau line January 14, 1904, and noted that it comprised: umbrella stands, jars and peds, vases, all with raised decorations on a matt green and buff background (Fig. 90). By April 28, 1904, the Art Nouveau shell vase with the lady in profile had arrived, and by May 26, Art Nouveau umbrella stands with raised flowers, fruit, dragons, and pheasants came into stock. Weller Pottery made Art Nouveau from about 1904 to 1907, in a matt green and pink finish as well as a glossy brown glaze (Fig. 91). The same shapes came with the matt finish and the gloss glaze, but the company developed fewer glossy Art Nouveau pieces.

The Weller potters borrowed styles and techniques from the French potters Auguste Delaherche and Clement Massier. The Matt Green line derived from the pottery of Delaherche, while the Sicard line adopted the Reflets Métalliques of Massier. Auguste Delaherche created a unique plant form of pottery in a matt glaze, with shapes suggesting pumpkins, pears, and flower cups. His display at the Exposition Universelle in Paris in 1889 introduced his work to the public and won immediate approval. The simple, graceful shapes of his vases suggested the naturalistic and oriental influences common to Art Nouveau. Sometimes, he decorated his ware with natural forms such as a rose, a clover, a thistle, or peacock feathers in a wreath.

Anna Leonard described "A Visit to the Pottery of Auguste Delaherche," in *Keramic Studio,* September 1900: "He obtains wonderful effects by using enamels or glazes that flow, in connection with a glaze that is permanent, thus using the softer glaze at the top and letting it flow down the vase over another color." Delaherche was famous for his drip glazes.

Fig. 89: *Impressed* Art Nouveau Weller shell vase 6" high. Collection: Lillian Saxe. Photo by Leach.

After she attended the Paris Exposition, Anna Leonard wrote an article on it for *Keramic Studio* in August 1900. She was impressed by the luster pottery of Massier and by the work of Delaherche and wrote of him: "His glazes are beautiful, not like glass, but soft, smooth and semi dull, like the shell of an egg. All the potters seem to be trying for that effect." The work of Delaherche influenced American potters, causing a bevy of imitations at Grueby, Rookwood, and Weller. Weller potters copied Delaherche's drip glazes, his embossed stylized flowers on stems, his embossed leaf designs in panels, putting them on various lines.

William Grueby of the Grueby Faience Company admired the pottery of Delaherche. He tried to buy models from Delaherche, who did send him sketches of models, but the price was too high for Grueby. Using the sketches, Grueby created a matt finish pottery, imitative of plant forms. He displayed his pottery in Boston in 1897, at the Paris Exposition in 1900, and at the St. Louis Expo in 1904.

Like Delaherche, Grueby rejected underglaze decoration and let the glaze and form serve as decoration on his vases. With its bold matt green glaze, its leaf motifs, pointed, blunt leaves set in double and triple rows, Grueby's pottery transformed the ceramic world. He used a variety of leaves: lily, mullein, plantain, narcissus, and arrowroot. He did not employ molds. Like other artists in the Arts and Crafts Movement, Grueby insisted on handwork, simple colors, and shapes. Craftsman Gustav Stickley used Grueby vases to enhance his famous oak furniture and decorated his model homes with Grueby tiles.

Introduced about the time that standard glaze pottery was at its apogee, Grueby pottery gave American potters a new direction. Shortly after 1900, all the major companies, including J. B. Owens, Rookwood, and Weller, began to imitate Grueby's matt glaze. The commercial potters, however, could mass produce the matt green pottery, while Grueby and his staff made each piece by hand. He had to charge $15 to $50 per vase to make a profit. Naturally, he was undersold by Weller and by the other potteries which used molds and faster production methods. Despite his success initially, his awards at the Paris Exposition in 1900 and at St. Louis in 1904, where he won the Grand Prize, Grueby abandoned the production of art ware around 1911.

To compete with Grueby, Weller introduced Matt Green and Weller Matt Ware. *American Pottery Gazette* wrote in April 1905 about "S. A. Weller's New Matt Glazes," and pictured several vases including one with a nude male molded in relief on one large vase. The *Gazette* noted that Weller admired the work of the Oriental potters, in particular the color and the texture of their glazes. Weller Matt Ware glazes were veined, streaked, or mottled, and the figures were modeled in high and low relief (Figs. 92, 93). Some vases had human figures, others had birds or foliage, according to the *Gazette*. On August 24, 1905, *C & G* described teapots shaped like frogs, and also candelabra, vases, jugs in shades of green, gray, or reddish brown with dark veins. Workers molded human figures, birds, frogs, mice, and fruit in relief on these new Weller Matt wares.

CGL noted the appearance of Matt Green in jars, peds, and umbrella

Fig. 91: *Impressed* Art Nouveau Weller: Glossy brown pitcher 12″ high, decorated with raised grapes and leaves. Collection: Ed Gisel.

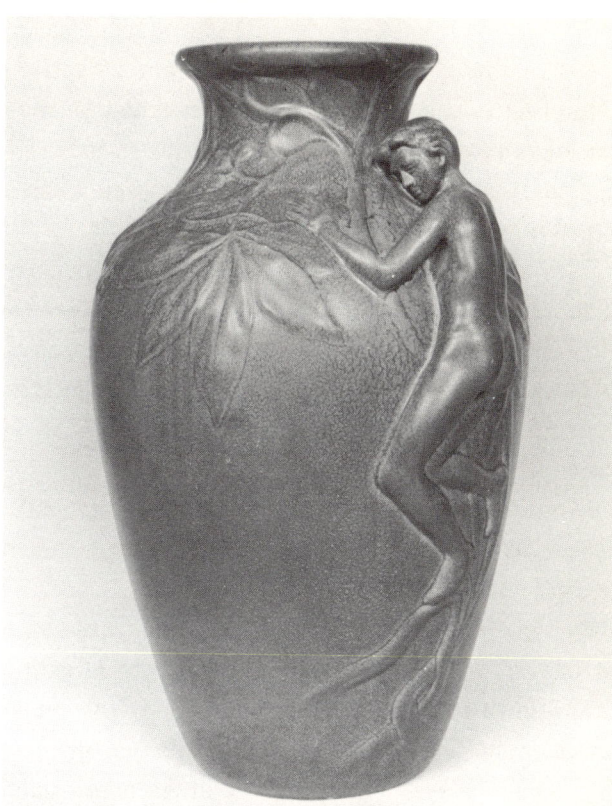

Fig. 93: Weller Matt Ware Man vase 18″ high, with a dark gray green matt finish, marked Weller on the side and the bottom of the vase. Collection: Gary Struncius.

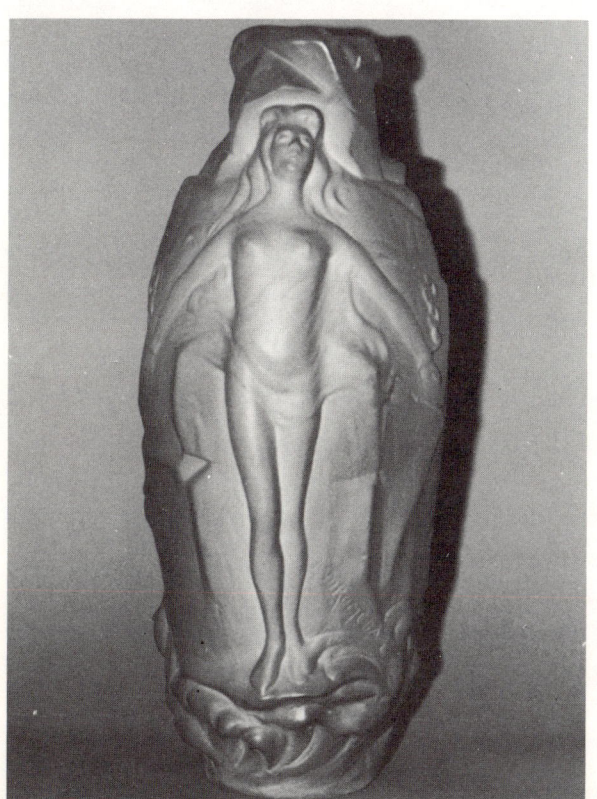

Fig. 92: *Incised* Weller Matt Ware: "Andromeda" vase 16″ high, artist signed by C.B. Upjohn and dated 1903, with a gray green matt finish. Collection: Jean and Richard Danielson. Photo by D.L. Hill.

Fig. 94: *Marked Weller:* Matt Green jardiniere and pedestal 27½″ high, with large, embossed hosta leaves. Collection: Norman Haas. Photo by Deb Nance.

stands on September 8, 1906: "The surface is not solidly green, but possesses a sort of crystalline appearance that is conspicuous without detracting in the slightest degree from the warmth and richness of its grass-like color. Some pieces are devoid of embossment, but others have frog, leaf and floral designs in fairly strong relief that are mighty attractive." (Fig. 94).

Weller advertised Matt Green in GPW in December 1906 and in February 1908. The 1908 ad proclaimed, "Matt Green Ware the Present Rage," and "The New Pottery LAMP Lines with colored art glass shades are radically different from anything on the market." In September 1908, GPW remarked that the greatest number of orders at the Weller factory were for Matt Green lamps.

From 1905 to 1913, Weller Matt Green sold well. Bedford Matt Green, discussed in C & G on December 12, 1907, came in sixteen different patterns. As late as June 12, 1913, C & G wrote about the Zanesville potteries: "The approach of summer has caused an increased demand for jardinieres and art pottery items for porch and outdoor purposes, and the plants in this district are simply loaded with business. The matt green treatments on jars are very popular this season."

Clement Massier attracted the attention of American potters with his iridescent pottery called Reflets Métalliques. On November 20, 1895, CGL described the painstaking process of making the ware, the colorings of purple, green, gold, and red, and the loss of pieces during firing. As early as 1889, Massier exhibited his Reflets Métalliques at the Paris Exposition.

Massier developed Reflets at Golfe Juan, near Cannes, France. William Jervis in his book *Rough Notes on Pottery* described the production of Reflets Métalliques. First, the vase or plaque was painted with metallic oxides, principally copper and silver. During firing, artificial air currents entered the kiln and caused a partial crystallization of the oxides in the pigments, which left a beautiful metallic deposit or iridescence. Motifs on the iridescent vases and jars ranged from starfish to peacock eyes, feathers, palm leaves, and thistles. Massier signed his work Massier or C. M.

Jacques Sicard, an employee of Massier, left France with Henri Gellée to come to America in 1901 (Fig. 95). To commemorate their departure he made a plaque which read: "The unknown awaits us. Go, and be happy. 10 o'clock in the evening, 24 December 1901. J. Sicard." Arthur Rose wrote in *House Furnisher,* October 5, 1903: "Mr. J. Sicard severed his connection with M. C. Massier and came to this country about two years ago, since which time he has been experimenting in this beautiful lustre work on Mr. Weller's pottery, and has now perfected a new ware, 'Sicardo,' which is destined to take its place among the highest grade art potteries of the world." He continued, "The specimens I had the pleasure of examining were equal to the very finest produced by Clement Massier, and many even surpassed them in beauty and lustre."

Mr. Rose described the process of making Sicard: "The vases are first treated all over with a secret metallic preparation, and then decorated in floral and other art effects, with chemically prepared metallic pigments, which, when fired at a great heat (by natural gas, instead of coal), are transformed into the most beautiful metallic lustres." Arthur Rose was the pottery expert for Tiffany and Company, which promoted and sold Sicard. Weller produced myriad items in the Sicard line: vases, candy dishes, umbrella stands, jars, star-shaped jewel boxes, plaques, candlesticks, figurines, and lamp bases.

Sam Weller yearned to know the formula for Sicard. He engaged Levi Burgess and Frank Ferrell to spy on Sicard as he made the pottery. Sicard did all that he could to preserve secrecy, working in a soundproof room lined with tin and locked with two locks. As a young man, decorator Charles Chilcote saw Sicard and Gellée work very fast turning pieces of Sicardo by hand on a projecting arm, rather than on a turn table. Sicard tried to keep the formula a secret, because he had heard that Sam Weller fired William Long, after he obtained the formula for making Lonhuda. Hence, Sicard refused to allow Ferrell or Burgess to assist him, and he locked them out.

Weller Sicard appeared on the market around 1903 and was actively promoted in 1905 in the trade journals. On May 18, 1905, *C & G* praised its superb luster effects in garnets, purples, greens, browns, and reds, which resembled metal rather than pottery. The journal remarked that the unique flower designs seemed to have eaten their way through the thin coating of color to become part of the metal body.

Sicardo or Sicard ware was iridescent pottery in shades of magenta, green, gold, silver, and purple, with designs of stars, flowers, seahorses, or

Fig. 95: Jacques Sicard on the left and Henri Gellée on the right. Sicard created Weller Sicard. Courtesy of Mose Mesre.

dolphins worked into the glaze. A few pieces had molded designs under the glaze; others had maple leaves, daisies, seaweed, and stylized lilies. The name Sicard, Weller Sicard, or Sicardo appeared on the side of each piece (Fig. 96 and C-13).

In Norris Schneider's notebook is a "Memo of a Conversation with Sicard" on Weller stationery, in which Sicard asked Weller if he could bring two assistants from France to help him make Sicard ware. He told Weller that one person could decorate twenty large vases per day, which would sell for $100 each. Small pieces could sell for $20, with a production of one hundred per day. Sicard assured Weller that he himself could make one hundred pieces a day, if he worked fast and did not use much care. "The success of the ware depends on the thickness of the glaze—a heavy glaze taking the metallic colors best," Sicard said. He admitted that he had worked so long without a contract that he did not care if he had one or not. He would continue to make the best ware possible. He assured Weller that his two assistants from France would not know the formula for Sicard and could not divulge it to the other potteries. They would receive the same pay as the other decorators. Probably, Weller refused Sicard's request to hire the French decorators.

From this "Memo of a Conversation with Sicard," we can infer: 1. that Sam Weller feared that J. B. Owens or Roseville would discover the formula for making Sicard; 2. that he wished to sell Sicard to a mass market; 3. that the expense of making the ware concerned him. Indeed, Sicardo cost so much to produce that Weller sought alternatives to his dependence on Jacques Sicard.

In 1906 Sam Weller tried to buy the formula for Reflets Métalliques from Clement Massier and his son Achille. On August 10, 1906, Achille Massier wrote Weller quoting a price of $4000 for the formula: "For all this important information I ask twenty thousand francs (dollars 4000) a sum

Fig. 96: Three *marked* Weller Sicard vases: Magenta vase 6½" high, purple and green vase 8" high, and magenta vase 4¼" high. Photo by Leach.

far from exorbitant in comparison to the yearly salaries that you have paid to Messrs. Sicard and Henri Gelée who manufacture reflets for your firm with such unsatisfactory results." Massier further informed Weller that Sicard was using an enamel rejected by Massier years ago because it caused so many failures. Now he used a green glaze enamel to assure successful firing.

Weller replied to Massier's letter on October 15, 1906, and refused the $4,000 offer because the price was too high. He asked if Massier had a lower price for the Reflets formula. If so, he needed to know it at once, since Sicard's contract had to be renewed. Undoubtedly, Massier did not answer Weller's letter or reduce his price for the Reflets Métalliques formula. Sicard continued to work for Weller until 1907. His tenure at the Pottery cost Weller $50,000 in salaries and materials. The conversation with Sicard and the letter to Massier are preserved in Norris Schneider's notebooks at the Ohio Historical Society.

On July 4, 1907, the Zanesville Times Signal reported: "J. W. Sicard, who for the past ten years has been a valued employee in the art department of the S. A. Weller Pottery, will with members of his family depart in a few days for his old home in France. During his residence in this city Mr. Sicard has made many friends who will miss him sadly. He has added much to the potter's art here and his work has never failed to win him recognition." A few errors arose in this account: Sicard was at Weller from 1902 to 1907, not a decade. Also, he was unmarried and had no family. In 1907 Sicard returned to France, where he ran a pottery at Amiens, until the Germans invaded the city during World War I. After he left Amiens, Sicard started a small pottery at Golfe Juan on the Mediterranean. He died in 1923.

In 1917 C. H. Taylor devoted one whole table in his Fifth Avenue building to display the Sicard line, a sign of its durability (Fig. 97). On December 12, 1918, PGB reported that Wanamaker's Department Store in New York had a big Sicardo display, with large and small vases arranged on a purple velvet drape. The store announced that they had taken over a collection of Sicardo to sell at prices much lower than those at the Pottery. The vases cost from $2.50 to $150 each.

Letters from Frederic Grant and Walter Hughes to Norris Schneider indicated that the company may have made Sicardo after Jacques Sicard left Weller. Hughes claimed in August 1956 that Weller continued to produce Sicardo, even after Sicard's departure. Frederic Grant said that in 1924 he found complete notes on Sicard's formula in French in a safe at the Pottery. He translated the notes and tried some of the simpler formulas for the ware. Former employees claimed that Sam Weller hired John Lessell in 1920 to make a metallic luster ware like Sicardo, but instead he created LaSa.

With its peacock feathers, female forms, and lilies on long stems, Art Nouveau made quite an impact on Weller Pottery in the early years of the twentieth century, reflected in such lines as Art Nouveau, Matt Green, and Sicard. The presence of Jacques Sicard and Henri Gellée at Weller Pottery served to increase the enthusiasm for things Gallic and to cement the French connection.

Fig. 97: Two marked Weller Sicard vases: Green and purple vase 5″ high, and magenta vase 6″ high, with maple leaves.

Chapter X

New Weller Lines 1906-1910

Between 1906 and 1910, Weller Pottery introduced many new lines: Bells of San Juan, Burnt Wood, Claywood, Dresden, Fru Russet, Fudzi, Greenaways, Narona, Norwood, Souevo, and Teakwood. They continued, however, to offer their old popular lines like Louwelsa, as they tried out their new repertoire.

Around 1905, Sam Weller enticed Japanese artist Gazo Fudji away from the Roseville Pottery, where he had created Rozane Woodland and Fujiyama. At Weller Pottery, Fudji developed the Fudzi line. The company included Fudzi in the Weller pottery on display in Richmond, Indiana in June 1906. The *Catalog of the Tenth Annual Exhibition of the Art Association, Richmond, Indiana* listed Fudzi along with nine other lines from S. A. Weller: Art Nouveau, Aurelian, Eocean, Fudzi Ware (five vases), Glazed Dickens, Jap Birdimal, Louwelsa, Matglaze Line, Matt Dickens, and Sicardo.

Gazo Fudji made Fudzi ware by a laborious process. After molding, while the clay was moist, he incised flowers or leaves into it and added tiny dots for further ornamentation, so that the vase had a pinprick effect. Then he colored the designs with rich orange, green, or brown enamels. Since the matt background was softly shaded, the enameled flowers stood out in stylized designs. On the vase pictured here, the zinnia appears to be cut in half at the top of the vase (Fig. 98). Note the exaggerated swirl of the petals and the leaves. The dark orange of the zinnia itself was complimented by orange enamel lining the inside of the vase. Fudzi resembled Rozane Woodland, but fewer pieces of Fudzi exist.

Another new line, Fru Russet was mentioned breifly in *CGL*, October 5, 1907, in a review of Weller ware at the Jamestown Exhibition: "The Weller Pottery, of Zanesville, has a very fine case of its various glazes. Most noticeable is the Sicardo ware in the huge lustre effects, over which are light fantastic tracings. There are some very pretty Louwelsa vases. Several pieces in the Dresden blue-gray effect make a fine showing. The mats are very good, indeed, and so also is the latest glaze, the Fru Russet, in gray with russet-like spots." Shown here are two vases which may be Fru Russet (Figs. 99, 100). They both have embossed or raised designs, one of seahorses, the other of horse chestnuts. Both have matt backgrounds with dark gray and deep red speckling throughout. Both are signed with the tiny Weller block mark impressed in the base, which was used in the early pre-1910 period. It is possible that these mystery vases are Fru Russet.

The Dresden line appeared in *C & G,* August 1, 1907. Against a blue or

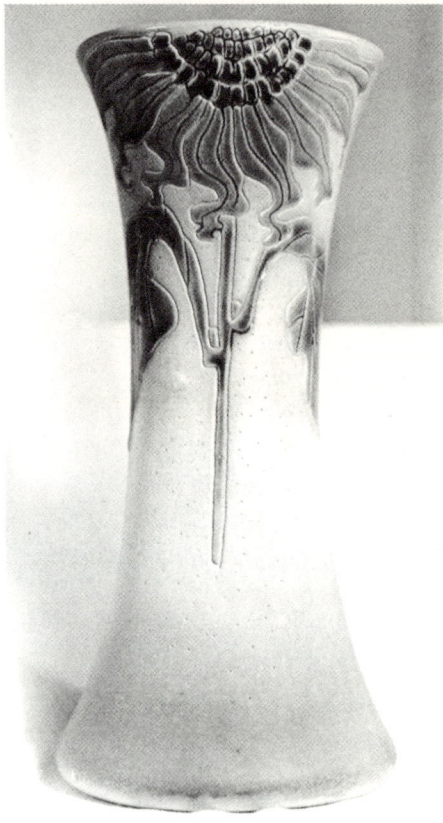

Fig. 98: *Marked Weller:* Fudzi vase 8½" high. Collection: Sheila Amdur.

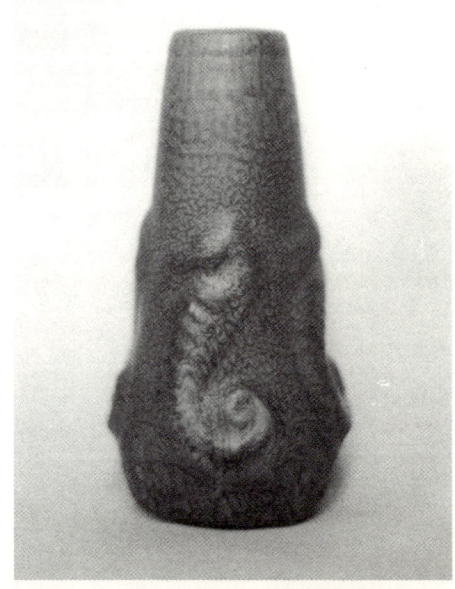

Fig. 99: *Marked Weller:* Fru Russet vase 5½" high, with embossed seahorses. Collection: Robert Newton.

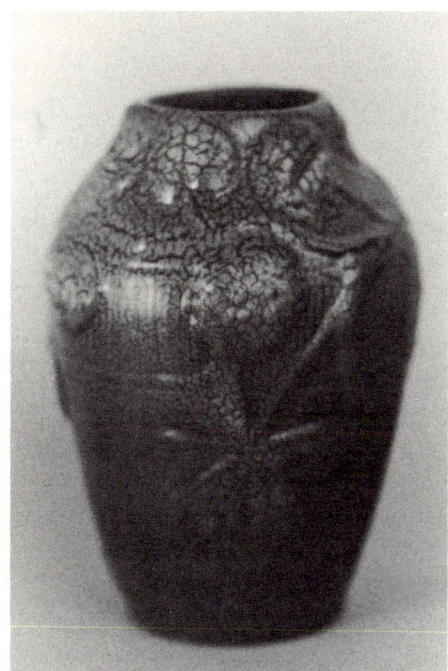

Fig. 100: *Marked Weller:* Fru Russet vase 8½" high, with embossed horse chestnuts. Photo by D.L. Hill.

Fig. 101: *Marked Weller:* Dresden vase 9" high, artist signed L.J.B. Collection: Paul and Rosemary Enoch. Photo by Ralph Crowell Associates.

green matt finish, artists slip painted dark blue windmills, sailboats, and Dutch boys and girls (Fig. 101). Occasionally, the decoration included a seascape fading into the distance behind the windmill or the Dutch boy. Mugs, vases, pitchers, and jardinieres were made and shown in the Weller catalogs. *P & G* discussed the Dresden line in November 1909, noting its low prices and active sales. Artist Levi Burgess painted and signed several Dresden vases.

The Dutch motif emerged also on Greenaways, described with Dresden in *P & G,* March 1909: "Some other novelties . . . were the so-called 'Greenaways' and 'Dresden'. The first named is decorated in grayish and pinkish tints—mostly displaying landscapes with windmills, also sea scenes with sailboats. The Dresden ware is similarly decorated, but the coloring is light blue." While Dresden was limited to shades of blue and green, Greenaways came in gray, pink, orange, green, and yellow shades, with slip decoration.

Pictured here is a Greenaways jardiniere (Fig. 102). The back of the jar has a gray windmill adjoining a small house. The front of the jar, as shown, has a much larger house with an orange roof. Two-thirds of the jar is grayish green; the top third is pale yellow green. Impressionistic, bushy green trees crowd the horizon, the decoration thickly applied. The factory often did not mark Greenaways. So far, collectors have found only jardinieres in this line. While both Dresden and Greenaways used the Dutch motif, the two lines differed greatly in shape and in color.

Souevo or Indian Ware was popular from 1907 to 1910. It came in thirty-six different shapes, from vases to pitchers, covered jars, wallpockets, and hanging baskets (Fig. 103). Made from porous red clay, Souevo was left unglazed. Decorators painted black and white decorative Indian designs on it, which contrasted well with the red clay background (Fig. 104). Each

Fig. 102: Greenaways jardiniere 10" high. Courtesy of Allan Wunsch. Photo by Leach.

Fig. 103: Weller catalog page of Souevo Ware. Courtesy of Ohio Historical Society.

piece had a glossy black interior. "It is truly characteristic of the old Indian clayworker whose hands were about the only tool he used in fashioning his wares," wrote *C & G* of Souevo, on January 28, 1909. Souevo sold well in the far West, where visitors bought it, thinking that it was made by the Indians. Invariably unmarked, crude, and primitive in design, Souevo might have been made to deceive.

Burnt Wood, Claywood, Norwood, and Teakwood resembled each other in texture and decoration, with their dark brown to tan backgrounds, their stippling, and their relief designs. Called Dechiwo at first, Burnt Wood came out in 1908. The name Dechiwo was derived from the first two or three letters of its designs: devils, children, and women. Since few persons could remember the name Dechiwo, the Pottery decided to call it Burnt Wood, according to *GPW*, November 20, 1908.

Three pieces of Dechiwo invite examination: a Woman vase, a Children vase, and a Devil-Satyr jardiniere. The Woman vase portrayed an elegant woman picking fruit in an orchard. Dressed in a flowing robe, her hair in a chignon, she held a basket in one hand and with the other hand reached up to pick an apple from the tree above. The look of carved wood, the dark coloring, and the raised figure, all suggested the Burnt Wood line. Both the Woman and the Children vases had stylized trees with apples set against a wreath of leaves. Unfortunately, the decorators applied a green glaze to the Children vase, which obfuscated its dark, carved wood appearance. Dechiwo was, however, a line in transition. Shown here, the Children vase depicts two little girls in long dresses blowing bubbles on the grass, and a small girl and boy tossing a ball back and forth (Fig. 105). The young boy is dressed in knickers and high button boots, his clothes dating from the 1908 period.

Fig. 104: Souevo vase 5″ high. Collection: Dick and Nancy Sigafoose.

Fig. 105: *Marked Weller:* Dechiwo vase 6½″ high, with children playing ball and blowing bubbles. Collection: Dora Betts.

Fig. 106: *Marked Weller:* Dechiwo jardiniere 10½″ high, artist signed by Rudolph Lorber. Collection: Dora Betts.

Fig. 109: Decorated Burnt Wood vase 10″ high: Egyptians plowing with oxen. Collection: Dora Betts.

Fig. 110: *Marked Weller:* Decorated Burnt Wood vase 9″ high: The Wise Men. Collection: Dora Betts.

Rudolph Lorber may have developed the Dechiwo line. Note here the Devil-Satyr jardiniere signed R. Lo, for Rudolph Lorber (Fig. 106). The satyr was a mythological creature, half goat half man, with horns on his head, cloven hooves, and goat's legs with thick shaggy hair. There was a close connection in Christian Art between the satyr and the devil. The illustrious satyr Pan, a Greek fertility god, who gamboled in the woods and played his pipe with the other satyrs (as on the Lorber jardiniere), became after 1000 A. D. a prototype of the devil. Robert Hughes in *Heaven and Hell in Western Art* discussed Pan's transition from fertility god to Satan, from satyr to devil. He explained how the attributes of Pan were transferred to the devil. Iconographically, the devil in art was often represented by the goat man with horns on his head, hairy flanks, and cloven hooves. The satyrs on the Lorber jardiniere looked like a set of dancing devils. The jar had all the characteristics of Dechiwo and Burnt Wood.

The Lorber jar and a matching vase embodied the devil side of Dechiwo, the line noted for its devils, women, and children. It resembled the Woman vase and the Children vase discussed above. Undoubtedly, Lorber and his assistants designed and modeled the Dechiwo line, which then evolved into Burnt Wood.

Burnt Wood had the textured appearance of a wood carving (Fig. 107). The designs seemed to be incised on a stippled background, or raised in relief. Subject matter included flowers, berries, pine cones, birds, and fish. A dark brown band on the rim and the base of each pot, and a honey colored, glossy interior typified the line. The early Dechiwo pieces were so expensive and so laborious to make, that the Pottery abandoned them in favor of the simpler Burnt Wood wares with their more prosaic designs.

Not all Burnt Wood was brown, black, and tan in coloring. Some vases sported bright colors. The gourd-shaped vase here has bright red flowers on the front, with green and white ones on the back of the vase, and the stippled background, the dark rim and base typical of Burnt Wood (Fig. 108).

Fig. 107: Three Burnt Wood Wares: Candlestick 8″ high, low bowl 3″ high, and vase 5½″ high. Collection: Dick and Nancy Sigafoose.

Fig. 108: *Marked Weller*: Burnt Wood vase 5¾″ high, with red, green, and white flowers. Collection: Dora Betts.

A variation of the Burnt Wood line, Decorated Burnt Wood had hand colored, raised figures in relief on a textured background. Exotic, often Middle Eastern scenes embellished this line. Note the vases on page 71, the Egyptians Plowing with Oxen, and the Wise Men (Figs. 109, 110). The latter has two Wise Men on camels with a child leading one camel, and stars overhead in the sky. The vase was marked Weller in large block letters. With its nubby background and graceful figures in full relief, Decorated Burnt Wood possessed great charm and beauty.

Dark, parallel bands separating the decorations distinguished Claywood from Burnt Wood (Fig. 111). The Weller catalogs showed Claywood mugs, candlesticks, bowls, and vases with raised brown panels between each design. Decorations included stylized flowers, spider webs, running mice, butterflies, ducks, and fish, etched in deep brown lines against a stippled background. The Pottery offered Claywood in 1909 and 1910.

Like Claywood, the Norwood line came out in 1909. "The patterns of Nouveau Art are carried out in strong lines and surfaces against a stippled background which send them out in distinct and strong relief. This is further enhanced by the color treatment of strong yet soft blues, reds, etc.," wrote *P & G*, August 1909. As on Claywood, the designs on Norwood were incised and outlined, then painted in dark colors, separated from each other by panels. The article in *P & G* pictured two Norwood jars, one with incised, long stemmed roses, the other with stylized leaves and flowers, both on stippled backgrounds, with dark panels, and bands at the rim and the base of each jar (Fig. 112).

A new line that imitated the look of teak, Teakwood emerged in *C & G*, May 6, 1909. It had a black background with a high relief tan decoration. Raised grapes and leaves, or apples graced the rims of some jardinieres, while full length, stylized apple trees and winged lions adorned the umbrella stands, as shown in the Weller catalogs. Sometimes, the modelers separated the tree and fruit designs by panels. Teakwood had a strong masculine look to complement the gentleman's study with its leather couch and mahogany desk.

Fig. 111: Claywood and Burnt Wood Wares: Claywood vase 3½" high, with flowers; Claywood vase 3" high, with butterflies; Burnt Wood vase 7" high, with winged lions; Claywood vase 9" high, with berries; Burnt Wood mug 4" high, with an elderly man. Collection: Dorothy Daniel, Kathryn Powell. Photo by Leach.

NEW JARDINIERES, FLOWER POTS, ETC.

NEW styles of jardinieres, flower pots, etc., are coming out seasonably.

Two new lines from the S. A. Weller potteries at Zanesville, Ohio, are attracting much attention at their New York showrooms at the corner of West Broadway and Park Place. They have been named the "Norona" and the "Norwood."

THE PATTERNS OF NOUVEAU ART ARE STRONG IN LINE AND SURFACE AGAINST A STIPPLED BACKGROUND 🌻 🌻 🌻 🌻 🌻 WELLER

THE CLASSIC "NORONA" LINES OF THE S. A. WELLER POTTERIES 🌻 🌻 🌻

The Norona line embraces many ornamental and useful articles including jardinieres, umbrella stands, vases, etc., all of a tendency toward that simplicity of shape which best suits the classical sculptured designs of art figure modelling. These are very properly interpreted in strong enough relief to insure good proportion and effect and to avoid the apparent distortion so often noticed in bas-relief work of too flat treatment. The soft ivory, wax finish, too, has been well chosen, and is of great value to the general classic atmosphere which this line of pottery is designed to furnish. These articles are water-proof and are therefore easy to keep clean.

The other new Weller line, the Norwood, runs into jardinieres, pedestals, vases, etc. The patterns of Nouveau Art are carried out in strong lines and surfaces against a stippled background which sends them out in distinct and strong relief. This is further enhanced

ANOTHER EXAMPLE OF THE "NORWOOD" LINE FROM THE S. A. WELLER POTTERIES 🌻 🌻

Fig. 112: Weller Narona and Norwood, pictured in an article in *Pottery and Glass*, August 1909. The line Narona is misspelled Norona in the article. Collection: Library of Congress.

An imitation of classical bas relief Greek sculpture, Narona appeared in 1909. The catalog showed clay jars and vases with winged creatures, warriors with swords and spears in hand to hand combat, dancing maidens with wreaths, harp players, Amazons fighting soldiers with cross bows. Narona had an unglazed, rough exterior finish with a glazed interior. The Weller catalogs said Narona, "has the appearance of untanned leather with a darker tint in the deep parts, making a pleasing contrast, and bringing out the details of the modeling—finished with a wax treatment."

"Bells of San Juan is a line modeled after the old buildings of California," wrote C & G on January 13, 1910. The line resembled both Burnt Wood and Claywood, having dark brown panels like Claywood. High relief designs of the old mission churches of California embellished the ware. The jar pictured here measures 8½ inches high by 10 inches in diameter and has four scenes, each captioned in block letters: 1. Bells San Juan Capistrano: a view of four church bells set in an archway, in the interior courtyard of a church; 2. San Luis Rey de Francia, Cal.: a scene with archways in the foreground and behind them a mission church, trees, meadows, and clouds; 3. Santa Barbara, Cal.: a scene of a mission church with trees and a monk by the fountain in the foreground; 4. Santa Ines, Cal.: a mission church on a grassy knoll with clouds behind it (Fig. 113). The scenes represented the actual mission churches of California. The decorators labeled each scene in capital letters inside a dark band at the rim of the jar, and they molded cobblestones at the base. Bells of San Juan was a unique line, reminiscent of Owens' Mission Ware, but done in a totally different style.

I have examined two Bells of San Juan jardinieres, the one pictured here with its deep brown and tan relief designs, and one with a glossy green glaze covering the entire jar. The latter measured 7 inches high by 9 inches in diameter. While neither jar had a Weller mark, both came from the Pottery.

From 1906 to 1910, several new lines emanated from Weller Pottery. Some like Bells of San Juan and Souevo were destined for the tourist trade, while others like Burnt Wood, Dresden, and Fudzi made a positive, new creative statement.

Fig. 113: Bells of San Juan jardiniere 8½" high by 10" diameter. Collection: Harold Nichols. Photo by Leach.

Chapter XI
Weller Hudson and the Cream Colored Wares

The years from 1910 to 1920 saw the flowering of Weller Hudson, perhaps the most beautiful artist-decorated line in the history of American pottery. In the same decade, Weller introduced several lines with a cream colored background: Crystalline, Dupont, Eclair, Eldora-Chelsea, Ethel, Florala, Ivory, Noval, Pearl, Roma, Tivoli, and Tupelo.

Weller Hudson first appeared in 1917 and continued to be sold until about 1934. The company produced a variety of Hudson wares: White and Decorated, Blue and Decorated, Pictorial, and Rochelle. Weller artists hand decorated each piece with flowers, birds, horses, tigers, cowboys, snow scenes, sailboats, soldiers, Arabs, and fishermen. The matt backgrounds ranged from white to dark blue.

White and Decorated Hudson appeared in C & G on August 9, 1917, described as a line of vases and wallpockets in a rich, matt ivory finish with decorations of apple blossoms and lilacs. Both White and Decorated and Blue and Decorated Hudson used the apple blossom motif frequently, sometimes in a heavy slip, with the blossoms trailing from the rim down into the body of the piece.

On November 13, 1919, *PGBS* described a hand decorated Weller ware painted with scenes of the three wise men and the star of Bethlehem, oriental princes in silks and jewels with dromedaries resting under palm trees, jungle scenes with crouching tigers, all the pieces "done in heavy raised colors." Although *PGBS* gave the line no name, the description fitted Hudson Pictorial. These Pictorial vases were truly spectacular, ranging from 8 to 27 inches high, with scenes of mountains, sailboats, cranes, swans, owls in the moonlight, cowboys in the Grand Canyon, decorated by Sarah McLaughlin, Hester Pillsbury, and Mae Timberlake (Fig. 114 and C-9).

The Weller artists also painted flowers on Hudson vases. They worked on shaded wares, with colors verging from pink to gray as on the 13 inch high vase with dogwood blossoms, decorated by Lillie B. Mitchell, pictured here (Fig. 115). Some vases shaded from gray to blue or blue to pink, with slip painted irises, chrysanthemums, lilies of the valley, fruit, and pine cones. The artists usually signed both the floral and the Pictorial Hudson vases.

PGBS noted the advent of Blue and Decorated Hudson on August 14, 1919: "Another new showing is an assortment of hand-painted vases. On a rich dark blue base color appear hand-painted lifelike sprays of fruit blossoms and flowers, so true to nature that one almost expects the odor of a delicate perfume." In an interview with Lucile Henzke in *Pottery Collectors Newsletter*, June 1973, Naomi Walch discussed decorating Blue Hudson:

Fig. 114: *Marked Weller*: Hudson Pictorial vase 9½" high, with a sailboat scene, artist signed McLaughlin. Collection: Larry and Mary Swaney.

"The dark blue Hudson line with the pink and blue decoration was the most difficult to decorate. The greatest care, in every detail, had to be exercised in order to secure perfection." (Fig. 116). Occasionally, a bright parrot or an owl stood out against the navy blue background. To the touch, some of these vases felt smooth as satin. Note here the small vase with dogwood berries and the stick type vase with the pale blue band decorated with red blossoms (Fig. 117). Both have the satin finish.

Fig. 115: *Marked Weller*: White and Decorated Hudson vase 8″ high; Hudson vase 13″ high, decorated with dogwood flowers and signed L.B.M., and gray on gray Hudson vase 7½″ high, with lilies of the valley. Photo by Leach.

Fig. 116: *Marked Weller*: Hudson vase 8″ high, signed Hood; Blue and Decorated Hudson vase 9½″ high, with pine boughs, and Blue and Decorated Hudson vase 8½″ high. Photo by Leach.

Fig. 117: *Marked Weller:* Blue and Decorated Hudson vase 4" high, Blue and Decorated Hudson vase 9" high, and pink Hudson vase 6" high, with dogwood flowers, artist signed H.P. Photo by Leach.

In a series of letters to me during 1980, artist Ruth Axline described how Hudson was made. The artists decorated Hudson in a semi-damp condition and handled it very carefully or fingerprints would show. If the vase became too dry, the slip decoration would not adhere to it. Therefore, Hudson vases resided in a specially built damp room, until they were decorated. "Hudson ware was semi-dry with the background color already sprayed on. The pieces were placed on 5 to 6 foot boards about a foot wide and kept in what they called a damp room. The back of our tables had a shelf or ledge. The board boy brought us a board full of vases as we needed them. We'd have several of these to do in a day depending on the vase sizes. The board boy kept track of how much ware we received, etc. These vases had to be sprayed with glaze and then they were fired," Ruth wrote, on June 14, 1980.

The artists slip decorated the vases freehand on a clay body which had been sprayed with the basic body color, blue, pink, or gray. Ruth began to decorate Hudson vases with dogwood leaves and berries, under the tutelage of decorator Sarah McLaughlin. After she mastered the leaves and berries, Ruth learned how to draw irises on Hudson vases. She came to work for Weller on the Hudson line in 1929.

While White and Decorated Hudson vases resembled the Blue and Decorated in shape and motif, occasionally they had a high gloss glaze and were called Glazed Hudson. The Weller catalogs pictured Glazed Hudson vases of all sizes, with cream backgrounds and bands of dark colors at the rim, with fruit blossoms covering the back and the front of the vases. Another type of Glazed Hudson ware, dogs and cats in slip design, appeared in *C & G* in August 1934. Illustrated here is a Pekingese dog on a vase with a glossy white background, skillfully painted in heavy slip by Hester Pillsbury (Fig. 118).

The following artists decorated Weller Hudson: Ruth Axline, Dorothy Laughead, Claude Leffler, Sarah McLaughlin, Lillie B. Mitchell, Hester

Fig. 118: *Marked Weller*: Glazed Hudson white vase 7″ high, with a Pekingese dog, artist signed H.P. Photo by Leach.

Fig. 120: *Marked Weller*: Hudson basket 14″ high. Collection: Dora Betts.

Fig. 119: Weller catalog page of Rochelle, a line of slip decorated, brown Hudson vases. Courtesy of Mose Mesre.

Pillsbury, Eugene Roberts, Mae and Sarah Timberlake, and Naomi Walch. Mae Timberlake did the best work. "Everyone conceded that Mae Timberlake was the most talented artist in our department and was given the largest and most difficult pieces to decorate. She and her sister Sarah had a small niche all their own in which to work," Naomi Walch told Lucile Henzke in *PCN,* June 1973.

A color page from the Weller catalogs showed a line of brown Hudson vases called Rochelle (Fig. 119). Appearing in the twenties, Rochelle used typical Hudson shapes on backgrounds which shaded from dark brown at the rim to light brown at the base. Artists slip decorated Rochelle with roses, dogwood, tulips, lilies, and grapes.

The line collectors call Copra was a branch of the Hudson line. Found mainly in vases, baskets, and jars, this Hudson variant had a smear glaze effect with irregular, horizontal bands of dark green, brown, and black, shading into each other. Colorful large red, white, and yellow tulips, roses, or poppies adorned each piece (Fig. 120).

Some Hudson vases used dark and light shades of the same color: gray on gray, blue on blue, maroon on maroon. The factory made hundreds of gray on gray Hudson vases with gray green leaves setting off pale white flowers, trillium or lilies of the valley, on a background shading from light to dark gray, as in Figure 115. Often confused with the earlier, entirely different Delta line, the blue on blue Hudson vases featured pale blue and white flowers on a medium blue background. Prettiest of the three, the maroon vases had a flower, often a long stemmed light maroon narcissus, on a dark maroon background. The artists rarely signed these vases.

Between 1917 and 1934, the company displayed myriad Hudson vases in the New York show room. From the Pictorial vases to the ubiquitous Blue and Decorated pieces, the Hudson line represented some of the best work ever done by the Weller artists.

The cream colored wares appeared during the same decade in which Weller Hudson developed and flourished, 1910 to 1920. A departure from the dark glazed Louwelsa line, the cream wares from Ivory to Tupelo were molded and hand colored.

Ivory appeared in January 1910 at the annual Pittsburgh Glass and Pottery Exhibition. With decorations in bas relief, the line comprised hanging baskets, window boxes, fern dishes, jars, peds, vases, cuspidors, and umbrella stands (Fig. 121). In its catalog description of Ivory, the Pottery noted that it had "a cast design on which a brown filler or paint was sprayed, rubbed off and the brown was allowed to remain in the indented parts which gave an ivory effect." The designer of Ivory, Rudolph Lorber chose classical motifs: gods in chariots, cupids with arrows, nudes, as well as flowers, fruit, and foliage. Since Ivory borrowed molds from other lines, the embossed decorations also included swans, squirrels, and Art Nouveau maidens. The company offered Ivory as late as 1927, when *PGBS* described jars 22 inches in diameter, January 13, 1927. Hotel lobbies, apartment house lobbies, and automobile show rooms displayed these huge jardinieres.

Rudolph Lorber also created Roma, a cream colored ware with red,

Fig. 121: *Marked Weller:* Ivory jardiniere 6½" high, with raised squirrels on an oak tree. Collection: Dora Betts.

Fig. 123: Eldora-Chelsea vase 5" high, shown on the Weller catalog page of Eldora-Chelsea.

blue, and green fruit and floral decorations, described in *P & G*, May 1912. The Weller catalogs showed a variety of Roma wares: a raised compote with arches, flower form compotes with raised pond lilies, a tobacco jar with pipes, low bowls with roses, grapes, or birds in relief bands, jars and peds, baskets, hanging planters, and smoking sets. *PGBS* wrote about Roma, July 4, 1912: "In the Roma ivory line several new designs have been brought out. . . . The rose, grape (fruit and foliage), dogwood blossom and pine cone are the subjects which the craftsmen at the Weller plant have skillfully worked up into artistic panel designs. An umbrella stand with panels of plain ivory divided by narrow bars of a raised pattern is another item worthy of comment." (Fig. 122).

The Pottery offered Eldora-Chelsea sometime before 1920 (Fig. 123). The catalog pictured tall candleholders, vases, jars, baskets, and bowls. Each item had a series of raised red and blue rosettes in the midsection with beading above and below. The bottom half of each piece had tinted green, vertical ribs. A thin, dark green band often accented the top and the bottom rim of each piece. Note here the catalog page of Eldora-Chelsea (Fig. 124), p. 82.

The Weller catalogs pictured Crystalline in a series of jardinieres measuring from five to ten inches in diameter, with a cream background with vertical panels of leaves which looked like feathers in relief stacked on top of one another. The catalogs also showed matching Crystalline pedestals.

Dupont emerged in *P & G* in January 1915, with a relief design of a Marie Antoinette basket filled with flowers, encircled by flowing ribbons

Fig. 122: *Marked Weller*: Three Roma paneled vases: 9" high, 7" high, and 5" high. Collection: Dorothy Daniel. Photo by Leach.

Fig. 124: Weller catalog page of Eldora-Chelsea. Courtesy of Ohio Historical Society.

Fig. 128: Weller catalog page of Florala console sets. Courtesy of Ohio Historical Society.

which formed a wreath around it, a popular motif in pottery and glass designs. The Dupont vase here has three panelled scenes of birds perched on a bucket holding a rose tree (Fig. 125). Behind the colorful red and green rose tree stands a white net backdrop, almost like a window screen. The background and panels are pale green. Dupont came in bowls, planters, vases, and jars, some with the rose tree and bird motif, others with the Marie Antoinette basket.

Named for Weller's youngest daughter Ethel, the line Ethel had a colorful medallion of a young girl smelling a rose at the top of each vase. Vertical bands of stylized flowers on a cream background surrounded the medallion. At the top and the bottom of each vase stood raised, diagonal bands of diamonds. Note the Ethel vase in the color section (C-18). *PGBS* described Ethel on January 27, 1916, as a line with the cameo of a girl's head. The company offered large and small vases, some without the cameo of Ethel.

Eclair and Noval appeared around 1920. Both lines had either molded apples and grapes, or roses in full relief. Illustrated here are a Noval chalice vase with a red rose, and a console set with a fruit bowl and two tall candlesticks (Fig. 126). In the Weller catalogs Noval came in vases, compotes, bowls, covered compotes, and candlesticks. The line was glossy white with glossy black bands in vertical ribs, and bands at the top and the bottom of each piece.

Eclair used the same shapes as Noval, but it lacked the decorative black bands. It was monochromatic, coming in glossy black, white, or red. Pictured in the Weller catalogs, the two lines seemed nearly identical. Occasionally, Eclair appeared in dark colors with a white band at its rim and base and white handles. Note the handled, black Eclair vase shown here (Fig. 127). Full relief red roses usually decorated Eclair.

Florala had colorful panels of flowers on a cream and blue background. Bright yellow, white, and red cosmos flowers alternated with panels of

Fig. 125: *Marked Weller:* Noval chalice vase 6″ high, Ivory jardiniere 6″ high, and Dupont vase 6½″ high. Photo by Leach.

Fig. 126: *Marked Weller:* Noval console set, with a bowl 4″ high, and candlesticks 9½″ high. Collection: Dorothy Daniel. Photo by Leach.

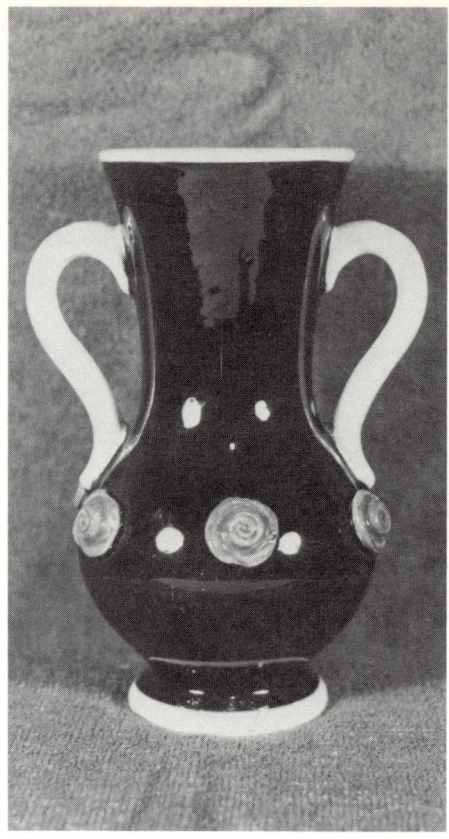

Fig. 127: *Marked Weller:* Eclair vase 6″ high. Collection: Dick and Nancy Sigafoose.

Fig. 129: *Marked Weller:* Tivoli bowl, and Florala vase 8″ high. Collection: H.M. Dietrich.

Fig. 130: Tupelo candlestick 7½″ high, shown on the Weller Tupelo catalog page as #15.

diamonds and vertical white ribs. Sometimes, only the vertical ribs separated each panel as on the console sets illustrated here from the Weller catalogs (Fig. 128), p. 82. How delightful to see the console sets, with bowls filled with flowers and candles in matching candleholders, all set for a festive dinner party! Florala was one of the prettiest cream colored wares.

A close relative of Eclair and Noval, Tivoli featured a glossy white or red background and subdued decoration (Fig. 129). It had only a small colorful band, one or two inches wide, of red roses and purple grapes, set off by a tiny black band. Often, the decor embellished only the top or the bottom of the piece. The Tivoli line included vases, bowls, candlesticks, compotes, and wallpockets.

Tupelo came in low bowls, wallpockets, vases, and two to three branched candlesticks. Shown here, the two branched candlestick has bands of beads and diamonds tinted light blue, with a red orchid-like flower embossed near the base (Fig. 130). With its cream background and raised flowers, Tupelo resembled Roma and appeared before 1920.

Designed by Rudolph Lorber, Pearl came out April 17, 1922, in *CGL*: "The background is a white glaze and each piece has from 60 to 240 pearls or beads, which are decorated in colors. Also included in the decorations are floral designs of roses and other flowers with leaf and spray effects." Festooned with strings of dark pearls on a glossy white background, Pearl comprised vases, bowls, wallpockets, baskets, candlesticks, and fern dishes (Fig. 131). Decorators interspersed red roses with the pearls, which were colored lavender, blue, yellow, or deep pink.

Weller offered the cream colored wares from about 1910 to 1927. They were versatile, from smoking sets to jardinieres, brightly colored, and amenable to any decorative scheme in the home.

Fig. 131: *Marked Weller:* Pearl vase 6″ high and Tivoli basket 8½″ high. Collection: Dorothy Daniel. Photo by Leach.

Chapter XII

From Baldin to Woodcraft

In addition to Hudson and the cream colored wares, Weller produced a number of other lines in the decade from 1910 to 1920. They included: Baldin, Blue Ware, Bo Marblo, Denton, Fairfield, Flemish, Forest, Fra Bel Ita, Fruitone, Morocco, Muskota, Rosemont, Voile, and Woodcraft. Naturalistic designs predominated, with hand colored, raised decorations of owls, squirrels, pheasants, and apple trees.

PGBS first noted Voile with its soft yellow, matt background and embossed apple trees laden with ripe red apples, on July 20, 1911. Long slender trunks of apple trees reached from the base of each piece up to the rim, where the full boughs of apples spread out abundantly on vases and jardinieres (Fig. 132).

Morocco Carvo, called Morocco by collectors, appeared in *C & G*, February 6, 1913, with a rich brown decoration simulating carved or embossed leather, on jars, peds, and vases. Like Narona, Morocco was rough or granite-like to the touch. Morocco used molds from other lines, in particular Roma molds (Fig. 133).

Like Voile, Baldin employed the apple motif. On a brownish green or a navy blue background, red apples, molded in relief, decorated vases, jars, and bowls. *PGBS* mentioned Baldin on December 13, 1917, as a line with Flemish coloring and apple decoration. Sometimes, magnolia leaves adorned Baldin vases.

Designed by Rudolph Lorber, Blue Ware emerged August 22, 1918, in *C & G*. With its deep blue or tan background, Blue Ware came in vases and

Fig. 132: *Marked Weller:* Bo Marblo bowl 2" high, Blue Ware vase 10" high, Voile vase 7" high, and Baldin vase 6" high. Collection: Dorothy Daniel. Photo by Leach.

jars decorated with raised, ivory colored ladies, who wore Grecian tunics. This was the age of Isadora Duncan, who recreated classical Greek dances. She wore a Greek tunic and danced barefoot, often out of doors, like the ladies on the Blue Ware vases and jars. Crowds acclaimed her in New York and Paris in 1917 and 1918, about the time these pieces were made. The dancers on Blue Ware leapt amid the trees, marched, played the flute or lyre, and carried garlands or grapes. The vases often had small floral bands at the rim and base. Variants in the line included jars with winged ladies like figureheads on a ship, lamps with flower bands centered around a tiny bird, and large vases with panels of roses.

The Denton line came out July 13, 1916, in C & G: "The new patterns include exceptionally attractive floral and bird designs in relief work on a glazed black background in vases and other items." The Pottery offered Denton in either a black or a white gloss glaze with colored birds and flowers. Note here the black umbrella stand with the pheasant and the bluebird (Fig. 134). The umbrella stand appeared in the Weller catalogs with another decoration: two peacocks on a magnolia tree. Denton was a colorful, dazzling line.

Rosemont resembled Denton, but was less ornate. The Weller catalogs showed glossy black jardinieres, with either bluebirds or red roses, in the Rosemont line. The company made vases and jars, often with raised, colored bluebirds on branches with pink blossoms. Like Denton, the line had either a black or a white gloss glaze. Illustrated here is a Rosemont urn with a bluebird staring up at a butterfly (Fig. 135).

Described as a line which imitated Italian marble and onyx, Bo Marblo appeared in P & G on January 7, 1915. The line was glossy with tinted, veined patterns representing marble, onyx, and agate. Collectors call it Marbleized, but the Pottery introduced it as Bo Marblo in a variety of items: low bowls, jars, large and small vases, all with a glossy marbleized finish blending deep black with purple and white, or golden amber with deep brown, or red with white and brown.

Fig. 134: Denton umbrella stand 23″ high. Collection: Richard A. Harmer.

Fig. 133: *Marked Weller*: Bo Marblo vase 5″ high, Morocco vase 10″ high, on a Roma mold, and Forest jardiniere 4½″ high. Collection: Lee Dietrich.

Responding to the popularity of Roseville's Donatello line, the Weller modelers created Fairfield around 1916-1917. It featured cherubs playing instruments or reclining on the grass. Set off by a row of beads, the cherubs embellished the upper half of each piece. Below them stood rows of vertical ribs outlined in green. Shades of brown to deep green behind the white cherubs, brown bands at the rim and the base, and brown glazed interiors enhanced the effect of Fairfield. The company offered vases, fern dishes, wallpockets, and jardinieres (Fig. 136).

Designed by Rudolph Lorber, Muskota was one of the most popular Weller wares. Naturalistic in detail and coloring, the line offered a plethora of flower inserts: birds, fish, animals, and nudes. The Weller catalogs pictured several Muskota wares: the kingfisher, the crow, the goose, the blackbird wallpocket, the turtle with a blossom on his back, the squirrel perched on a bowl, and the elephant.

Fig. 136: Fairfield wallpocket, #2B on the Weller Fairfield catalog page. Collection: Lee Dietrich.

Fig. 135: *Marked Weller:* Blue Ware vase 10″ high, Rosemont urn 7″ high, and Rosemont vase 6″ high. Collection: Dorothy Daniel. Photo by Leach.

Fig. 137: *Marked Weller:* Hobart Bathing Beauty insert 6″ high, in a footed glossy black Muskota bowl 2½″ high. Photo by Leach.

Fig. 138: *Marked Weller* Muskota: Fisher Boy 6½″ high, Toadstool with Bee insert 2″ high, and Muskota Frog with Waterlily insert 4½″ high. Collection: Kathryn Powell. Photo by Leach.

Fig. 139: *Marked Weller*: Muskota Three Cupids flower insert 8" high. Collection: Dorothy Daniel.

The Pottery offered matt or glossy Muskota bowls and compotes in pink, yellow, red, blue, green, purple, and black. As illustrated in the Weller catalogs, these 4 to 11 inch diameter bowls accompanied Muskota flower inserts. Pictured here and in the catalogs is a glossy black Muskota bowl with three feet and a raised red and white flower in a square panel (Fig. 137). The catalogs showed many flower inserts: butterflies, dragonflies, bees, crabs, starfish, swans, mushrooms, fish, frogs, and birds (Fig. 138).

Muskota bathing girls stood, sat, or posed gracefully on the edge of bowls in the Weller ads in the trade journals. Some wore dresses but no shoes; others wore swimsuits. Little cupids sat, kneeled, and waded in the bowls (Fig. 139). The cupids and the bathing girls appeared in *PGBS*, November 9, 1916.

Muskota birds could stand alone or serve as flower inserts. Well modeled and colored, the birds included stately kingfishers and gray woodpeckers (Fig. 140). The Weller catalogs pictured two Muskota kingfishers, the crane with the twisted neck, two canaries on one perch, the gray woodpecker with orange breast, and two spread-winged geese.

The Weller modelers created Muskota birds and butterflies, measuring only one or two inches long. "Miniature birds, ducks, fish and butterflies, which may be used to decorate lily bowls, are shown in excellent modeling and lifelike colors," wrote *PGBS* on July 13, 1916. Since the factory did not mark these, collectors often confuse them with the tiny creatures made by the McCoy and Roseville Potteries. The Weller catalogs pictured and labeled the miniature birds and butterflies. The company produced small place cards with birds or molded butterflies in one corner and a place to insert a card and a flower. Three sizes of Chanticleer roosters appeared also.

As early as December 16, 1915, Weller Pottery placed an ad for Muskota in *C & G*: "We are now presenting a line of Birds, Bowls and other items for Table Decoration unequalled by an American or Foreign Factory." The same journal noted the Muskota inserts on July 13, 1916: "In perforated flower holders are new conceptions and finishes, including lobsters, crabs,

Fig. 140: *Marked Weller*: Muskota lobster flower insert 2" high; Glendale nest with eggs insert 3" high, and Muskota gray woodpecker 5½" high. Photo by Leach.

fish, toadstools, star fish, etc. Also small flying birds and perch birds for decorating flower bowls and other purposes." The Muskota line included figural elephants; two cats sitting on a fence; a fisherboy in a boat or on a stump; a fisherboy with a stand for a goldfish bowl; a washerwoman; a girl in a long white dress and picture hat, and some nudes (Figs. 141, 142). Leaning or sitting on rocks, the Muskota nudes looked sculptural and serene.

In addition to the figurines and flower frogs or inserts, the Pottery made Muskota book racks and doorstops simulating pottery baskets filled with brightly colored flowers or fruit. Bird feeders of red earthenware, which resembled miniature houses, sat on posts or garden walls.

The 1928 Price List mentioned several Muskota products: Gloss Kingfisher in two sizes, 6 and 8 inches high; Two Birds on Base; Frog; Flying Geese; Girl and Swan on Rock; Girl on Rock; Gloss Woman Lidded Bonbon, 9 inches; Single Fisherboy; Fisherboy on Stump; Flying Swan Bowl; Crane, and Matt Kingfisher, 6½ inches high. The diversity of shapes, designs, and colors of Muskota enchanted collectors in 1916, and still does today.

Weller Woodcraft appeared in 1917. *Pottery for the Florist* described the line: "Pieces are modelled as if made from trees." Notable for its brown tree bark surface, Woodcraft came not only in vases, but also in lighting devices, discussed in Chapter VII. Typical of the line are the pieces shown here: the Tree Trunk vase, the Three Foxes vase, and the Log planter (Fig. 143). The Weller catalogs pictured these and an acorn decorated bowl with a squirrel on the rim; a vase with an owl on a branched cherry tree; a log ashtray; candlesticks, compotes in tree forms; a wallpocket with an owl peering from a hole in a tree trunk; a jar with a full figure woodpecker

Fig. 141: *Marked Weller*: Muskota Fisher Boy stand for fish bowl 12″ high. Collection: Robert Miller and Glen Vogt.

Fig. 142: *Marked Weller*: Muskota Nude insert 8″ high; Forest basket 9½″ high; Muskota blue butterfly 3½″ wide, and Muskota red flower insert 2″ high. Collection: Dorothy Daniel.

on a tree trunk, and an umbrella stand with a fox and chicken. All these shared the textured, tree bark finish in shades of matt brown and green. The Three Foxes vase had the most appeal, with the curious baby foxes peering out from their secure haven inside the tree trunk.

PGBS introduced Woodcraft on April 5, 1917, and August 2, 1917. The journal noted the jardiniere in the shape of a log with the woodpecker and the flying squirrel. It called Woodcraft a line imitative of bark and wood, with raised animal figures, squirrels, owls' heads, birds, leaves, and fruit.

Woodcraft borrowed some molds from Voile. A color page from the Weller catalogs pictured Woodcraft in Voile shapes, but the background color was brown shading to green. Witness the vases in the color section here, the Voile vase with the yellow background, and the Woodcraft vase in greenish brown, both using Voile molds. (C-19).

PGBS described Forest on April 10, 1919, as a line with babbling brooks, streams, woods, and mountains, on vases, fern dishes, jars, and peds. Forest was another naturalistic line like Woodcraft with trees and forests in relief, colored in wood tones of orange, brown, green, and blue. The catalog depicted jars and peds, fern dishes, baskets, hanging baskets, and vases. Designed by Rudolph Lorber as he rode on a train to a pottery show in the East, Forest evoked scenes of late summer or early fall.

Inspired perhaps by the popularity of the Sylvan line, offered by the Brush McCoy Pottery in the fall of 1915, Weller's Forest surpassed Sylvan in design and coloration. Sylvan had trees in relief on a cream colored background. The overall effect was rather bland when contrasted with the rich natural coloring of Forest.

The Flemish line resembled Forest and Woodcraft. *Pottery for the Florist* described Flemish: "A mild pastel polychrome treatment, the floral modeling

Fig. 143: *Marked Weller* Woodcraft: Tree Trunk vase 10″ high; Three Foxes vase 5½″ high, and Log planter 4″ high. Collection: Kathryn Powell. Photo by Leach.

Fig. 144: *Marked Weller:* Flemish squirrel bowl 3″ high and Flemish reeded planter 4½″ high. Photo by Leach.

Fig. 145: *Marked Weller:* Flemish flower form compote 9″ high, with the flower shading from green to dark blue to deep rose. Shown as #51 in the Weller Flemish catalog. Collection: Phyllis Larson.

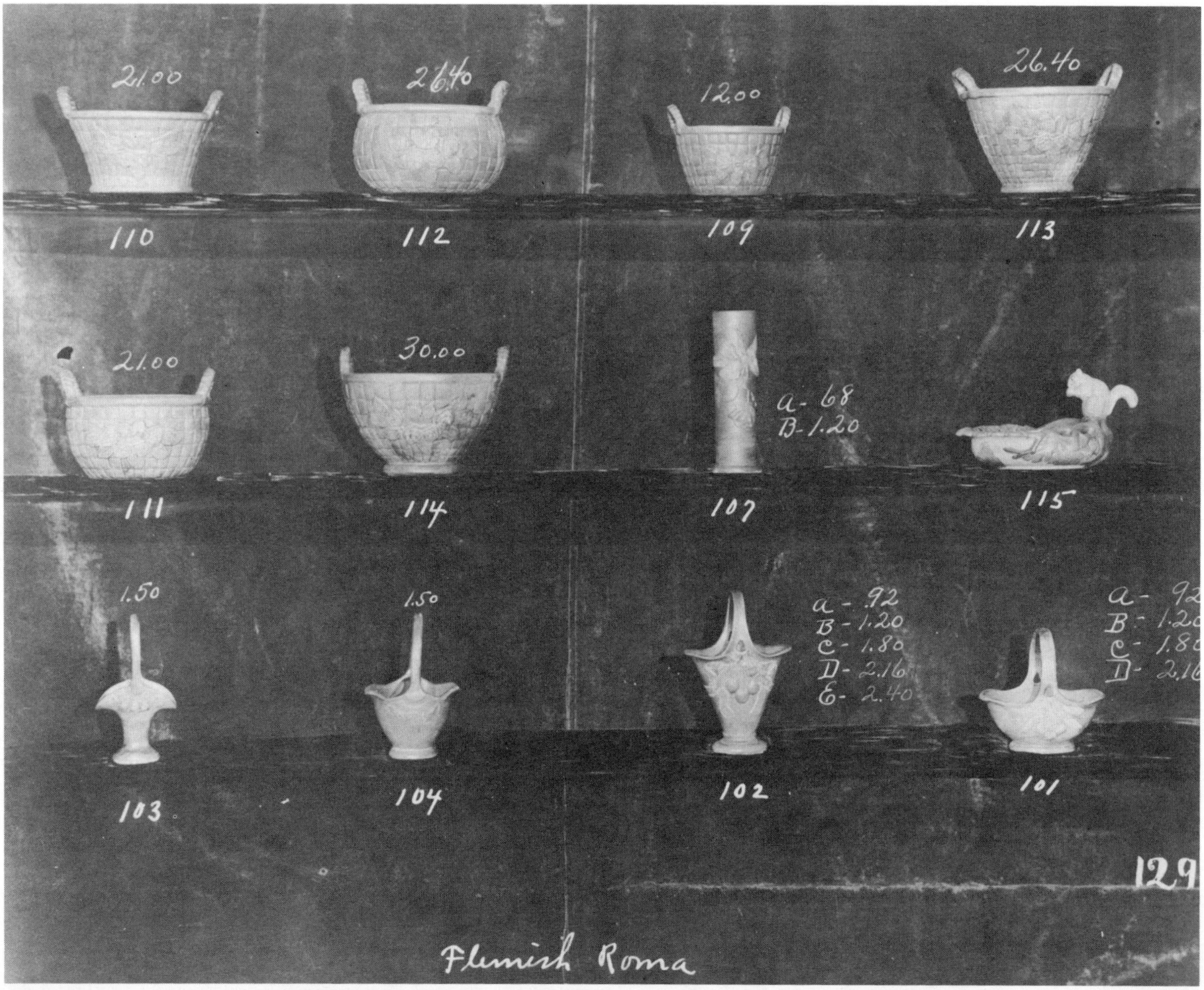

Fig. 148: Weller catalog page of Flemish. Courtesy of Ohio Historical Society.

is brought out by being tinted in bright harmonious colors." Although it was more colorful and dramatic than Woodcraft, Flemish did have the greenish brown background and the woodlike tones. By August 9, 1917, C & G noted the appearance of Flemish jars and peds, fern dishes, and window boxes.

The Weller catalogs showed Flemish jars and peds decorated with bright cockatoos and parrots in lush, flowered gardens; apples in relief; grapes in relief; squirrels in trees, and foxes gazing up at birds in a tree. Rudolph Lorber and his assistants either embossed or incised the designs and hand colored them. One jar had incised birds on a wire between two trees. The quartet squirrel bowl displayed four raised squirrels sitting on their haunches, between panels of trees in the forest (Fig. 144).

There was such beauty and imagination in Flemish! One extraordinary compote resembled a Tiffany flower form vase. The bowl was shaped like a flower set on a twisted green stem (Fig. 145). Ornate red roses in relief topped covered, ivory colored compotes and powder jars. Birds and roses adorned wallpockets and inkwells. The Flemish line endured for over a decade.

The 1928 Price List enumerated the following Flemish wares: Footed Grape and Fruit Jar, Parrot Jar and Ped, Squirrel Bowl, Vase Cosmo and Lattice, Hanging Basket Cosmo and Lattice, Jar Ribbed and Roses, Umbrella Stand (Apple, Woman, Rose), Bowl Bulrushes, Bowl Vine and Leaf, Jar Children in the Woods, Jar Tulip. The prettiest was the Children in the Woods Jar with the children, so delicately colored they looked alive, strolling through the woods.

Weller Pottery boasted in an ad in *PGBS*, December 12, 1918: "The Flemish Art Pottery is one of the more recent pronounced successes in increasing favor." Around 1925 the Pottery made some additions to Flemish, including planters and bowls resembling a reeded basket. Other additions after 1917 included the towel bar with bluebirds and the toothbrush holder (Figs. 146, 147). Pictured here is a page from the Weller catalogs with Flemish reeded planters, the squirrel on the bowl, and some attractive baskets with raised flowers or cherries (Fig. 148).

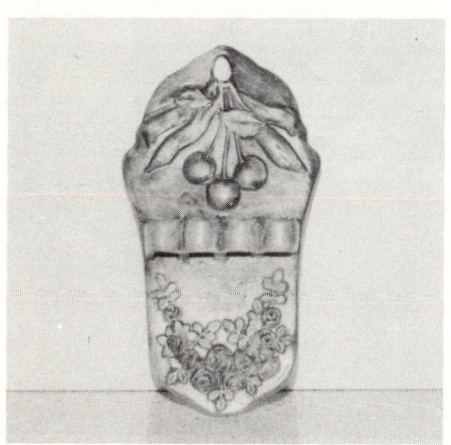

Fig. 147: *Marked Weller:* Flemish toothbrush holder 7" high. Collection: Arthur and Rita Townley.

Fig. 146: *Marked Weller:* Flemish towel bar 12" long. Collection: Robert Miller and Glen Vogt.

Devised as a wartime tribute to the Allies, Fra Bel Ita came out January 9, 1919, in *PGBS*. The line combined the decorative arts of France, Belgium, and Italy. Its acronymic title derived from the first three letters of each country's name. "A raised treatment features a variety of flowers, fruits, animals, turtles, and other objects on a plain background. It is in these various objects that the arts of the countries named in the title are designed. So far flower holders only have been produced, yet the variety of these runs the gamut of sizes, from the largest to the smallest cabinet pieces." I have not identified any examples of Fra Bel Ita.

Fruitone appeared July 17, 1919, in *C & G,* which noted its soft matt body in shades of terra cotta, burnt orange, rose, and dark red, blending into lighter tones like crushed fruit. The company offered vases, candlesticks, footed bowls, and pictured them in the catalogs. Frequently, the colors, green and brown, brown and yellow, or green and pink, blended to form a striated effect (Fig. 149 and C-21).

Except for the fine Weller Hudson line, the wares offered from 1910 to 1920, described here and in Chapter XI, were molded and hand colored on a variety of backgrounds. Hudson marked the apogee of artist decoration at Weller. Successive wares, from the cream colored to the wood tone lines, showed the triumph of the modeler's art. Colorful, naturalistic, imaginative, the lines from Forest and Muskota to Denton and Rosemont attract and enchant collectors today.

Fig. 149: *Marked Weller:* Fruitone vase 5″ high. Collection: Dorothy Daniel.

Chapter XIII

The Twenties at Weller

The twenties was a prolific period for Weller Pottery. It introduced several new lines, from the classic Blue Drapery and Louella, to the woodsy Glendale, Knifewood, Selma, Warwick, and Wood Rose. In this period of glaze experimentation, the luster glaze enhanced Lamar, LaSa, and Marengo, while the drip glaze distinguished Mottled Ware and Nile.

To reflect the soft folds of drapery, Rudolph Lorber created Blue Drapery, mentioned January 20, 1921, in *PGB*. Simulating a rich blue fabric hanging in easy folds, the line included baskets, vases, wallpockets, jars, hanging baskets, candlesticks, and fern dishes (Fig. 150). Each piece featured raised, molded red roses. Inspired by the success of Blue Drapery, the company introduced Louella. On Louella, decorators painted the flowers in slip and varied the background colors from blue to silver gray, wine red, or dark blue.

CGL introduced Melrose on February 26, 1923: "It is a grey rose tint, decorated with raised flowers and vines and berries. This type of creation is indeed in vogue at present, coming in the face of the spring buying season, inasmuch as the mere sight reminds one of spring and summer." On a matt, gray-rose background, Melrose had raised red roses, apples, cherries, and grapes, with tree boughs as handles and decoration. Shapes included candlesticks, baskets, bowls, vases, and pitchers (Fig. 151).

Arcola resembled Melrose in its shapes and in its embossed designs of roses, grapes, and cherries. The two lines differed in the glaze. Melrose

Fig. 150: *Marked Weller*: Blue Drapery vase 4″ high and Louella powder jar 3″ high. Collection: Kathryn Powell. Photo by Leach.

Fig. 151: *Marked Weller:* Melrose basket 8½″ high. Collection: Esther and Martin Myers.

Fig. 152: *Marked Weller:* Arcola basket 8½″ high. Collection: Esther and Martin Myers.

had a matt, rose glaze, and Arcola a gloss glaze which shaded from dark green to cream to brown (Fig. 152). The Weller catalogs pictured Arcola with grapes and cherries in high relief, with twining branches and scalloped rims, in baskets, bowls, jars, candlesticks, and vases. Arcola and Melrose were well modeled, subtly colored, and beautifully designed.

Naturalistic motifs reappeared in the twenties with Glendale, Knifewood, Selma, and Warwick. Knifewood made its debut August 25, 1921, in *PGB*, which remarked that it looked as if it were carved out of wood with a sharp knife. Indeed, it had a matt background similar to Burnt Wood. Swans, dogs, squirrels, and peacocks were molded in relief, then colored (Fig. 153). The Weller catalogs showed large and small jars, vases with long tailed peacocks, and a flying squirrel, low bowls with swans, and a tobacco jar with hunting dogs. The catalogs also pictured Knifewood umbrella stands, hanging planters, jars, peds, bowls, and vases.

With pastel colors and a gloss glaze, the Knifewood line became Selma. *PGB* discussed Selma on July 26, 1923: "C. H. Taylor . . . has just received from the S. A. Weller Company . . . samples of two new lines of art pottery made by the concern. One of these is the 'Selma'. This is a carved ivory effect and is shown in a full line of ornamental table pieces." The Weller catalogs pictured Selma bowls and vases. Selma utilized many of the Knifewood molds, but it had lighter colors than Knifewood, with pale creamy swans or daisies on an amber, textured, glossy background (Fig. 154). Knifewood featured white swans or tan squirrels and dogs on a dark black or a gray matt, textured background. Color and glaze differentiated the two lines, designed by Rudolph Lorber.

The 1928 Weller Price List described Glendale as a "New Line, Modeled Birds and Forest Scenes. Decoration in tinted colors. Matt Glaze. Vases, wallpockets, Gate Bud Vase, Double Bud Vase, Candlesticks, etc." (Figs. 155, 156). The Weller catalogs showed Glendale console sets with flower

Fig. 153: *Marked Weller:* Knifewood swan vase 5″ high, Knifewood owl and squirrel vase 7″ high, and Selma daisy vase 7¼″ high. Collection: Dorothy Daniel. Photo by Leach.

Fig. 154: *Marked Weller:* Knifewood goldfinch vase 5″ high and Selma swan planter 3″ high.

Fig. 155: *Marked Weller:* Glendale double bud vase 7″ high, and Glendale wallpocket 12½″ high. Collection: Robert Miller and Glen Vogt.

Fig. 156: *Marked Weller:* Glendale parrot vase 9″ high, Glendale nest with eggs insert 3″ high, and Glendale thrush vase 5″ high. Collection: Kathryn Powell. Photo by Leach.

inserts; a nest with three eggs sat in a bowl encircled with seagulls. The vases in the catalog had colorful molded goldfinches, thrushes, and bluebirds on their nests, and long tailed parrots. The modelers favored the thrush above all the other birds. With its spotted, cream colored breast and brown feathers, the thrush epitomized the naturalistic colors and fine modeling of Glendale. The birds perched, flew, or sat in natural settings: cherry trees, meadows with timothy grass, daisies, and thistles, or the shore of a northern swamp.

Another nature effigy was Warwick, discussed September 5, 1929, in *PGB*. Each piece had a suggestion of slight decay in the rich and still beautiful woodland, according to *PGB*. Warwick possessed a distorted, tree shaped body with a soft matt glaze. The line comprised vases, bowls, twisted flower inserts, baskets, tree trunk vases, and small jars (Fig. 157). Warwick had an autumnal look, with flowers and leaves in relief.

Noted for its oak bucket effect, Wood Rose appeared January 8, 1925, in *C & G*. Each piece of Wood Rose resembled a wooden bucket with the soft brown grain of the wood modeled in relief by designer Rudolph Lorber (Fig. 158). Simulated iron bands surrounded the buckets, and clusters of red roses emerged in relief. Wood Rose came in bowls, wallpockets, and vases.

In the twenties, several lines appeared which depended on glaze effects for decoration: Bronze Ware, Colored Glaze Ware, Coppertone, Frosted Matt, Mottled Ware, Nile, and Underglaze Blue Ware. The company advertised Colored Glaze jardinieres in *C & G*, December 13, 1923. The catalogs pictured the jars, from Roma or Ivory molds, with embossed flowers and panels, glazed in two-tone shades of brown and green, or maroon and green. Note the jar here which shades from green to maroon (Fig. 159). Colored Glaze jars also came in monochromatic colors, green, blue, or pink, as noted in *Pottery for the Florist*.

The catalogs showed Mottled Ware, a drip glaze line with a hand-turned surface like Ansonia. Concentric, horizontal ridges surrounded each

Fig. 158: *Marked Weller:* Wood Rose vase 7" high. Collection: Dorothy Daniel. Photo by Leach.

Fig. 157: *Marked Weller:* Warwick vase 4½" high, Warwick flower insert 5½" high, and Warwick bud vase 7" high. Collection: Kathryn Powell. Photo by Leach.

Fig. 159: *Marked Weller:* Colored Glaze jardiniere 9" high, shading from green to maroon. Collection: Robert Miller and Glen Vogt.

Fig. 160: *Marked Weller:* Mottled Ware handled vase 6" high. Collection: Barbara Watson. Photo by Leach.

vase. Illustrated here is a heavy Mottled Ware vase with a rolled over rim, rope handles, and a pale lavender background (Fig. 160). A brown tint highlighted the ridges, accented by a glossy blue drip glaze below the rim. The factory marked the vase Weller on the base in black crayon.

Weller mounted a big display of Frosted Matt at the Pittsburgh Glass and Pottery Exhibition of 1921. It had a mottled or splotchy surface in light and medium green, blue, pink, brown, gray, or yellow. Often, a two-tone effect occurred, with gold on green, or red on mottled beige. The company made Frosted Matt vases, electric lamps, and bowls in a textured finish, which felt rough to the touch (Fig. 161).

In May 1929 *House and Garden* pictured a Coppertone bowl, filled with roses, and a matching candlestick. The ad stated: "Here the bowl in its shape and texture resembles a piece of ancient copper that centuries have mottled with green." *Pottery for the Florist* described Coppertone as "a glaze the color of Old Bronze, showing irregular through a verdant green matt." On February 4, 1980, Ruth Axline explained how Coppertone was made: "The brown or tan finish was brushed on lightly and then the green was applied with a sponge." Ruth pointed out that Coppertone, a Lorber creation, was such a popular line in the twenties that the Weller employees often put the Coppertone frogs in their pockets and took them home. The company produced vases, frog ashtrays, pitchers with fish handles, candleholders, console sets, and frogs and turtles in several sizes (Fig. 162). It also made Coppertone garden ware, including a frog sprinkler with the sprinkler mounted in the head of the frog.

Fig. 161: *Marked Weller:* Frosted Matt vase 7½" high and Cloudburst vase 5" high. Collection: Dorothy Daniel. Photo by Leach.

Fig. 162: *Marked Weller:* Top row: Coppertone candleholders 2" high; Coppertone frog 4" high. Bottom row: Coppertone turtle 4½" long; Coppertone turtle 6" long, and Coppertone frog cigarette stand 5" high. Collection: Kathryn Powell. Photo by Leach.

The catalogs illustrated a mystery line called Underglaze Blue Ware. It looked like blue Coppertone, with a blue sponged on surface instead of a green one. It came in mottled shades of black, dark blue, light blue, and gray, in vases, bowls, candlesticks, jars, and peds. I could not find or identify a piece of Underglaze Blue Ware.

Greora resembled Coppertone. With a textured, brown-rust background with bright green splotches all over, the line included pyramid flower inserts, vases, and strawberry pots. Greora, Mirror Black, and Nile are pictured in the color section (C-21).

Mirror Black emerged February 26, 1923, in CGL: "A beautiful mirror black has also been added to the line, and this is indeed a beauty. It is finished in such a manner as to give a slight silver lustre when the light strikes at a certain angle." Strawberry jars, vases, and wallpockets appeared in Mirror Black.

Bronze Ware was a line which resembled corroded antique bronze vessels, according to CGL, March 12, 1923. Colors varied from red to purple, gold, and green, treated with a simulated bronze finish and a metallic luster. The catalogs showed Bronze Ware vases and lamp bases. Most pieces had a nubby texture and iridescence, with a deep reddish purple coloring (Fig. 163).

PGB mentioned Nile on July 4, 1929: "It is made in various shades of green which, flowing together, form a harmonious maze of color irregularly matched." Nile was heavy and massive, with a gorgeous blue green glaze that looked silky as the hair of a cat, and varied from a deep green to a teal blue. The thick glaze dripped down over the bottom of the white clay base and was sheared off. Pitchers, large vases with curved handles or scalloped rims, bowl-shaped vases with triangular handles typified the line which was rarely marked. Witness the Nile vase in the color section (C-14).

John Lessell became head of the Weller decorating department in 1920. He created the luster lines, Chengtu, Lamar, LaSa, and Marengo, assisted by his wife Jennie, Art Wagner, and Carl Weigelt. LaSa had a white clay body decorated in red, gold, and green overglaze luster, with tropical landscapes or landscapes of trees, mountains, and lakes. Very complicated to produce, the line required several firings. Mrs. Lessell wrote to Norris Schneider on September 5, 1956, and explained that her husband was the sole creator of the overglaze luster. She claimed that Art Wagner, supervised by John Lessell, drew designs on LaSa, and that Carl Weigelt fired the kiln. PGB praised LaSa on November 2, 1922, for its metallic luster effects, its landscapes, forest, and water scenes in vivid colors. When Lessell left the Pottery in 1924, Wagner and Weigelt continued to make LaSa and to sign each piece on its side, Weller LaSa.

Called Chinese Red, Chengtu also came from John Lessell, who bequeathed it to Wagner and Weigelt. Ruth Axline watched Weigelt make Chengtu and described the process on May 12, 1980: "The vase received a light coating of oil or varnish and then he dusted with the silk bag the entire surface with the orange color . . . a finely ground overglaze color. I believe he put more than one coat on—firing between coats and I think the last coat may have been blown on. This orange was dangerous—poisonous

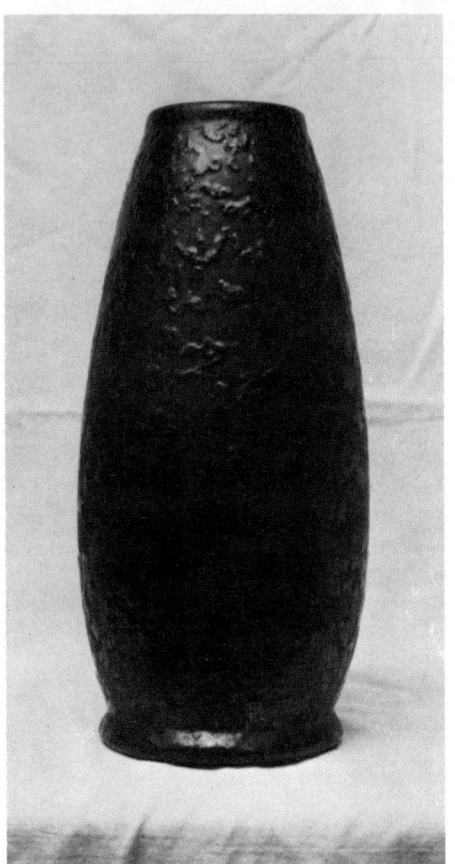

Fig. 163: Weller Bronze Ware vase 11½" high. Collection: Lee Dietrich.

I should say. Sometimes he wore a mask." An orange-red luster ware, Chengtu derived from ancient Chinese pottery its classic shape vases and covered jars.

An ad in *House and Garden* in June 1929 described Chengtu: "Duplicating ancient shapes with the old gentleness of color, or giving those shapes a full bright richness and clear lustre—such is Weller Pottery. A Coppertone vase . . . Or a bowl in Chengtu red to offset startlingly the milky white of gardenias."

The Luster line appeared in 1922 in a panorama of pastels, orange, blue, green, pink, and yellow. Note here the two vases with identical shapes, one LaSa, one yellow Luster (Fig. 164). The Weller catalogs illustrated several shapes and sizes of Luster: low bowls, tall candlesticks, baskets, stick vases, and comports.

Cloudburst arrived October 6, 1921, in *PGB*. In a poetic description, the journal wrote: "As the sun bursts through the clouds it creates an effect that nothing in nature can duplicate . . . the general effect is mottled and somewhat suggestive of agate. While no two pieces are alike, there are three tones particularly in evidence and which predominate. These are a red, a blue and a green, all being of the agate type of coloring. The ware itself is thin and very pleasing." Cloudburst vases and bowls had a porcelain-like quality, light and delicate, not clay heavy at all. *C & G* rhapsodized about Cloudburst on October 13, 1921: "The body is in an artistic crackled effect, in rich shades of green, blue, red, buff, etc., with a very lovely iridescent finish which seems to fairly radiate every color of the rainbow, just as the sun when it breaks through the clouds floods everything with light and color." Myriad intersecting dark lines gave Cloudburst a picture puzzle effect.

In addition to Chengtu, Cloudburst, LaSa, and Luster, Weller created Besline, Lamar, and Marengo, to surpass them in luster decoration. Besline had an acid-etched design of leaves and berries, placed either over or

Fig. 164: Marengo vase 8" high; *marked Weller:* LaSa vase 4" high, yellow Luster vase 4" high, and blue Luster vase 5½" high. Collection: Dorothy Daniel. Photo by Leach.

underneath a bright orange luster. Collectors first identified this rare, unmarked line through a paper label found on the base of a candlestick, marked Weller Besline and priced $11.00. On January 8, 1925, *C & G* described it as orange luster pottery with finely etched in line decoration of sprays of blossoms, berries, and leaves (Fig. 165). The journal commented that the large vases made good lamp bases, and that Besline came in two sizes of small handled baskets, three sizes of bowls, one comport, candlesticks, and several sizes of vases, with twenty-six pieces in the assortment. Pictured in the color section is a Besline candlestick and a Chengtu vase (C-20, C-21).

Marengo emerged April 8, 1926, in *PGB* as a new line with a luster glaze and a freehand decoration of palm trees. The Weller catalogs depicted Marengo in orange, lavender, blue, green, and pink luster with stylized trees in darker colors. Dark blue trees stood out against light blue backgrounds, with the trees outlined in white. Landscapes of mountains and lakes, with trees in the foreground, typified the line. The trees had puffs of leaves outlined in white. With its stylized trees and leaves, Marengo had a Deco look.

CGL noted the appearance of Lamar, August 20, 1923: "Lamar is a fine adaptation of the long famous 'Old Sung Glaze' by the Doulton Company of England. The feeling is American which possibly explains why it enjoys such demand." The Weller catalogs pictured Lamar with a red luster background and black decorations of pine trees, mountains, and lakes (Fig. 166). Some vases had palm trees near the ocean; others had herons feeding at a lake, or bears by the lake with mountains towering above. One vase depicted three tepees on a lake shore. Of all the overglaze luster lines, Lamar exhibited the most imaginative decorations.

John Lessell created several luster lines at Weller. Undoubtedly, he developed Besline, Cloudburst, and Luster, as well as Chengtu, Lamar, LaSa, and Marengo. The Pottery displayed some of these luster lines in February 1922 at the annual meeting of the American Ceramic Society in St. Louis. "S. A. Weller of Zanesville, Ohio . . . sent a wide range of ornamental pottery, including lustres, matte glazes, enamels, molded birds, etc.," wrote Frederick H. Rhead in the *Bulletin of the American Ceramic Society*, May 1922. Weller joined Rookwood, which showed its famous Tiger Eye glaze, Fulper, Newcomb, and Paul Revere Pottery, in the first exhibition of pottery held by the American Ceramic Society.

For a brief period in the mid twenties, after he left Weller, John Lessell began to make LaSa and Marengo for Camark Pottery in Camden, Arkansas. The LaSa twin was called Le-Camark. The Camark version of Marengo differed from Weller Marengo, in that the lines around the trees and the mountains were wider than those on Marengo. Camark occasionally marked these wares Lessell or Le-Camark. In style and decoration, however, Weller Marengo and LaSa surpassed Camark's imitations.

Designed by Rudolph Lorber, the Zona line endured from 1911 to 1936. The trade journals mentioned it often during the twenties, hence its inclusion in this chapter. On May 8, 1922, *CGL* noted the Zona Cottage Sets, decorated with apples and leaves, in sets including four plates, one

Fig. 165: Besline vase 9″ high, marked with a paper label. Collection: Dorothy Daniel.

Fig. 166: *Marked Weller:* Lamar vase 13½″ high. Collection: Dorothy Daniel.

sugar, creamer, teapot, handled basket, comport, and footed bowl. This famous apple dinnerware later became Franciscan Ware at Gladding, McBean and Company of California. Called Zona Utility Ware, the line sported red apples on a cream gloss background. Shown here are a vase, creamer, and milk pitcher in the famous apple pattern (Fig. 167).

On July 16, 1925, *C & G* announced another Zona tea set with embossed purple grapes, autumn leaves, and red flowers peeping through a lattice (Fig. 168). Fruit clusters formed the knobs on the teapots and sugar bowls. The journal also described Zona Baby Ware. The Baby Ware sets included a rolled rim dinner plate, bowl, cup, and pitcher, decorated with ducks, squirrels, bunnies, or Mary and her lamb (Fig. 169). Zona Baby Ware sold well for over a decade. It was still offered on the January 1, 1936 Price List.

The 1928 Price List had several Zona items: Persian Jar 10"; Jar bottom ribbed, narrow floral band at top; Jar ribbed wide floral band at base; Jar willow basket, roses, green and blue filling; Stand 20" Dancing Woman, all in a white gloss glaze with decoration in tinted colors. The Price List included the kingfisher and the duck pitchers, and Zona Utility Ware:

Fig. 167: *Marked Weller:* Zona Utility Ware: Vase 9" high, creamer 3½" high, and milk pitcher 6" high. Collection: Kathryn Powell. Photo by Leach.

Fig. 168: *Marked Weller:* Zona teapot 6" high. Collection: Robert Newton.

Fig. 169: *Marked Weller:* Zona Baby Ware dinner plate 7" diameter, and Zona Baby Ware pitcher 3½" high. Photo by Leach.

creamer, sugar and lid, teapot and lid, plate 10¼″, cup, saucer, plate 12½″, plate 9″, bowl, dessert 5½″, all with apple decoration.

The Weller catalogs illustrated several Zona pieces: white pitchers decorated with colored kingfishers or chrysanthemums, glossy white umbrella stands with dancers carrying colorful garlands of flowers, and flower and lattice jardinieres (Fig. 170). *PGB* described these jars on April 24, 1924: "The Zona line is in a white glaze with perpendicular inset blue lines, and is trimmed with rose bands finished with black borders." Zona resembled Flemish in its shapes and decorations.

Parian vases and wallpockets appeared in the mid twenties. They had the rough Graystone background with a sprightly decoration of a diamond-shaped flower within a diamond, cut into the surface and then tinted white and blue (Fig. 171).

In the twenties, gift shops and florists sold most of the pottery formerly offered by department stores and specialty china and glass shops. The emphasis was on the flowers, the gardenias in the Chengtu bowl. Nonetheless, Weller Pottery continued to offer beautiful vases, in Knifewood, Lamar, or Nile, which stood alone with or without flowers, as objects of virtu.

Fig. 171: Parian wallpocket 7¼″ high. Collection: Nick Pedotto. Photo by Tom Turnquist.

Fig. 170: *Marked Weller:* Zona jardiniere 6½″ high; Zona apple pitcher 7″ high; Zona floral pitcher 7½″ high; Zona duck pitcher 7½″ high, and Zona kingfisher pitcher 8″ high. Collection: Lee Dietrich.

C-1: Top left: *Impressed* Lonhuda Faience vase 11″ high, with a portrait of a lady, artist signed A.D.F. Top right: *Incised* Eocean Weller vase 10½″ high, with two storks in flight, artist signed Chilcote. Bottom left: *Incised* Eocean Rose Weller vase 6½″ high, with two fish, artist signed and painted by Charles Chilcote at age 16. Bottom center: *Impressed* Lonhuda Faience vase 11½″ high, with two elks, artist signed by Elizabeth Ayers. Bottom right: *Incised* Eocean Weller vase 5″ high, with a swan, artist signed by Levi J. Burgess. Courtesy of Dick Downey, Mose Mesre, and the Zanesville Art Center. Photo by Tullius.

C-2: Top left: *Impressed* Louwelsa Weller pitcher 12″ high, with an Indian portrait, artist signed by Anthony Dunlavy. Top right: *Impressed* Louwelsa Weller pitcher 13″ high, with an Indian portrait, artist signed by Levi J. Burgess. Bottom left: *Impressed* Dickensware Weller First Line vase 12″ high, with a portrait of a lady. Bottom center: *Impressed* Lonhuda Faience vase 14″ high, with a portrait of Aphrodite rising from the waves. Bottom right: *Impressed* Louwelsa Weller handled vase 10½″ high, with a portrait of a cavalier, artist signed by R.G. Turner. Courtesy of Dick Downey, Mose Mesre, and the Zanesville Art Center. Photo by Tullius.

C-3: Top left: *Impressed* Dickensware Weller Second Line pitcher 12" high, with the title incised on the back of the vase: "Mr. Weller dispelling the feverish remains of the previous evening's conviviality. *Pickwick Papers*," artist signed L.S. Top right: *Incised* Floretta Weller pitcher 14" high, decorated with apples. Middle row: Dickensware Weller Second Line vase 11" high, with the title incised on the back of the vase: "God Bless Me! What's the Matter? *Pickwick Papers*." Bottom left: *Marked Weller:* Woodcraft vase 7" high, with an owl on a tree trunk. Bottom right: *Impressed* Dickensware Weller Second Line vase 10" high, with an Indian portrait, artist signed by L.J. Burgess and dated 1901. Courtesy of Dick Downey, Mose Mesre, Harold Nichols, and the Zanesville Art Center. Photo by Tullius.

C-4: The Weller Dickensware Second Line Circus Vase 20" high, dated 1902 and artist signed with Latin abbreviations: C. B. Upjohn Sc. (Sculptor); G. Mull del. (Designer), and L. Knaus Pinxt (Painter). Courtesy of the National Road/Zane Grey Museum. Photo by Tullius.

109

C-5: The back side of the Weller Dickensware Second Line Circus Vase 20 inches high, with the magician, the young blond performer, and the dogs. Dated 1902, the vase is artist signed by C. B. Upjohn, Gordon Mull, and L. Knaus. Courtesy of the National Road/Zane Grey Museum. Photo by Tullius.

C-6: Top row left to right: *Impressed* Dickensware Weller, Glazed Dickensware mug 6″ high, with a seated clown, artist signed by L. J. Burgess. *Impressed* Louwelsa Weller mug 6″ high, with an Indian portrait, artist signed by Karl Kappes. *Impressed* Dickensware Weller, Glazed Dickensware mug 6″ high, with a female circus performer. Bottom row left to right: *Impressed* Dickensware Weller Second Line mug 5½″ high, with the title incised on the back: "Mr. Micawber impressing the names of the streets. *David Copperfield*," artist signed by C. B. Upjohn. *Incised* Eocean Weller mug 5½″ high, with a cat portrait, artist signed by Elizabeth Blake. *Incised* Dickens Weller, Dickensware Third Line mug 5¼″ high, titled "Wackford Jr.," and artist signed L.P. Courtesy of the Zanesville Art Center. Photo by Tullius.

C-7: *Impressed* Louwelsa Weller vase 20″ high, with a portrait of a lady, artist signed by Karl Kappes. *Incised* Dickens Weller, Dickensware Second Line vase 19″ high, taken from a painting by Emanuel Leutze in the Metropolitan Museum of Art, titled "Washington Crossing the Delaware." Artist signed by C. B. Upjohn and E. L. Pickens, and dated 1902. *Incised* Aurelian Weller vase 16″ high, with four ducks, artist signed by John J. Herold. Courtesy of the Zanesville Art Center. Photo by Tullius.

C-8: *Impressed* Louwelsa Weller pitcher 12¼" high, artist signed by L.J. Burgess, with a portrait of a smiling cavalier, reminiscent of Shakespeare's character of Sir John Falstaff in *Henry IV*, Part I and Part II. *Impressed* Louwelsa Weller vase 14" high, with a portrait of French artist and landscape painter of the Barbizon school Jean François Millet, who lived from 1814 to 1875 and painted scenes of French peasants at work in the fields: "The Angelus," "The Gleaners," and "The Sower." Both the title of the vase "Jean Francois Millet" and the artist signature of L.J. Burgess are done in yellow slip. Photo by Leach.

C-9: Top row left to right: *Marked Weller:* Hudson Pictorial vase 9″ high, with a girl and two rabbits, artist signed Timberlake. *Incised* Weller Rhead Faience vase 9″ high, with a geisha holding a parasol, artist signed C.M.M. *Impressed* Louwelsa Weller: Delta vase 8″ high, shown on the Weller Delta catalog page. Bottom row left to right: *Marked Weller:* Hudson Pictorial vase 8″ high, with three ships in full sail, artist signed by Hester Pillsbury; Hudson Pictorial vase 6¼″ high, with a fox in the snow, artist signed by Hester Pillsbury. *Impressed* Dickensware Weller Second Line vase 9″ high, with a cowboy and his horse and their reflection in a stream, artist signed by C. B. Upjohn. Courtesy of Dick Downey, Mose Mesre, and the Zanesville Art Center. Photo by Tullius.

Cover Photo & C-10: *Marked Weller:* Hudson Pictorial vase 16″ high, with a peacock in the snow, artist signed Timberlake; Second Line Dickensware vase 17″ high, with two cats and a butterfly, and Hudson Pictorial vase 16″ high, with two bluebirds and a butterfly. Courtesy of Dick Downey, Mose Mesre, and the Zanesville Art Center. Photo by Tullius.

C-11: *Marked Weller:* Rhead Faience vase 6⅝" high, with barren trees along a stream, artist signed R. at the base of one tree; Rhead Faience teapot 7" high, artist signed Rhead on the base, described in Chapter VIII; Auroro blue pinched neck vase 4½" high, with two daisies. Matt Green vase 13" high, with two molded semi-nude women with flowing skirts, on either side of the vase. This vase was pictured with four Weller Matt Ware vases in *Pottery and Glass* in August 1908. *Marked Weller:* Fudzi vase 8½" high, described in Chapter X. Courtesy of Sheila B. Amdur. Photo by Stephen J. McCabe.

C-12: Top row: *Marked Weller:* Narona jardiniere 9½″ high; Dickensware Third Line vase 8″ high, with a portrait of Sam Weller, and the title tube lined on a disc on the back of the vase: "Mr. Weller, Sr., *Pickwick Papers.*" Bottom row: *Impressed* Dickensware Weller Glazed Dickensware vase 13″ high, with three circus scenes: clown with hoop, two bareback riders, and female bareback rider; *marked Weller* Lasa vase 12½″ high, with a portrait of a Portuguese sailor smoking a pipe, and *incised* Auroral Weller candlestick 14½″ high. Courtesy of Dick Downey, Mose Mesre, Zanesville Art Center, and Zane Grey/National Road Museum. Photo by Tullius.

C-13: *Marked Weller* Sicard: Pillow vase 5½″ high; large pinched neck vase 16″ high, called the most perfect piece of Sicard ever made, and a Sicard vase 9½″ high, with a ruffled rim. In the foreground is a Weller Sicard tile 4″ wide by 8″ long, made by Henri Gellée, and artist signed on the back: H. Gellée 1905. A typed inscription on the back of the tile states: "Presented to Mr. Young, head of Roseville Pottery, as a sample in 1905 by the artist, who was late employed at Weller." Courtesy of the Zanesville Art Center. Photo by Tullius.

C-14: Back row: *Incised* Aurelian pitcher 22½" high, artist signed by E. Roberts and by modeler Coyleone. Coyleone molded the spout of the pitcher to resemble the head of an animal. Handled Nile vase 17" high, marked with a paper label. *Impressed* Dickensware Weller Second Line vase 17" high, titled "The Winemaker," artist signed by C. B. Upjohn and E. L. Pickens, and dated 1902.

Front row: *Impressed* Louwelsa Weller vase 11" high, with a portrait of an Irish setter, artist signed L. Blake. Marked Weller: Rosemont II vase 11½" high, with two calla lilies molded in full relief. Courtesy of Bob Bettinger and Kathryn Powell. Photo by Leach.

C-15: *Marked Weller:* Dickensware Third Line mug 5″ high, artist signed L.P., with the title tube lined on a disc on the back of the mug: "Young Bolber, *Nicholas Nickleby*." *Impressed* Turada Weller mug 6″ high. Perfecto vase 8″ high, artist signed by William H. Stemm. *Marked Weller* Sicard vase 6½″ high. *Impressed* Dickensware Weller Second Line vase 7″ high, with a gladiator. St. Louis World's Fair souvenir teapot 4¼″ high, slip decorated with a little girl holding a hanky and a stick. Courtesy of Bob Bettinger. Photo by Leach.

C-16: Orris vase 10½″ high, with a daffodil. *Impressed* Louwelsa Weller: Blue Louwelsa vase 11″ high. *Marked Weller:* Barcelona handled vase 9¼″ high; Melrose vase 12″ high, and Dickensware Third Line vase 13″ high, with the title tube lined on a disc on the back of the vase: "Carker, *Dombey and Son*." Courtesy of Bob Bettinger and Allan Wunsch. Photo by Leach.

C-17: Row 1: *Marked Weller:* Eclair vase 5″ high, Velvetone pitcher 11½″ high, Bells of San Juan jardiniere 8½″ high, Glazed Hudson vase 9″ high, with ruffled rim, and *incised* Eocean mug 5¼″ high, with cherries.
Row 2: Souevo vase 4″ high. *Marked Weller:* Atlas vase 4½″ high, Mottled Ware vase 6″ high. *Incised* Eocean Rose Weller vase 5″ high. *Impressed* Lonhuda Pottery Company vase 4½″ high, dated 1892 and artist signed by Jessie R. Spaulding. Courtesy of Bob Bettinger, Dorothy Daniel, Harold Nichols, and Barbara Watson. Photo by Leach.

C-18: Back row: *Marked Weller:* Muskota washerwoman 7½″ high, Florala vase 6¾″ high, Ethel vase 10″ high, Eldora-Chelsea vase 8″ high, and Muskota Leda and the Swan insert 7″ high.
Front row: *Marked Weller:* Florenzo vase 4″ high and Roma planter 4″ high. Courtesy of Dorothy Daniel. Photo by Leach.

C-19: Row 1: *Marked Weller*: Woodcraft vase 7″ high, in Voile mold; Voile vase 7″ high; Geode vase 8½″ high; Sydonia vase 9″ high; Lavonia vase 7″ high, and Tutone basket 7½″ high.

Row 2: *Marked Weller*: Hobart Girl with Flowers insert 8½″ high, in blue Muskota bowl; Lido vase 6½″ high; Muskota Kingfisher insert 9″ high, with a Muskota butterfly on the rim of the Muskota bowl; Glazed Hudson White and Decorated vase 7″ high, and Clarmont bowl 3″ high. Courtesy of Dorothy Daniel and Ann McDonald. Photo by Leach.

C-20: Row 1: Besline candlestick 10½" high. *Impressed* Dickensware Weller, Second Line vase 10¼" high, with a monk, holding a baton and singing. Greenbriar vase 10" high. *Marked Weller:* Hudson vase 9½" high, artist signed Morris; Loru vase 7¾" high; Breton vase 8" high, and Marvo vase 7" high.

Row 2: *Marked Weller:* Selma vase 7¼" high; Malvern vase 8½" high; Klyro U.C.T. souvenir vase 7" high; Silvertone vase 8" high; Floretta vase 6½" high; Forest basket 9½" high, and Ardsley vase 7½" high. Courtesy of Bob Bettinger and Dorothy Daniel. Photo by Leach.

C-21: Row 1: *Marked Weller:* Juneau vase 6½" high; Nile vase 7¾" high; Evergreen console bowl 5" high; Colored Glaze jardiniere 6" high, and Turkis vase 7½" high.

Row 2: *Marked Weller:* Chengtu vase 3½" high; Fruitone vase 6" high; Greora vase 4½" high; Evergreen goose 6" high; Mirror Black vase 5½" high; Fruitone stick vase 9" high, and Blossom vase 6" high. Courtesy of Bob Bettinger and Dorothy Daniel. Photo by Leach.

Back Cover and C-22: *Marked Weller:* Woodcraft vase 18" high, with a squirrel and an owl; Foxy Grandpa Incense Burner 5" high, and Gnomes on Toadstool 17" high. Courtesy of Mose Mesre. Photo by Tullius.

C-23: *Marked Weller:* Woodcraft wallpocket 15" high, with two bluebirds, one sitting on a nest and the other perched on an adjacent branch. This is the most detailed, elaborate, and beautiful of all the Weller wallpockets. *Impressed* Etna Weller pitcher 10½" high. Courtesy of Mose Mesre and the Zanesville Art Center. Photo by Tullius.

C-24: Three Weller Birds: The Dozing Duck 14" high; The Rooster 9½" high, and the Pelican 12" high. Courtesy of Dick Downey, Mose Mesre, and the National Road/Zane Grey Museum. Photo by Tullius.

C-25: Row 1: White Bulge-Eyed Dog 10″ high. *Marked Weller:* Black Bulge-Eyed Pup 4½″ high, and white CAT 10″ high. Row 2: Parrot with a Chengtu glaze 14″ high, and Elephant 10″ high. Courtesy of Dick Downey, Mose Mesre, and the Zanesville Art Center. Photo by Tullius.

Chapter XIV

The Twenties: Art Deco and Weller

Synonymous with the twenties was the Art Deco movement. It invaded art, dance, architecture, even art pottery. Finding its genesis in the Ballets Russes' productions in Paris in 1909, with their Oriental designs and bright colors, the movement reached a peak with the Paris Exposition of 1925. Art Deco was a reaction against the romanticism of Art Nouveau, the exaggerated curves, the asymmetrical forms, the lily, the peacock, and the flowing haired maiden. It was also an expression of classical and geometrical form, reflective of the speed, the modern inventions, and the liberated life styles of the twenties.

A major influence on the Art Deco movement was the discovery in 1922 of the tomb of King Tutankhamen in Egypt. The pyramid shapes, scarab motif, hieroglyphics, sphinx heads, Egyptian cats, all appeared in the art of the 1920s. Another influence, Mexican art and architecture, the stepped forms of the Aztec temples, for example, found expression not only in glass perfume bottles, but also in art pottery lines like Roseville Futura and Weller Lorbeek.

At the 1925 Paris Exposition, a smorgasbord of Art Deco designs emanated from European workshops. Art, architecture, even industry embraced it. Functional forms, clean lines, cubism predominated. Art Deco was angular, stylized. The geometric rose or chrysanthemum supplanted the Art Nouveau lily, with flowers outlined in darker colors to stress their angularity.

Women in the twenties began to assert their independence. They shortened their skirts and cut their hair. The Art Deco flapper upstaged the Art Nouveau lady with her flowing gown and flying hair. The flapper appeared everywhere: in posters, in paintings, and even in pottery figurines made by Cowan and by Weller.

Art Deco transformed American pottery. Roseville introduced Falline, Futura, and Morning Glory. The stepped shapes, pyramid effect, and geometric designs of Futura manifested several Deco styles. With their short hair, scarves, and illusion of speed, the nude figurines of Cowan Pottery epitomized Art Deco. Brush McCoy Pottery presented Matt Green Egyptian jardinieres, with the sphinx and the pyramids in relief. Always quick to recognize a trend, Weller Pottery brought out several Deco lines: Clarmont, Hobart, Lavonia, and Lorbeek in the twenties, and Atlas, Geode, and Stellar in the thirties. The strong geometrical shapes of Lorbeek and the flapper-like figurines of Lavonia and Hobart, all reflected Art Deco influences.

This chapter will explore not only the Deco lines, but also the other

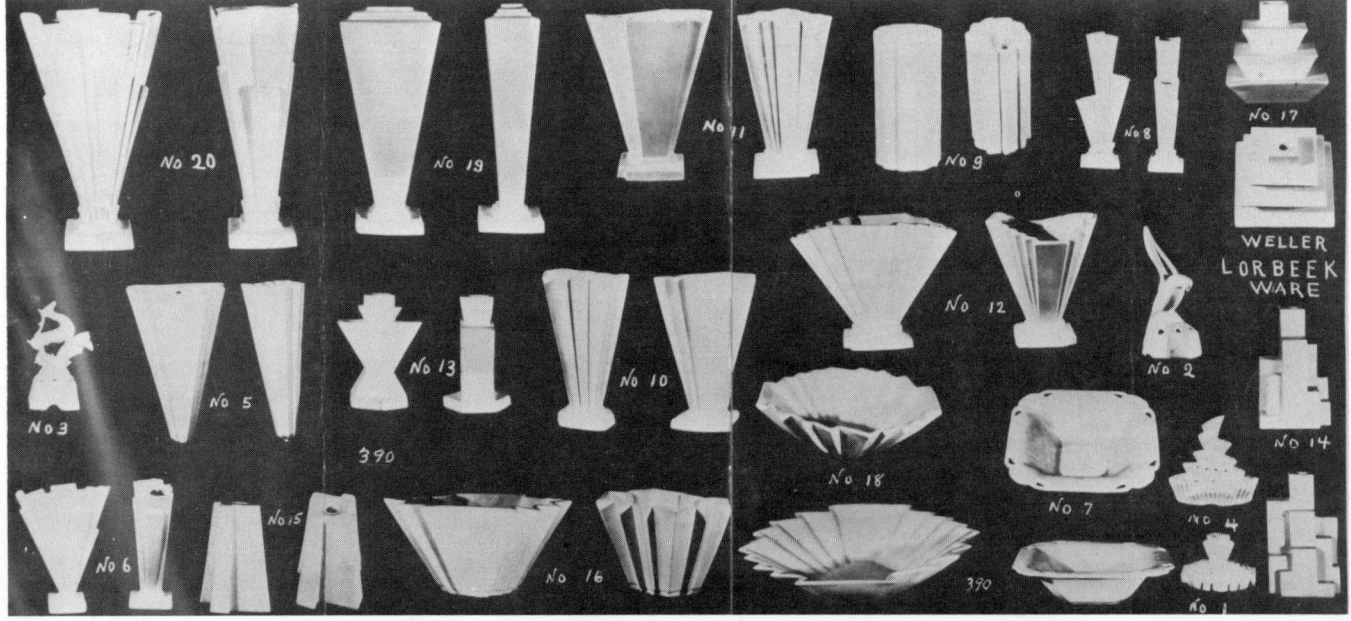

Fig. 172: Weller catalog page of Lavonia. Courtesy of Ohio Historical Society.

Fig. 176: Weller catalog page of Lorbeek Ware. Courtesy of Ohio Historical Society.

All About Weller
Price Guide

by
Ann Gilbert McDonald

No part of this book may be reproduced or used in any form or by any means, electronic or mechanical, including photocopying and recording, or by any information storage or retrieval system, without permission in writing from the publisher:
Antique Publications, P.O. Box 553, Marietta, Ohio 45750.

The Weller market has climbed high and dipped low like a roller coaster during the last fifteen years. From 1975 to 1981, prices rose. In 1982 they declined with the recession. From 1988 to 1990, prices climbed again. The Weller animals, Hudson Pictorial and Sicard vases showed strong appreciation. Vases, jars, planters, or pitchers, decorated with animals, birds, butterflies, or people, brought high prices. Today the Weller market is strong and viable.

As a dealer in Weller pottery for nearly twenty years, I watched the market rise and fall, then rise again. The price fluctuations have made it difficult to compile a Weller price guide. Many hours went into the preparation of this *Guide*. I examined catalogs, noted the prices of Weller pottery at shows and in shops, and read the trade journal ads. I called dealers all over the country to inquire what prices they had received for Weller. I consulted with several persons who buy and sell Weller pottery: George Alig, Bob Bettinger, Bernice Lyons, Mose Mesre, Esther Myers, Mike Smith, Don Treadway, and Bunnie Walker. I appreciate their kind assistance.

Knowing the current market for Weller was not enough. I had to evaluate each piece shown in *All About Weller*. I considered the measurements of each piece, realizing that the larger and taller vases bring higher prices. I looked at the art work, noted the artist who executed the piece, and considered the quality of the decoration. With the molded items, such as Cameo or Glendale, I looked for imaginative design, sharp detail and bright colors. I emphasized the aesthetics of each piece, asking: Is this a work of art? Did it take time an effort to produce it? Is it pleasing to the eye? Some lines, such as Warwick, charmed me by their ingenuity and absence of beauty. Finally, I considered rarity: the rarer the piece, the higher the price, usually.

The items priced here are presumed to be in perfect condition, with no chips, cracks, or repairs. Prices reflect this "mint condition." Some of these prices will seem too high, others too low. Take what you like and leave the rest.

This *Price Guide* is written only as a guide. Antique Publications and I are not responsible for any loss that may ensue as a result of using this *Guide*. I recommend supplementing the *Guide* with published auction results, for Weller pottery, and other established price guides.

Certain items in this *Guide* have no valuation. I have not assigned prices to pottery other than Weller/and Lonhuda, nor have I attempted to price such rare pieces as the large Aurelian vases exhibited at the St. Louis World's Fair in 1904, shown in Chapter VI.

At times, the height of the vases described in the captions of *All About Weller* will not correspond to the height given in the *Price Guide*. Since the book was already in press, I was unable to make the needed revisions. Therefore, please use the *Price Guide* for the most accurate measurement of each piece.

If a collector wishes to report a price he paid for Weller pottery, he can write to me at: P.O. Box 7321, Arlington, Va. 22207, and include a self addressed stamped envelope, if a reply is desired. Since I anticipate revising the *Price Guide* in a few years, I would like to receive reports on current prices. **I cannot appraise or identify any piece of pottery by mail, however.**

I am grateful for the interest and enthusiasm generated by the publication of *All About Weller* and for all the help given to me by Weller collectors throughout the United States.

Chapter I, pp. 1-11

Fig. 2:	Louwelsa Weller pitcher 12 1/4" high	$275-325.
	Louwelsa Weller vase 13" high	$275-325.
Fig. 3:	Dickensware II mug 5 1/2" high	$450-550.
	Dickensware II pitcher 7" high	$350-400.
	Dickensware II pillow vase 5 1/2" high	$300-350.
Fig. 4:	Dickensware II vase 15" high	$750-850.

Chapter III, pp. 21-15

Fig. 21:	Lonhuda/Weller vase 5" high	$700-800.
Fig. 22:	Lonhuda/Weller vase 5 3/8" high	$250-300.
Fig. 23:	Lonhuda/Weller bowl 9 1/2" long	$275-325.
Fig. 24:	Lonhuda/Denver vase 6" high	$275-325.
Fig. 25:	Lonhuda/Denver vase 8 1/2" high	$275-325.

Chapter IV, pp. 26-32

Fig. 26:	Louwelsa Weller vase 11" high	$1100-1300.
Fig. 27:	Louwelsa Weller vase 14" high	$2000-2500.
Fig. 28:	Louwelsa Weller vase 6" high	$1600-1900.
Fig. 29:	Louwelsa Weller vase 5" high	$120-130.
	Louwelsa Weller vase 6" high	$130-150.
	Louwelsa Weller jug 4 1/2" high	$120-130.
Fig. 30:	Louwelsa Weller vase 6 1/2" high	$110-125.
	Louwelsa Weller ewer 6 1/4" high	$150-175.
	Louwelsa Weller vase 6 1/2" high	$110-125.
Fig. 31:	Louwelsa Weller clock 8 3/4" high	$500-600.
Fig. 32:	Louwelsa Weller jardiniere and pedestal 33" high	
		$1850-2000.
Fig. 33:	Blue Louwelsa vase 11" high	$850-950.
	Matt Louwelsa pitcher 12" high	$400-500.
	Blue Louwelsa vase 11" high	$850-950.
Fig. 34:	Perfecto Weller vase 12" high	$900-1100.
Fig. 35:	Perfecto Weller pillow vase 10 1/2" high	$7000-8000.

Chapter V, pp. 33-42

Fig. 37:	Dickensware II mug 5 1/2" high	$600-700.
	Dickensware II vase 10 1/4" high	$650-800.
	Dickensware II vase 7" high	$500-600.

Fig. 38: Dickensware Admiral Tobacco Jar 7" high .... $700-800.
Dickensware Turk Tobacco Jar 7" high .... $700-800.
Dickensware Chinaman Tobacco Jar 6" high ... $600-700.
Fig. 39: Dickensware Irishman Tobacco Jar 6 1/2" high ....
$600-700.
Fig. 41: Dickensware II vase 10" high .... $850-950.
Glazed Dickensware vase 10" high .... $1600-1800.
Fig. 42: Dickensware II vase 10 1/2" high .... $850-1000.
Fig. 43: Dickensware II vase 13" high .... $1200-1500.
Fig. 44: Dickensware II vase 10" high .... $900-1100.
Fig. 45: Dickensware III Carafee with Cup .... $1200-1400.
Fig. 48: Etched Floral vase 12 1/4" high .... $300-400.
Fig. 49: Etched Matt vase 8 1/2" high .... $500-600.
Fig. 50: Glazed Dickensware vase 15" high .... $1000-1250.
Fig. 51: Dickensware I jardiniere 6" high .... $250-350.
Fig. 52: Hunter mug 6" high .... $400-500.
Fig. 53: Dickensware II vase 9" high .... $550-650.
Dickensware II souvenir vase 8" high .... $350-400.
Dickensware II golfer vase 12" high .... $750-850.
Dickensware II vase 12" high .... $600-700.

Chapter VI, pp. 43-47

Fig. 58: World's Fair souvenir mug 5 1/4" high .... $250-350.
Fig. 59: McKinley presidential plaque .... $75-85.
Fig. 60: Washington presidential plaque .... $95-125.
Jackson presidential plaque .... $75-85.
Grant presidential plaque .... $75-85.
Fig. 61: Lincoln presidential plaque .... $95-125.
Fig. 62: Roosevelt presidential plaque .... $85-95.
Map plaque .... $90-120.
Parker plaque .... $50-75.
Fig. 63: World's Fair souvenir vase 3 1/2" high .... $150-200.

Chapter VII, pp. 48-51

Fig. 64: Louwelsa Weller oil lamp 26" high .... $800-900.
Fig. 66: Louwelsa Weller electric lamp 13" high .... $475-575.
Fig. 67: Roma chandelier 22" diameter .... $800-1000.
Fig. 68: Woodcraft candelabra lamp 13 1/2" high .... $400-500.

Figs.69, 70: Brighton parakeet floor lamp 5 1/2' high ..$1200-1400.
Fig. 71: Blue Ware lamp base 8" high ....$200-250.
Louwelsa lamp base 10" high................................$300-400.
Hudson lamp base 8" high ....$300-400.

Chapter VIII, pp. 52-59

Fig. 72: Matt blue vase 10" high...$450-550.
Fig. 73: Turada Weller mug 6" high ....$250-300.
Fig. 74: Aurelian umbrella stand 23 1/2" high ....$1200-1500.
Fig. 75: Aurelian jardinieres and pedestals 37 1/2" high. Each......
$1200-1500.
Fig. 76: Eocean vase 14" high ....$700-900.
Fig. 77: Eocean stork vase 8" high ....$800-900.
Fig. 78: Late Eocean vases 6" high, 7" high. Each ....$110-130.
Fig. 79: Aurora vase 6" high..$350-400.
Fig. 80: Etna vase 10 1/2" high ....$200-250.
Fig. 81: Cameo Jewel umbrella stand 20" high ....$500-700.
Fig. 82: Cameo Jewel vase 14" high.......................................$350-450.
Fig. 83: Cameo Jewel vase 11 1/2" high.................................$400-600.
Fig. 84: Floretta vase 7" high..$80-100.
Floretta ewer 4 3/4" high ....$80-100.
Floretta vase 14" high...$150-200.
Fig. 85: Jap Birdimal vase 7" high...$700-900.
Fig. 86: Weller Rhead Faience vase 4 1/2" high...............$500-600.
Fig. 87 Weller Rhead Faience tea set ....$950-1250.

Chapter IX, pp. 60-67

Fig. 88: Art Nouveau vase 15" high..$400-500.
Fig. 89: Art Nouveau shell vase 6" high...........................$250-300.
Fig. 90: Art Nouveau jardiniere 9" high............................$400-500.
Fig. 91: Art Nouveau brown pitcher 12" high ....$150-250.
Fig. 92: Weller Matt Ware "Andromeda" vase 16" high ....
$2000-2500.
Fig. 93: Weller Matt Ware Man vase 18" high ....$900-1000.
Fig. 94: Matt Green jardiniere and pedestal 27 1/2" high................
$600-800.
Fig. 96: Sicard vase 6 1/2" high...$700-800.
Sicard vase 8" high ....$650-750.

Sicard vase 4 1/4" high	$650-700.
Fig. 97: Sicard vase 5" high	$600-675.
Sicard vase 6" high	$650-700.

Chapter X, pp. 68-75

Fig. 98: Fudzi vase 8 1/2" high	$800-900.
Fig. 99: Fru Russet vase 5 1/2" high	$150-175.
Fig. 100: Fru Russet vase 8 1/2" high	$175-200.
Fig. 101: Dresden vase 9" high	$700-800.
Fig. 102: Greenaways jardiniere 10" high	$500-600.
Fig. 104: Souevo vase 5" high	$95-120.
Fig. 105: Dechiwo vase 6 1/2" high	$450-600.
Fig. 106: Dechiwo jardiniere 10 1/2" high	$600-800.
Fig. 107: Burnt Wood candlestick 8" high	$65-85.
Burnt Wood bowl 3" high	$65-75.
Burnt Wood vase 5 1/2" high	$40-60.
Fig. 108: Burnt Wood vase 5 3/4" high	$90-120.
Fig. 109: Decorated Burnt Wood vase 10" high	$350-450.
Fig. 110: Decorated Burnt Wood vase 9" high	$350-450.
Fig. 111: Claywood vase 3 1/2" high	$35-45.
Claywood vase 3" high	$40-50.
Burnt Wood vase 7" high	$85-125.
Claywood vase 9" high	$50-60.
Burnt Wood mug 4" high	$85-125.
Fig. 113: Bells of San Juan jardiniere 8 1/2" high	$500-600.

Chapter XI, pp. 76-85

Fig. 114: Hudson Pictorial vase 9 1/2" high	$1200-1500.
Fig. 115: White and Decorated Hudson vase 8" high	$250-300.
Hudson vase 13" high	$650-750.
Gray Hudson vase 7 1/2" high	$100-140.
Fig. 116: Hudson vase 8" high	$250-300.
Blue and Decorated Hudson vase 9 1/2" high	$200-275.
Blue and Decorated Hudson vase 8 1/2" high	$195-225.
Fig. 117: Blue and Decorated Hudson vase 4" high	$125-150.
Blue and Decorated Hudson vase 9" high	$175-225.
Hudson vase 6" high	$250-300.
Fig. 118: Glazed Hudson white vase 7" high	$1600-1800.

Fig. 120: Hudson basket 14" high ....$200-300.
Fig. 121: Ivory jardiniere 6 1/2" high ....$50-75.
Fig. 122: Roma vase 9" high ....$55-65.
 Roma vase 7" high ....$45-55.
 Roma vase 5" high ....$40-50.
Fig. 123: Eldora-Chelsea vase 5" high ....$55-65.
Fig. 125: Noval vase 6" high ....$75-85.
 Ivory jardiniere 6" high ....$50-75.
 Dupont vase 6 1/2" high ....$65-75.
Fig. 126: Noval console set ....$225-250.
Fig. 127: Eclair vase 6" high ....$90-110.
Fig. 129: Tivoli bowl ....$75-95.
 Florala vase 8" high ....$85-95.
Fig. 130: Tupelo candlestick 7 1/2" high ....$50-60.
Fig. 131: Pearl vase 6" high ....$75-85.
 Tivoli basket 8 1/2" high ....$100-125.

Chapter XII, pp. 86-94

Fig. 132: Bo Marblo bowl 2" high ....$50-60.
 Blue Ware vase 10" high ....$150-175.
 Voile vase 7" high ....$55-65.
 Baldin vase 6" high ....$65-75.
Fig. 133: Bo Marblo vase 5 1/2" high ....$75-85.
 Morocco vase 10 1/2" high ....$85-95.
 Forest jardiniere 4 1/2" high ....$75-85.
Fig. 134: Denton umbrella stand 23" high ....$1000-1200.
Fig. 135: Blue Ware vase 10" high ....$150-175.
 Rosemont urn 7" high ....$250-325.
 Rosemont vase 6" high ....$250-300.
Fig. 136: Fairfield wallpocket 9" high ....$95-125.
Fig. 137: Hobart Bathing Beauty insert 6" high ....$150-165.
 Muskota bowl 2 1/2" high ....$50-75.
Fig. 138: Muskota Fisher Boy 6 1/2" high ....$150-175.
 Toadstool with Bee insert 2" high ....$65-75.
 Muskota frog 4 1/2" high ....$120-130.
Fig. 139: Muskota Three Cupids insert 8" high ....$250-300.
Fig. 140: Muskota Lobster insert 2" high ....$90-110.
 Glendale nest with eggs insert 3" high ....$120-130.

Muskota Woodpecker 5 1/2" high ....$150-175.
Fig. 141: Muskota Fisher Boy fish bowl stand 12" high...$400-500.
Fig. 142: Muskota Nude insert 8" high ....$225-275.
Forest basket 9 1/2" high ....$125-150.
Muskota blue butterfly 3 1/2" wide ....$95-110.
Muskota flower insert 2" high ....$55-65.
Fig. 143: Woodcraft Tree Trunk vase 10" high ....$50-60.
Woodcraft Three Foxes vase 5 1/2" high ....$160-180.
Woodcraft Log planter 4" high ....$45-55.
Fig. 144: Flemish squirrel bowl 3" high..................................$75-85.
Flemish reeded planter 4 1/2" high ....$65-75.
Fig. 145: Flemish Flower Form Compote 9" high ....$200-250.
Fig. 146: Flemish towel bar 12" long....................................$500-700.
Fig. 147: Flemish toothbrush holder 7" high.....................$350-450.
Fig. 149 Fruitone vase 5" high..$55-65.

Chapter XIII, pp. 95-104

Fig. 150: Blue Drapery vase 4" high.......................................$40-50.
Louella powder jar 3" high ....$40-50.
Fig. 151: Melrose basket 8 1/2" high ....$175-200.
Fig. 152: Arcola basket 8 1/2" high ....$175-200.
Fig. 153: Knifewood swan vase 5" high............................$175-225.
Knifewood vase 7" high..$275-325.
Selma vase 7 1/4" high ....$100-125.
Fig. 154: Knifewood vase 5" high.......................................$150-200.
Selma planter 3" high ....$175-225.
Fig. 155: Glendale double bud vase 7" high....................$200-250.
Glendale wallpocket 12 1/2" high.........................$250-275.
Fig. 156: Glendale parrot vase 9" high..............................$350-400.
Glendale nest with eggs insert 3" high ....$120-130.
Glendale vase 5" high ....$160-190.
Fig. 157: Warwick vase 4 1/2" high.....................................$50-60.
Warwick flower insert 5 1/2" high...........................$55-75.
Warwick bud vase 7" high..$50-60.
Fig. 158: Wood Rose vase 7" high ....$65-75.
Fig. 159: Colored Glaze jardiniere 9" high......................$100-125.
Fig. 160: Mottled Ware vase 6" high ....$75-85.
Fig. 161: Frosted Matt vase 7 1/2" high.............................$65-75.

Cloudburst vase 5" high ....$65-85.
Fig. 162: Coppertone candleholders 2" high ....$40-60.
Coppertone frog 4" high ....$125-150.
Coppertone turtle 4 1/2" long ....$135-165.
Coppertone turtle 6" long ....$150-175.
Coppertone frog cigarette stand 5" high ....$95-125.
Fig. 163: Bronze Ware vase 11 1/2" high ....$150-200.
Fig. 164: Marengo vase 8" high ....$250-300.
LaSa vase 4" high ....$175-200.
Luster vase 4" high ....$35-45.
Luster vase 5 1/2" high ....$35-45.
Fig. 165: Besline vase 9" high..$325-400.
Fig. 166: Lamar vase 13 1/2" high.....................................$300-400.
Fig. 167: Zona Utility Ware vase 9" high............................$50-60.
Zona Utility Ware creamer 3 1/2" high ....$30-40.
Zona Utility Ware pitcher 6" high.............................$50-60.
Fig. 168: Zona teapot 6" high ....$95-125.
Fig. 169: Zona Baby Ware dinner plate 7" diameter.............$45-55.
Zona Baby Ware pitcher 3 1/2" high........................$35-45.
Fig. 170: Zona jardiniere 6 1/2" high ....$100-125.
Zona apple pitcher 7" high......................................$110-140.
Zona floral pitcher 7 1/2" high ....$110-140.
Zona duck pitcher 7 1/2" high ....$100-125.
Zona kingfisher pitcher 8" high ....$150-175.
Fig. 171: Parian wallpocket 7 1/4" high..............................$85-110.

Color Section, pp. 105-126

C-1:	Lonhuda Faience vase 11" high	$1400-1500.
	Eocean vase 10 1/2" high	$1000-1200.
	Eocean Rose vase 6 1/2" high	$800-900.
	Lonhuda Faience vase 11 1/2" high	$1900-2000.
	Eocean vase 5" high	$600-700.
C-2:	Louwelsa Weller pitcher 12" high	$1200-1400.
	Louwelsa Weller pitcher 13" high	$1400-1600.
	Dickensware I vase 12" high	$800-1100.
	Lonhuda Faience vase 14" high	$2000-2400.
	Louwelsa Weller vase 10 1/2" high	$1200-1400.
C-3:	Dickensware II pitcher 12" high	$1200-1400.
	Floretta pitcher 14" high	$500-550.
	Dickensware II vase 11" high	$900-1100.
	Woodcraft vase 7" high	$450-550.
	Dickensware II vase 10" high	$1000-1200.
C-4:	Dickensware II Circus Vase 20" high	$7000-8000.
C-6:	Glazed Dickensware mug 6" high	$650-700.
	Louwelsa Weller mug 6" high	$700-800.
	Glazed Dickensware mug 6" high	$650-700.
	Dickensware II mug 5 1/2" high	$750-800.
	Eocean mug 5 1/2" high	$700-900.
	Dickensware III mug 5 1/4" high	$450-500.
C-7:	Louwelsa Weller vase 20" high	$2000-2200.
	Dickensware II vase 19" high	$2000-2500.
	Aurelian vase 16" high	$2000-2500.
C-8:	Louwelsa Weller pitcher 12 1/4" high	$1400-1600.
	Louwelsa Weller vase 14" high	$2000-2500.
C-9:	Hudson Pictorial vase 9" high	$2000-2400.
	Weller Rhead Faience vase 9" high	$1200-1500.
	Delta vase 8" high	$450-550.
	Hudson Pictorial vase 8" high	$2000-2200.
	Hudson Pictorial vase 6 1/4" high	$1800-2000.
	Dickensware II vase 9" high	$1100-1300.
C-10:	Hudson Pictorial vase 16" high	$2400-2800.
	Dickensware II vase 17" high	$2300-2800.
	Hudson Pictorial vase 16" high	$2000-2400.

C-11:	Weller Rhead Faience vase 6 5/8" high	$750-850.
	Weller Rhead Faience teapot 7" high	$650-750.
	Aurora vase 4 1/2" high	$300-400.
	Matt Green vase 13" high	$850-1000.
	Fudzi vase 8 1/2" high	$800-900.
C-12:	Narona jardiniere 9 1/2" high	$400-500.
	Dickensware III vase 8" high	$900-1100.
	Glazed Dickensware vase 13" high	$2000-2200.
	LaSa vase 12 1/2" high	$1800-2000.
	Auroral candlestick 14 1/2" high	$350-450.
C-13:	Sicard pillow vase 5 1/2" high	$850-900.
	Sicard vase 16" high	$4000-5000.
	Sicard vase 9 1/2" high	$900-1000.
	Sicard tile 4" by 8"	$1200-1500.
C-14:	Aurelian pitcher 22 1/2" high	$1400-1500.
	Nile vase 17" high	$300-400.
	Dickensware II vase 17" high	$1200-1500.
	Louwelsa Weller vase 11" high	$1100-1300.
	Rosemont II vase 11 1/2" high	$350-400.
C-15:	Dickensware III mug 5" high	$500-600.
	Turada mug 6" high	$250-300.
	Perfecto vase 8" high	$650-800.
	Sicard vase 6 1/2" high	$700-800.
	Dickensware II vase 7" high	$500-600.
	World's Fair souvenir teapot 4 1/2" high	$150-200.
C-16:	Orris vase 10 1/2" high	$50-60.
	Blue Louwelsa vase 11" high	$850-950.
	Barcelona vase 9 1/4" high	$150-175.
	Melrose vase 12" high	$150-200.
	Dickensware III vase 13" high	$1000-1300.
C-17:	Row 1:	
	Eclair vase 5" high	$75-95.
	Velvetone pitcher 11 1/2" high	$90-120.
	Bells of San Juan jardiniere 8 1/2" high	$500-600.
	Glazed Hudson vase 9" high	$150-175.
	Eocean mug 5 1/4" high	$150-175.

	Row 2:
	Souevo vase 4" high ....$85-100.
	Atlas vase 4 1/2" high ....$65-75.
	Mottled Ware vase 6" high ....$75-85.
	Eocean Rose vase 5" high ....$275-325.
	Lonhuda Pottery vase 4 1/2" high ....$300-350.
C-18:	Back row:
	Muskota washerwoman 7 1/2" high...................................$150-175.
	Florala vase 6 3/4" high ....$75-85.
	Ethel vase 10" high ....$125-150.
	Eldora-Chelsea vase 8" high...$65-75.
	Muskota Leda and the Swan insert 7" high.......................$250-300.
	Front row:
	Florenzo vase 4" high ....$35-45.
	Roma planter 4" high ....$35-45.
C-19:	Row 1:
	Woodcraft vase 7" high ....$45-55.
	Voile vase 7" high ....$55-65.
	Geode vase 8 1/2" high..$250-300.
	Sydonia vase 9" high ....$55-65.
	Lavonia vase 7" high..$50-75.
	Tutone basket 7 1/2" high ....$85-95.
	Row 2:
	Hobart Girl with Flowers insert 8 1/2" high ....$25-150.
	Blue Muskota bowl ....$25-35.
	Lido vase 6 1/2" high ....$30-40.
	Muskota Kingfisher insert 9" high ....$150-250.
	Muskota butterfly..$90-110.
	White Muskota bowl ....$25-35.
	Glazed Hudson White and Decorated vase 7" high ....
	$250-300.
	Clarmont bowl 3" high..$40-50.
C-20:	Row 1:
	Besline candlestick 10 1/2" high ....$250-300.
	Dickensware II vase 10 1/4" high ....$450-600.
	Greenbriar vase 10" high ....$80-90.
	Hudson vase 9 1/2" high..$300-350.
	Loru vase 7 3/4" high ....$50-60.

Breton vase 8" high .... $75-100.
Marvo vase 7" high .... $30-40.
Row 2:
Selma vase 7 1/4" high .... $100-125.
Malvern vase 8 1/2" high .... $40-50.
Klyro vase 7" high .... $50-60.
Silvertone vase 8" high .... $125-150.
Floretta vase 6 1/2" high .... $90-100.
Forest basket 9 1/2" high .... $125-150.
Ardsley vase 7 1/2" high .... $45-50.

C-21: Row 1:
Juneau case 6 1/2" high .... $60-75.
Nile vase 7 3/4" high .... $70-80.
Evergreen console bowl 5" high .... $40-50.
Colored Glaze jardiniere 6" high .... $85-95.
Turkis vase 7 1/2" high .... $40-50.
Row 2:
Chengtu vase 3 1/2" high .... $40-60.
Fruitone vase 6" high .... $50-60.
Greora vase 4 1/2" high .... $50-60.
Evergreen goose 6" high .... $65-75.
Mirror Black vase 5 1/2" high .... $60-75.
Fruitone vase 9" high .... $50-60.
Blossom vase 6" high .... $30-40.

C-22: Woodcraft vase 18" high .... $1500-1600.
Foxy Grandpa Incense Burner 5" high .... $650-750.
Gnomes on Toadstool 17" high .... $2000-2400.

C-23: Woodcraft wallpocket 15" high .... $1200-1500.
Etna pitcher 10 1/2" high .... $250-350.

C-24: The Dozing Duck 14" high .... $900-1100.
The Rooster 9 1/2" high .... $750-850.
The Pelican 12" high .... $1200-1500.

C-25: White Bulge-Eyed Dog 10" high .... $1800-2000.
Black Bulge-Eyed Pup 4 1/2" high .... $500-700.
White Cat 10" high .... $1500-1600.
Parrot on perch 14" high .... $900-1200.
Muskota Elephant 10" high .... $1200-1400.

Chapter XIV, pp. 127-138

Fig. 173: Hobart flower bowl 6 3/4" high ....$150-175.
Hobart Woman Vase 11" high ....$160-200.
Fig. 174: Hobart Bathing Beauty insert 6" high ....$150-165.
Hobart Girl with Flowers insert 8 1/2" high ....$125-150.
Fig. 175: Hobart Cupid and Duck insert 4 1/2" high.............$75-95.
Fig. 177: Lorbeek vase 6 1/2" high.........................$50-70.
Lorbeek yellow bird 8" high ....$140-160.
Fig. 178: Clarmont ginger jar 6" high......................$50-60.
Fig. 179: Brown Kenova vase 6" high ....$85-95.
Brown Kenova vase 8" high ....$95-110.
Fig. 180: Orris planter 2 1/2" high ....$35-45.
Orris vase................................$40-50.
Orris planter 3" high......................$35-45.
Fig. 181: Orris vase 10 1/2" high ....$50-60.
Orris vase 12" high.....................$65-75.
Fig. 183: Klyro planter 4" high ....$30-40.
Fig. 184: Alvin double bud vase 7" high.................$40-65.
Barcelona ewer 6 1/2" high.................$120-140.
Silvertone vase 8" high.................$125-150.
Klyro souvenir vase 7" high.................$50-60.
Fig. 185: Pumila candleholders 2 1/2" high................$40-50.
Pumila flower form bowl 3 1/2" high ....$30-40.
Pumila bowl 4" high ....$45-65.
Fig. 187: Brown Ansonia vase 7" high ....$65-75.
Green Fleron pitcher 6 1/2" high.............$75-85.
Fig. 188: Fleron Console Set....................$125-150.
Fig. 189: Velvetone pitcher 11 1/2" high ....$90-120.
Hobart Bacchus 9" high ....$175-200.
Ardsley vase 7 1/2" high...................$45-50.
Lorbeek stag insert 7" high................$140-160.
Clarmont bowl 3" high.................$40-50.
Fig. 191: Brighton pheasant 7 1/2" high ....$300-350.
Fig. 192: Brighton Hanging Parrot 15" high ....$900-1200.
Fig. 194: Alpha vase 4 1/4" high..................$65-75.
Fig. 195: Alpha planter 3" high ....$40-50.
Alpha candleholder 5 1/2" high................$65-75.

Chapter XV, pp. 139-147

Fig. 196: Tutone basket 7 1/2" high ....$85-95.
Evergreen ginger jar 12 1/2" high ....$90-110.
Blo Red vase 6" high ....$50-70.
Fig. 197: Sabrinian pitcher 9" high ....$160-200.
Sabrinian planter 4" high ....$50-75.
Fig. 198: Tile Scene of Weller Pottery Log Cabin ....$2500-3000.
Fig. 199: Weller Art Tile 6" square ....$100-150.
Fig. 200: Weller Art Tile 6" square ....$100-150.
Fig. 201: Elberta vase 5 1/2" high ....$40-50.
Sydonia vase 6" high ....$40-50.
Fig. 202: Golden Glow vase 9" high ....$55-65.
Fig. 203: Ivoris vase 6" high ....$30-40.
Fig. 204: Bonito vase 5" high ....$65-75.
Bonito vase 7 1/2" high ....$100-125.
Bonito vase 6" high ....$95-120.
Bonito vase 5" high ....$65-75.
Fig. 205: Bonito vase 11 1/2" high ....$200-275.
Fig. 206: Patra basket 6" high ....$50-60.
Fig. 207: Neiska vase 5" high ....$30-40.
Seneca vase 6 1/2" high ....$30-40.
Paragon vase 4 1/2" high ....$75-85.
Fig. 208: Velva vase 9 1/2" high ....$85-110.
Neiska vase 5" high ....$30-40.
Cornish vase 6 1/2" high ....$35-45.
Terose teapot 6" high ....$95-110.
Fig. 209: Turkis vase 9" high ....$80-90.
Fig. 210: Greenbriar vase 5" high ....$50-60.
Juneau vase 5 1/2" high ....$50-60.
Fig. 211: Ragenda vase 6 1/4" high ....$40-60.
Fig. 212: Malvern vase 5 1/2" high ....$35-45.
Fig. 213: Dedonatis Ware vase 6 3/4" high ....$190-250.
Dedonatis Ware vase 6 3/4" high ....$190-250.
Fig. 214: Darsie vase 5 1/2" high ....$30-40.
Patricia vase 5" high ....$60-70.
Novelty Line ashtray 5" high ....$75-100.
Manhattan vase 6" high ....$40-50.

Fig. 215: Classic vase 7 1/2" high ....$35-45.

Chapter XVI, pp. 148-156

Fig. 217: Novelty Line ashtray 4 1/2" high ....$135-165.
Fig. 218: Novelty Line ashtray 6" long ....$65-75.
Fig. 219: Novelty Line Egyptian wallpocket 10" high ....$150-250.
Fig. 220: Stellar vase 5" high ....$150-200.
Fig. 221: Geode vase 3 1/2" high ....$150-225.
Fig. 222: Cretone vase 6 1/2" high ....$275-325.
Fig. 223: Raceme vase 9" high ....$350-400.
Fig. 224: Raceme Glossy vase 5 3/4" high ....$50-75.
Fig. 225: Decorated Novelty Utility Line sugar bowl 3 3/4" high and creamer 4" high ....$350-400.
Fig. 226: Pastel vase 6 1/2" high ....$30-40.
Fig. 227: Bouquet vase 5" high ....$30-40.
    Atlas star vase 7" high ....$65-85.
    Roba pitcher 6" high ....$40-50.
Fig. 229: Raydence fan vase 6 1/2" high ....$30-40.
    Senic vase 6 1/2" high ....$50-60.
    Floral vase 4 1/2" high ....$30-40.
    Roba vase 6 1/2" high ....$35-45.
Fig. 230: Mi-Flo vase 10" high ....$60-75.
    Rudlor vase 7" high ....$30-40.
    Panella ginger jar 6 1/2" high ....$65-75.
    Arcadia vase 5 1/2" high ....$30-40.
    Blossom cornucopia 6" high ....$30-40.
Fig. 231: Gloria vase 5" high ....$30-40.
Fig. 232: Loru vase 7 3/4" high ....$50-60.
    Softone cornucopia 3" high ....$25-35.
    Softone comport 5" high ....$30-40.
    Dorland vase 6" high ....$30-40.
    Lido vase 6 1/2" high ....$30-40.
Fig. 233 Blue Cameo rectangular vase 8 1/2" high ....$40-50.
    Blue Cameo handled vase 13" high ....$65-85.
Fig. 234: Blue Cameo footed bowl 4" high ....$35-45.
    Lido candleholder 2 1/2" high ....$25-35.
    Delsa pitcher 6" high ....$30-40.
Fig. 235: Wild Rose cornucopia 5 1/2" high ....$25-35.

Fig. 236: Oak Leaf vase 9" high .... $40-60.
Fig. 237: Regal cornucopia vase 7" high .... $35-45.
Fig. 238: Chase vase 6 1/2" high .... $150-225.
Fig. 239: Chase vase 9" high .... $225-275.

Chapter XVII, pp. 157-163

Fig. 240: Scottie Dog 12" high .... $1200-1500.
Fig. 241: Gnome on Tree Trunk 19" high .... $2200-2500.
    Gnome on Boulder 18" high .... $2200-2500.
Fig. 242: Rooster 12 1/2" high .... $2500-3000.
    Chicken Hen 7 1/2" high .... $600-900.
Fig. 243: Sitting Squirrel 12" high .... $1400-1600.
Fig. 244: Spaniel 10 1/2" high .... $1400-1600.
Fig. 246: Coppertone Frog Sprinkler 13" high .... $1600-1800.
    Coppertone frog 8" high .... $450-650.
    Coppertone frog 4" high .... $125-150.
    Coppertone frog 2" high .... $90-100.
Fig. 247: Coppertone Birdbath with Muskota Fisher Boy 54" high.
    $2500-3500.
Fig. 248: Two Weller Swans 18 1/2" high and 14 1/2" high ....
    $4500-6000.
Fig. 249: Pesca, Old Man with Fish, 12 1/2" high .... $350-450.
Fig. 250: Silva the Dancer 8" high .... $175-225.
Fig. 251: Cactus Frog 4" high .... $65-85.
    Cactus Elephant 4" high .... $75-95.
    Cactus Elephant 4" high .... $75-95.
    Cactus Snail 4" high .... $65-85.
Fig. 252: Cactus Pan with Lily 5 1/2" high .... $75-95.
Fig. 253: Three Face Dog planter 7 1/2" high .... $65-75.
    Duck-Rabbit-Penguin planter 6 1/2" high .... $50-65.
Fig. 254: Woodcraft Squirrel wallpocket 9" high .... $150-190.
Fig. 255: Woodcraft wallpocket 9 1/2" high .... $95-125.
Fig. 256: Wallpocket 8 1/2" high .... $85-95.
Fig. 257: Brown and White Cookware custard set .... $100-150.
Fig. 258: Cream Light Blue Banded bowls. Set of 4 .... $160-200.
Fig. 259: Kitchengem Egg Beating pitcher 5 1/2" high .... $40-50.
Fig. 260: Ollas Water Bottle 11 1/2" high .... $45-65.
Fig. 261: Pierre teapot 8 1/2" high .... $55-65.

Fig. 262: Gold Decorated teapot 5 1/2" high..........................$75-85.
Fig. 263: Terose teapot 7" high...$95-120.

Chapter XVIII, pp. 164-173

Fig. 266: Aurelian vase 13" high..$900-1200.
Fig. 268: Matt Louwelsa pitcher 12 1/2" high ....$450-550.
Fig. 269: Aurelian Oil Banquet Lamp 27" high ....$1200-1400.
Fig. 271: Marengo vase 8 1/2" high..$250-350.
Fig. 272: Slip decorated vase 17 1/2" high........................$850-950.
Fig. 273: Yellow Cretone vase 8" high................................$300-350.
        Hudson vase 10 1/2" high......................................$325-375.
        Hudson vase 9" high..$300-350.

Chapter XIX, pp. 174-180

Fig. 278: Jap Birdimal geisha vase 10" high ....$1200-1400.
Fig. 281: Dickensware II vase 10 1/2" high ....$650-800.
Fig. 282: Dickensware II Circus Vase 20" high ....$7000-8000.
Fig. 283: Ivory vase 10" high...$55-65.
Fig. 284: Ting Console Set...$150-250.
Fig. 285 Decorative Etched Ware floor vase 27 1/2" high................
        $2500-2800.
Fig. 286: Rabbit 8" high...$800-1000.

Chapter XX, pp. 181-183

Fig. 288: Dickensware I vase 6" high..................................$175-225.
        Glazed Dickensware vase 12" high................$1500-1800.
Fig. 289: Eocean Rose vase 6" high ....$275-325.
Fig. 290: Hudson Pictorial vase 6 1/4" high ....$1000-1250.
Fig. 291: Sicard vase 8" high ....$850-950.
Fig. 292: Etched Floral vase 13 1/2" high ....$190-250.
Fig. 293: Yellow vase 4 1/2" high..$95-125.
        Green vase 6" high...$125-150.
Fig. 294: Aurelian Oil Banquet Lamp 36" high ....$1600-1800.
Fig. 295: Dickensware I jardiniere 11" high.......................$250-350.
        Dickensware I jardiniere 9" high.........................$200-275.

lines of the twenties at Weller: Alpha, Alvin, Ansonia, Ardsley, Barcelona, Breton, Brighton, Euclid, Fleron, Florenzo, Kenova, Klyro, Malta, Marvo, Orris, Pumila, Silvertone, Velvetone, and Wayne Ware.

Created by Rudolph Lorber, Lavonia and Hobart shared the same molds. *PGB* described Lavonia on January 13, 1927, as a line in lilac shading to pistachio green. The coloring enhanced the effect of Lavonia and gave it a springtime look. The 1928 Price List enumerated Lavonia wares: Woman Vase and Wallpocket, Bowl Bulrushes, Footed Bowl, Vine and Leaf Bowl, Octagon Bowl, Fluted Bowl, Flat Ribbed Bowl, and Candlesticks. Note here the page from the catalog and the Lavonia vase in the color section (Fig. 172 and C-19).

The elegant Woman Vase came in both Hobart and Lavonia. Standing arms outstretched, the woman seemed to flaunt her independence, grace, and agility (Fig. 173). She came in a free standing vase, 6 x 8 or 8 x 11 inches, or a wallpocket 7½ by 11 or 7 by 12 inches. With her bobbed hair and uncorseted dress, she epitomized the flapper. Hobart differed from Lavonia with its blended colors, lavender shading to green, or pink to green. Hobart had monochromatic colors, white, green, or blue.

The 1928 Price List presented several Hobart items: Cupid and Duck, Woman Candlestick, Kingfisher Insert, Crane Insert, Woman Wallpocket, Woman Flower Vase, Bowl Flying Geese, Flying Geese Insert, Sea Nymph Insert, Bathing Beauty Insert, Wading Girl Insert, Lydia and Swan Insert. The Lydia and Swan Insert embodied the classical Greek myth of Leda and the Swan. The Bathing Beauty Insert was a graceful nude sunbathing on a large rock (Fig. 174). The Cupid and Duck Insert represented a nude boy, with long hair like a girl, poised on a river bank to watch a duck in the water (Fig. 175). The Lydia and Swan and Crane Inserts also came in Muskota. *PGB* praised Hobart on March 4, 1926, for its finely modeled

Fig. 173: *Marked Weller:* Hobart blue kneeling nude flower bowl 6¾" high, and Hobart blue Woman Vase 11" high. Photo by Leach.

Fig. 174: *Marked Weller:* White Hobart Bathing Beauty insert 6" high, and blue Hobart Girl with Flowers insert 8½" high. Photo by Leach.

figures suggestive of Greek sculpture. Hobart and Lavonia figurines attract both collectors and interior decorators today.

PGB commended Lorbeek on August 2, 1928, for its modern, cubist look. With its lavender or tan semi-gloss glaze, the line comprised bowls, console sets, candlesticks, vases, and lamps, in angular, pyramid shapes, as illustrated here in a page from the Weller catalogs (Fig. 176). Two flower inserts appeared, a leaping stag and a graceful bird with upturned wings (Fig. 177). Lorbeek represented Weller's deepest bow to Art Deco.

Clarmont also reflected Deco influences. Stylized roses and clusters of grapes adorned the vases and bowls. The Weller catalogs pictured covered jars, exotic bowls with attached curved candleholders, vases, and candlesticks with scalloped handles. With its reddish brown, matt finish, the line was festooned with beading, rosettes, and horizontal ribbing. (Fig. 178).

PGB discussed Kenova January 29, 1920, a line with a dark green or tan, leather-like background and raised decorations. The Weller catalogs pictured vases with relief designs of roses and daisies, cameos of birds or ladies in profile, all hand colored. In the cameo vases, small bands of fruit or flowers encircled the top of each vase, with the cameo portraits below. Extending from the top to the bottom of the vase, long stemmed flowers also decorated Kenova (Fig. 179).

Another twenties line, Barcelona had a gold background with hand painted, stylized red, blue, and yellow flowers, reminiscent of Pennsylvania Dutch designs. The Pottery made Barcelona candlesticks, vases, ewers, baskets, hanging baskets, and bowls, all with concentric ridges, which gave a hand turned effect. Note the tall Barcelona vase in the color section (C-16).

A line in matt green with an antique metal effect, Orris appeared in *PGB*, August 31, 1922. To each piece of Orris, the decorator applied a matt green glaze, sometimes heavily, sometimes ever so lightly, so that the

Fig. 175: *Marked Weller:* Blue Hobart Cupid and Duck insert 4½" high.

Fig. 178: *Marked Weller:* Clarmont ginger jar 7" high. Collection: H.M. Dietrich.

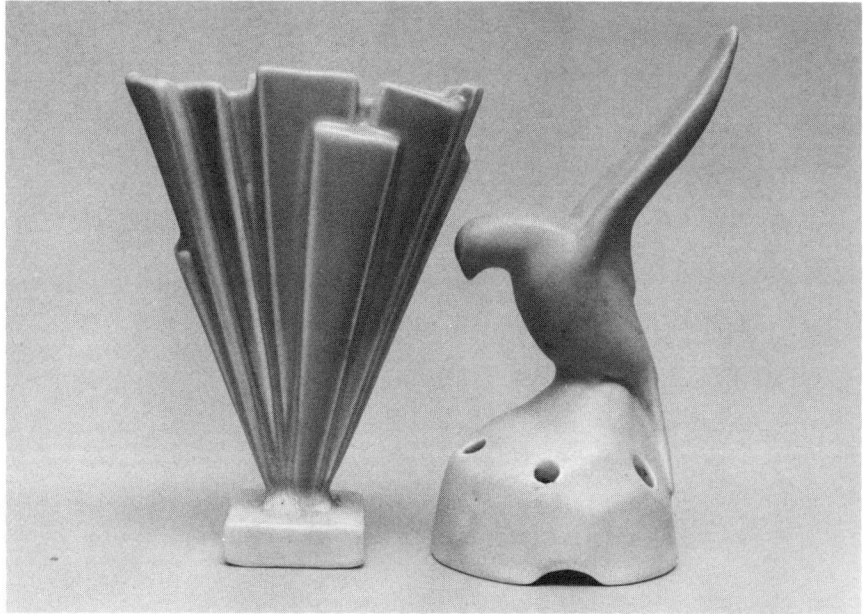

Fig. 177: *Marked Weller:* Lorbeek vase 6½" high in lavender, and Lorbeek yellow bird 8" high. Collection: Dorothy Daniel. Photo by Leach.

Fig. 179: *Marked Weller:* Brown Kenova vases: 6" high and 8" high. Photo by D.L. Hill.

Fig. 180: Green Orris wares: Raised leaf planter 2½" high, vase, and cosmos planter 3" high. Courtesy of Allan Wunsch. Photo by Leach.

Fig. 181: Green Orris wares: Vase 10½" high, with daffodil, and vase 12" high, with magnolias. Courtesy of Allan Wunsch. Photo by Leach.

Fig. 182: Weller catalog page of Orris. Courtesy of Ohio Historical Society.

outline of the molded design showed through to the red clay. The five pieces illustrated here have molded cosmos, magnolias, daffodils, and stylized flowers and leaves in relief (Figs. 180, 181). The cosmos planter was number 44 on the Orris catalog page, while the raised leaf planter was number 40. Note the catalog page here (Fig. 182). The factory rarely marked Orris. Collectors can identify it through a study of the shapes and designs in the catalogs: wallpockets, vases, bulb bowls, umbrella stands. Orris resembled the Moss Aztec line of Peters and Reed Pottery.

Crockery and Glass described Klyro July 16, 1925, as a line "done in Flemish finish in wide effect with cut out work and raised flowers and fruit." Klyro had a textured, vertical-striped white or light brown background (Fig. 183). It was often reticulated around the rim. The factory made Klyro vases, candlesticks, baskets, and planters, decorated with pink roses and blue grapes. They also created seven inch bud vases, souvenirs of the United Commercial Traveller's Convention. The paper label on these vases read: "Klyro Ware manufactured by the Weller Potteries, Zanesville, Ohio, Souvenir of the UCT Convention June 19 '26." The UCT was founded in Columbus, Ohio, as a protective fraternity for traveling salesmen.

PGB mentioned Alvin on January 13, 1927. The 1928 Price List described the line as "cream ivory with tinge of brown, matt finish, decoration in tinted colors." It listed the following items: Gate Bud Vase, Handled Bud Vase, Tree Bud Vase, Flower Basket, Fan Vase, Wallpocket, Oval Vase, and Double Bud Vase. The Alvin line looked like Woodcraft, with tree trunk vases, twining branches, and red apples in relief. The factory used some Woodcraft molds for Alvin. Alvin, however, was a lighter brown and had a bit more gloss than Woodcraft (Fig. 184).

With a crumpled surface like crushed paper, Silvertone emerged August 2, 1928, in *PGBS*. Raised, molded red poppies, yellow roses, or purple grapes stood out against the lavender to gray background. The factory made vases, wallpockets, bowls with flower inserts, and matching

Fig. 183: *Marked Weller:* Klyro planter 4" high. Collection: Dorothy Daniel. Photo by Leach.

Fig. 184: *Marked Weller:* Alvin double bud vase 7" high; Barcelona ewer 6½" high; Silvertone vase 8" high, and Klyro U.C.T. souvenir vase 7" high. Collection: Dorothy Daniel.

Fig. 185: *Marked Weller:* Pumila candleholders 2½" high, Pumila flower form bowl 3½" high, and Pumila bowl 4" high. Collection: Kathryn Powell. Photo by Leach.

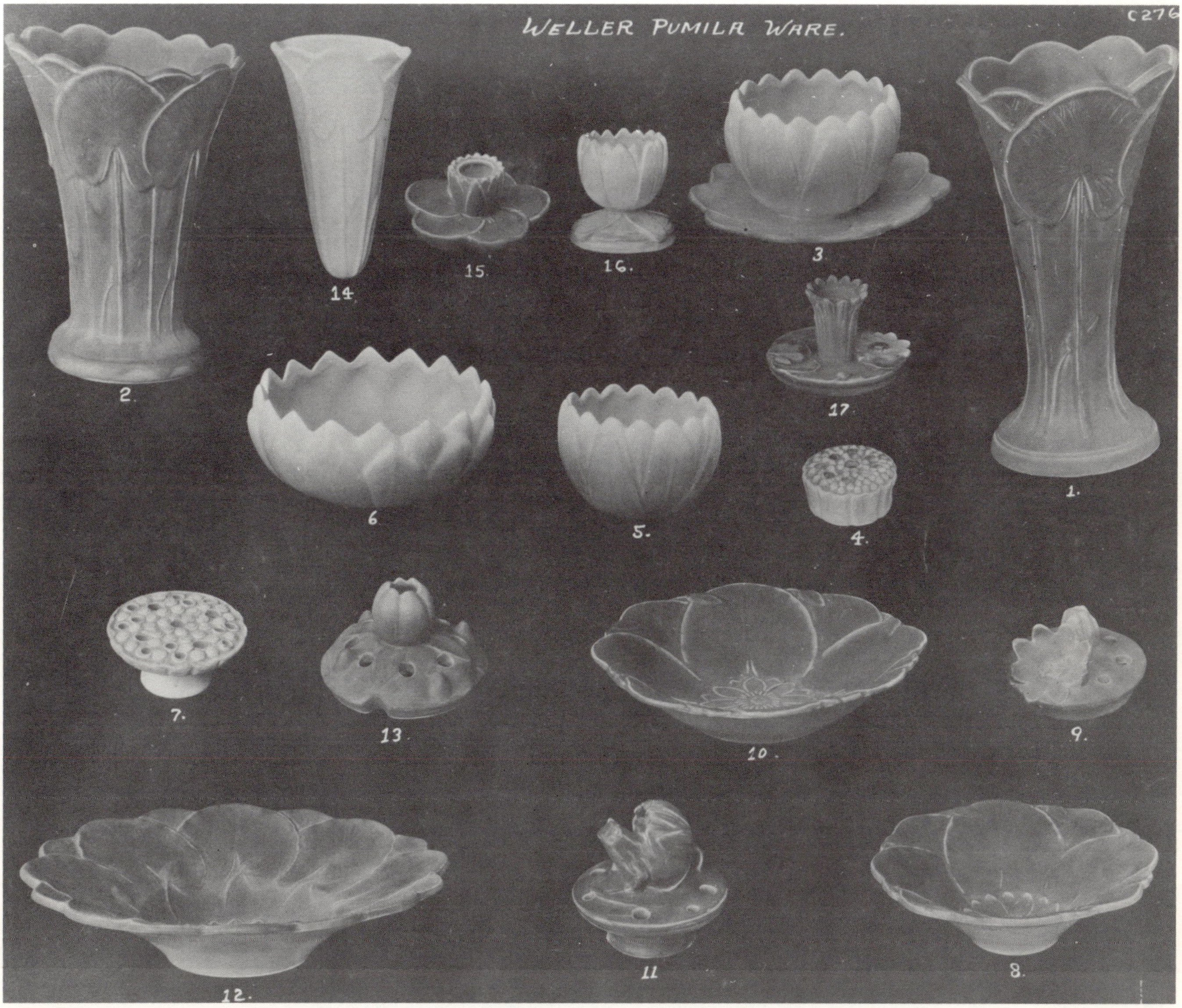

Fig. 186: Weller catalog page of Pumila Ware. Courtesy of Ohio Historical Society.

candleholders in Silvertone. At times, the overall effect was impressionistic, with pale colors and hazy decorations.

Molded water lilies enhanced the Pumila line, described January 12, 1928, in *PGBS*. Each piece portrayed a complete water lily in shades of pale to deep green. "The Lily Leaf is used as the decorative feature—finished in a blended green-tan gray mat glaze," wrote *Pottery for the Florist*. Pictured here are flower form bowls with yellow interiors and matching candleholders (Fig. 185). Pumila resembled ancient Chinese pottery from the Sung Dynasty, with its flower form bowls and vases. Witness the page of Pumila from the Weller catalogs (Fig. 186).

Ansonia appeared March 4, 1926, in *PGBS* which described it as pottery with a rough finish and a two-tone effect. With a dull brown or orange glaze and a hand turned surface, it looked as if it had just come off the wheel. The catalogs pictured Ansonia bowls, pitchers, candlesticks, and handled vases. The vases were shaped like urns (Fig. 187). The pitchers had primitive spouts, and the bowls had rolled-over rims. When the background changed from brown to green, a new line emerged in semi-gloss green called Fleron. The catalogs pictured both lines together and noted: "Ansonia . . . in green is Fleron." They shared the same molds.

Like Ansonia, Fleron had a hand turned effect, with an eye-pleasing glaze, a semi-gloss green with a rich raspberry interior and touches of

Fig. 187: Brown Ansonia vase and green Fleron pitcher, marked Weller. Collection: Lee Dietrich.

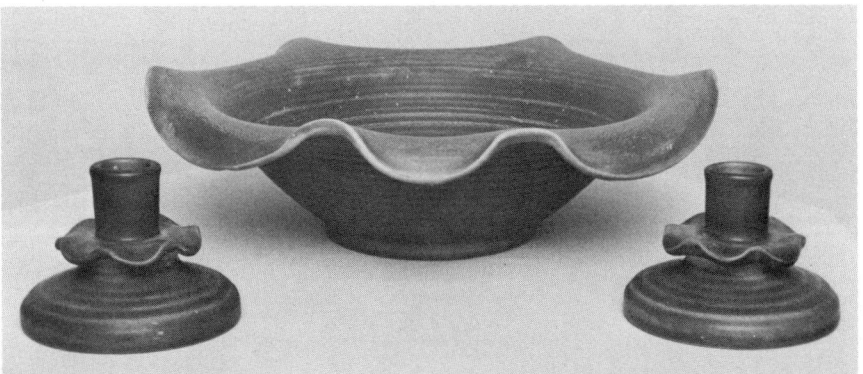

Fig. 188: *Marked Weller:* Fleron Console Set: Green bowl with maroon interior 4" high and green candleholders 3½" high. Collection: Dora Betts.

raspberry flowing into the green glaze, especially at the rim. Sometimes, the glaze had the look of silk with subtle striations. Note here the Fleron console set with the scalloped bowl and the matching candleholders (Fig. 188).

Closely related to Ansonia and to Fleron was Velvetone. The 1928 Price List described Velvetone: "New Styles all made from Hand Turned pieces. Ware comes in . . . Blended Green Pink, Yellow Pink, Brown Green, Matt Glaze." Unlike Fleron, the glaze on Velvetone had no gloss, but the colors were rich and dramatic: deep yellow-gold and pink (Fig. 189). Ansonia, Fleron, and Velvetone resembled ancient artifacts dug up from Greek or Roman ruins: antique jars, jugs, and pitchers. The factory usually marked these lines on the base: Weller Ware Hand Made.

A colorful line of bird figurines, Brighton endured from 1916 to 1923. The Weller catalogs showed Brighton and Malta together with the heading, "Malta Plain, Brighton Decorated." Note the catalog page (Fig. 190). The Brighton birds included: #1 the cardinal, #2 the bluebird, #3, 6, 8 the parrots (three of them in various sizes), #4 the two parakeets, #5 the pheasant, #12 the two geese with spread wings (Fig. 191). The Brighton birds comprised many colors. The bluebirds were glossy blue. The parrots were dark gray, maroon, orange, and yellow, and ranged in size from 7½ to 15 inches high, for the spread-winged, hanging parrot (Fig. 192).

Appearing on the same catalog page as Brighton, Malta was an undecorated, matt finish ware. "To fill a growing demand the Weller potteries have put out a new line of decorative ware called Malta. It is fancy plain glaze in assorted colors, exquisite shades and lines. There has been a call for the decorative birds in plain colors instead of the very conspicuous natural colorings. Weller has filled that demand most successfully. What the birds lack in coloring they make up in grace of line

Fig. 189: *Marked Weller*: Pink and gold Velvetone pitcher 11½" high; blue Hobart Bacchus 9" high; Ardsley vase 7½" high; Lorbeek leaping stag insert 7" high, and Clarmont bowl 3" high. Collection: Dorothy Daniel. Photo by Leach.

Fig. 191: *Marked Weller*: Brighton pheasants 7½″ high by 10½″ long. Collection: Nick Pedotto. Photo by Tom Turnquist.

Fig. 192: Brighton Hanging Parrot 15″ high. Collection: George and Judy Alig.

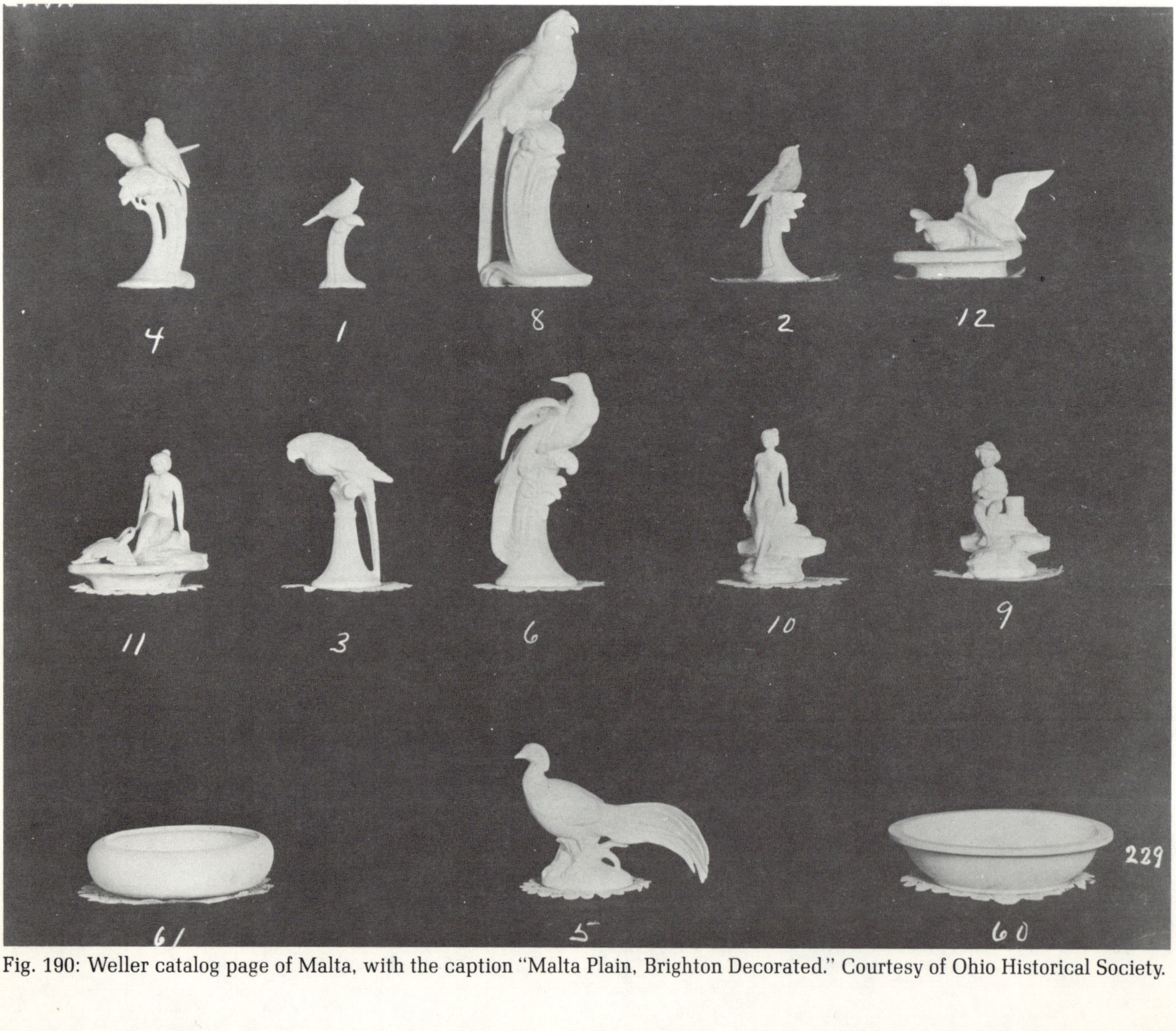

Fig. 190: Weller catalog page of Malta, with the caption "Malta Plain, Brighton Decorated." Courtesy of Ohio Historical Society.

Fig. 193: Weller catalog page of Breton. Courtesy of Ohio Historical Society.

and good workmanship," wrote *CGL* on August 20, 1923. Malta presented birds and figurines in solid, monochromatic colors.

Florenzo had a cream colored, "basket effect," described in *PGB*, January 12, 1928. Horizontal ribs extended from the top to the bottom of each piece, to simulate a basket. The top of each vase or planter was tinted green. Red roses, or grapes and roses stood out in relief. The factory made Florenzo baskets, planters, and vases.

The cattail line, Ardsley, emerged January 12, 1928, in *PGB. Pottery for the Florist* remarked that Ardsley was "produced in several pleasing tones of green. The design is partly tinted with dark color bringing out the modeling." The molded green cattails with their brown tips reached from the top to the bottom of each piece. White or blue water lilies ornamented the bases. Swaying in the breeze on curving stems, irises also decorated Ardsley vases, wallpockets, and baskets. The company produced fan vases, double vases, candleholders, bowls, and a kingfisher flower frog which sat in a cattail bowl. Ardsley, Florenzo, and Marvo appear in the color section (C-18, C-20).

Reflecting the thick growth of a tropical jungle, Marvo had raised, molded palm trees, ferns, and foliage which encompassed each piece. The 1928 Price List commended its free, hand carved look in four colors: green, rust, blue, and mauve. The line included vases, wallpockets, pitchers, jars and peds, bowls, and candlesticks.

The 1928 Price List described Wayne Ware as a line with "cream ivory, green filling, matt glaze." The company made large jars and peds in Wayne Ware, to decorate automobile show rooms, hotels, and clubs.

The Weller catalogs pictured Breton (Fig. 193). Usually unmarked, it came in matt brown, black, orange, or green, with a band of embossed flowers bisecting the upper half of each vase or bowl. Like Breton, Euclid was a monochromatic line. The Weller catalogs showed Euclid low bowls, vases, and candlesticks in classic shapes with a pastel matt finish.

The Weller catalogs illustrated a mystery line, a cream colored ware with reticulated rims and geometric designs. I will call it Alpha, although

Fig. 195: Alpha planter 3" high and Alpha candleholder 5½" high. Collection: Dorothy Daniel. Photo by Leach.

in the catalogs it bore no name. This line may have come from the Zanesville Art Pottery, purchased by Sam Weller in 1920 to become Plant III or the Ceramic Avenue plant. Ruth Axline and Dorothy Laughead thought that Alpha originated with this company. When Weller bought the Zanesville Art Pottery from David Schmid, he acquired not only the molds, but also the pottery stock and the employees. The catalog pictured hanging baskets, vases, comports, and planters with reticulated rims and designs of rampant lions and of classical women in profile. Decorators tinted the lightly incised lines green, yellow, blue, or black (Figs. 194, 195). Most pieces of Alpha lacked the Weller mark on the base.

I have allotted two chapters to the pottery produced at Weller in the 1920s. Use and re-use of the same molds with new glazes and decorations typified the wares of this decade. Spirited designs, hand coloration, and Art Deco styles characterized Weller pottery in the twenties.

Fig. 194: *Marked Weller:* Alpha vase 4¼" high. Collection: Phyllis Larson.

Chapter XV
The Thirties at Weller: 1930-1934

Prodigious output marked the thirties at Weller Pottery. From Atlas to Patricia, the modelers were ingenious, designing pieces shaped like stars, ducks, swans, and seahorses. These were the dark years of the Depression when Weller consolidated three plants into one at Ceramic Avenue. In a letter March 1, 1980, Ruth Axline recalled these hard times: "I remember most of the plant on Ceramic Avenue was laid off and some only worked half a day. I don't think it lasted more than two years." Working quickly to capture business, Weller introduced new lines, abandoned most hand decorating, and tried to keep prices low. The thirties saw the death of Harry Weller in 1932, and the successive presidencies of Frederic Grant from 1932 to 1933, Irvin Smith from 1933 to 1937, and Walter Hughes from 1937 to 1948.

"At Zanesville plants there today are more than 4000 different shapes and designs the Weller potters have turned out. They range the gamut from humble pots to table art pottery. Production is continuous. The whole nation knows Weller ware," wrote *C & G* in December 1931. The journal sagaciously noted the secret of Weller's success: "Handmade goods will always command a wide market but Weller early established the truth that art pottery can be manufactured on a wide commercial basis, be reasonable in price and still possess exceptional quality." Discussing current production at the Pottery, the journal stated: "Each piece passes through the hands of thirty men during production, only the finest clays are used, firing the ware has been regulated to a scientific degree that insures its perfection."

During the thirties, Weller created myriad new lines, from Blo Red to Patricia. *PGB* introduced Blo Red on July 10, 1930: "The new production is a fused color, with its lights and shades." The ware simulated a "blood redness," hence the name Blo Red. An orange glaze was superimposed over a red glaze, to give a mottled effect. The line shared molds with Turkis and Nile. With Blo Red, the colorful red glaze became the decoration (Fig. 196).

With its shells and seahorses, Sabrinian emerged in 1930, one of the best lines of the decade. *PGB* praised the line on January 2, 1930, noting that its billowing lines evoked the lazy waves of the sea. The factory made ashtrays, baskets, vases, pitchers, planters, wallpockets, and console sets. A pair of candlesticks with inverted dolphins, similar to those made at the Sandwich Glass Company a century earlier, accompanied a lavender shell shaped bowl with a seahorse flower insert. The stately pitcher had a semi-gloss scallop shell body, a shell shaped spout, and a life-like brown

Fig. 196: *Marked Weller*: Tutone basket 7½" high, Evergreen ginger jar 12½" high, and Blo Red vase 6" high. Collection: Dorothy Daniel.

Fig. 197: *Marked Weller*: Sabrinian pitcher 9" high and Sabrinian planter 4" high. Collection: Lillian Saxe. Photo by Leach.

seahorse handle. Pictured here are the Sabrinian pitcher and planter (Fig. 197).

Tiles and Tile Work advertised and pictured Weller tiles in April and in June 1930. Several tiles formed the vivid canal scene in Venice with a gondola and houses along the canal, in April 1930. Based on a design from Bolivia, Weller Inca tiles with strange gods and figures appeared in the journal in June 1930. Mae Timberlake painted a six tile scene of Weller Pottery as it looked in 1872, with the log cabin and the old horse Whitey (Fig. 198). Hester Pillsbury decorated other tiles with scenes of sailing ships and Germanic castles.

Fig. 198: Tile Scene of the 1872 Weller Pottery Log Cabin, artist signed Timberlake. Courtesy of Norris Schneider.

Fig. 199: Weller Art Tile: Windmill, 6″ square. Collection: The W.E. Lyons.

Fig. 200: Weller Art Tile: Lake and Mountains, 6″ square. Collection: The W.E. Lyons.

Illustrated here are two colorful Weller Art Tiles, one with a golden yellow and orange windmill set against a puffy white cloud, the other with green trees in the foreground, set against a blue lake and green mountains (Figs. 199, 200). Strong colors and raised designs enhanced the beauty of these tiles, which measured 6 by 6 inches square. They were made of buff colored clay, about one half an inch thick. The factory incised the mark WELLER ART TILES on the back of each tile, in wet clay, with a nail-like implement. Since the production of tiles was limited, few exist today. The Pottery also made several historical and classical plaques, some titled: "Cupid and Venus," "Hercules carrying Bear," "Adam and Eve in the Garden of Eden," "Bonaparte," "Dante," and "Homer."

Tutone appeared January 2, 1930, in *PGB* which noted the odd, original shapes and the raised, green designs which resembled oriental tree growths. In Tutone, embossed dart shaped flowers decorated maroon to pink, or green to tan backgrounds. Occasionally, a tiny white cluster of berries nestled near the leaf. The factory made wallpockets, console sets, vases, and baskets. Shapes were modern and geometrical, exemplified by the triangular console sets. Art Deco endured at Weller.

Sydonia and Elberta came out in 1931 (Fig. 201). Designed by Dorothy Laughead and Rudolph Lorber, they had diverse shapes and colorations. An ad in *C & G* in November 1931 pictured Sydonia wares: a double branched candleholder, a double vase, a quadruple vase, a console bowl, and three ribbed fan vases with scalloped tops. The appearance of Sydonia marked Weller's sixtieth anniversary, and the opening of a new office and plant. "Taking humble marsh plants as the inspiration and the model the potter has made bowls, jugs and vases of the broad, deeply-fluted leaves, from the tubular roots has conceived bud vases and candlesticks, from the open blossom of the marsh flower has devised cornucopias. In grayish blue or in light green this ware is equally delightful," wrote *C & G*, in December 1931. The embossed marsh mallow plant enhanced each piece of Sydonia.

Fig. 201: *Marked Weller*: Elberta vase 5½" high and Sydonia vase 6" high. Collection: Dorothy Daniel. Photo by Leach.

Fig. 202: *Marked Weller*: Golden Glow vase 9" high. Collection: Dorothy Daniel. Photo by Leach.

Elberta had a mottled glaze which shaded from pink to green, or from green to honey brown. An inch wide pink or green clay rope often encircled the vases. Sometimes, the shapes were grotesque, as in the twisted bowl vases with folded over rims and pointed edges. The company produced Elberta vases, bowls, and console sets.

Bonito, Evergreen, Golden Glow, and Ivoris appeared in 1932. Evergreen had a beautiful pale blue green glaze with a moire effect. Like many of the Weller lines, it appeared first at the annual Pittsburgh Glass and Pottery Exhibition. Oriental shapes predominated, reproductions of old Chinese pottery, bowls in petal form, covered urns, and ginger jars. The catalogs illustrated Evergreen ducks, geese, pelican planters, footed vases, console sets, petal bowls with inserts, hanging planters with horizontal fluting, and stepped pyramid candleholders. The factory incised the mark Weller Pottery in script on the base of most pieces.

PGB described Golden Glow and Ivoris on January 7, 1932, the former with its "golden yellow to sere brown" colors, the latter with its "embossed white ivory" finish. Golden Glow had raised, stylized green or brown leaves, and tiny curved handles (Fig. 202). The shapes evoked the art of the metal worker, according to *PGB*. The Pottery made covered jars, vases, and candleholders in Golden Glow. Ivoris borrowed the molds from several Weller lines: Flemish, Golden Glow, Ivory, Neiska, Sydonia, and Velva. The factory produced covered jars, candlesticks, bowls, planters, and vases, in a white semi-gloss glaze (Fig. 203). Simplicity was the hallmark.

Dorothy Laughead designed the shapes for Bonito, one of the few hand decorated wares of the thirties. Ruth Axline, Anna Jewett, Rose Langstaff, Margaret McGinnis, and Naomi Walch were all called back to the plant to work on Bonito. They decorated the line in mineral colors under the glaze, with dozens of flowers from columbine to daisies to wild roses. The artists matched certain flowers with certain shapes: for example, pansies on urn

Fig. 203: *Marked Weller*: Ivoris vase 6" high. Photo by Leach.

Fig. 205: *Marked Weller:* Bonito vase 11½" high.

Fig. 204: *Marked Weller:* Bonito vase 5" high, with blue daisy, signed N. for Naomi Walch; Bonito vase 7½" high, with tulips, signed N.C.; Bonito vase 6" high, with pansies, signed N.C.; and Bonito vase 5" high. Collection: Kathryn Powell. Photo by Leach.

shaped vases (Figs. 204, 205). Speed was essential. The factory assigned production quotas, so many vases a day per decorator. To pair the decorator with her vase and her quota of vases, the company insisted that she sign each piece with one or two initials on the bottom of it. Naomi Walch often signed her vases N.

Bonito had a cream colored background with contrasting lines of color at the top and the bottom of each piece. Ruth Axline used to apply these lines with a wedge-shaped brush, while the vase turned rapidly on a wheel. Bonito "was a freehand decoration on a bisque body which was later dipped in glaze. Designed as a cheap line . . . in the early thirties, it was made at the Ceramic Avenue plant when the company was only working part time," Ruth wrote, on February 4, 1980. Bonito came in vases, compotes, candlesticks, and bowls. C & G welcomed it in August 1932 and praised the decoration of naturally colored field and garden flowers and the jade green interior.

Bonito, Cretone, Geode, Raceme, and Stellar represented the end of hand decorating at Weller Pottery. "The inability to get decorators who could do freehand work fast was the reason Weller finally had to give up the better lines. And we did have to work fast to hold a job," Ruth Axline wrote on June 14, 1980. Today Bonito seems like a bright streak of light from the gloom of the Depression, when the diminished staff worked part time and often contributed two weeks of labor without pay to keep the plant open.

Made in the early thirties, Patra resembled an orange with its textured surface and its deep orange color (Fig. 206). Artists embossed stylized red, blue, and orange flowers on baskets, bowls, vases, jars, and nut dishes.

The oriental influence predominated in Neiska and Seneca, created by Rudolph Lorber. Weller advertised Neiska in C & G in August 1933: "Neiska, the new Weller Art Line . . . Smart with classical simple shapes and

Fig. 206: *Marked Weller:* Patra basket 6" high. Collection: Dorothy Daniel.

Fig. 207: Blue Neiska vase 5" high. *Marked Weller:* Green Seneca vase 6½" high, and maroon Paragon vase 4½" high. Collection: Dorothy Daniel. Photo by Leach.

interesting glazes . . . an unusual ceramic yellow and a clear warm blue softly stippled in green . . . the interiors strikingly lined in creamy ivory." Neiska had plain, undecorated shapes, ornamented with tiny oriental handles and dainty feet. Shown here is a blue vase with a white interior and three small curved feet (Fig. 207). In the Weller catalogs, Neiska came in candleholders, vases, and bowls, with a matt finish. Seneca and Neiska shared the same molds. The glaze on each piece determined the line. Seneca had a glossy glaze in light blue, green, and other pastels.

Cornish and Velva appeared in 1933 (Fig. 208). *C & G* described Cornish in August 1933, as a line with a mottled rust and rose glaze and raised leaves and berries. The modeler embossed tiny blue berries and green leaves on a blue, rust, or tan background. The factory offered vases, bowls, and candlesticks with prices beginning at 75¢. Velva had a rich green, a blue, or a shaded tan background, with the decoration in one oblong panel with sharp well defined edges, according to *PGB*, January 19, 1933. It sold for 50¢ to $3.00. Produced for the Pittsburgh Pottery Exhibition, Velva sported recessed panels with raised white or tan hydrangeas and green leaves. It was striking and very attractive.

Fig. 208: *Marked Weller:* Velva vase 9½" high, Neiska vase 5" high, Cornish vase 6½" high, and Terose teapot 6" high. Collection: Dorothy Daniel and Kathryn Powell. Photo by Leach.

Fig. 209: *Marked Weller*: Turkis vase 14" high. Collection: Lee Dietrich.

Fig. 210: Greenbriar vase 5" high, and Juneau vase 5½" high, marked Weller. Collection: Dorothy Daniel.

Fig. 211: *Marked Weller*: Maroon Ragenda vase 6¼" high. Collection: Dora Betts.

The January 1933 Price List noted Bonito, Evergreen, Golden Glow, Ivoris, Sydonia, and Turkis, at prices from 25¢ to $3.35. Bonito cost $1.50 per vase to $3.35 for the console sets. The October 1933 Price List mentioned Cornish, Neiska, Velva, and several cookware lines.

There were two Rosemont lines, the first discussed in Chapter XII, with its glossy black glaze and colorful bluebirds, the second with a tan matt finish. I will call the second one Rosemont II. Mentioned in *PGB*, January 19, 1933, Rosemont II had a tan glaze and appliqued flowers which stood out from the vase. Calla lilies, dogwood, and poppies were molded in full relief and hand colored to simulate real flowers. The catalogs pictured baskets, covered jars, vases, and console sets. Note the exquisite Rosemont II vase with calla lilies in the color section (C-14).

Greenbriar, Juneau, and Turkis all possessed a colorful, glossy, drip glaze. The January 1933 Price List noted Turkis (Fig. 209). It came in vases of all sizes, from large urns to small bowls. Turkis borrowed molds from Blo Red, Juneau, and Nile. Against a glossy red background, Turkis had a mottled, yellow green drip glaze. On Juneau the drip glaze, in red, yellow, blue, and green, pointed down into each vase like an arrow. The background was a glossy bright pink. *PGB* commended Greenbriar for its blended colors of lilac, purple, and bright green, on July 10, 1930 (Fig. 210). The gloss glaze highlighted its bright colors. All three lines are pictured in the color section (C-20, C-21).

The Ragenda line recalled Blue Drapery, with its raised designs suggesting fabric. Ragenda came in a dark maroon, a pink, or a blue matt finish, with molded drapes knotted at the side or in the middle of the vase. It was a sculptural line with pleasing shapes and colors (Fig. 211).

Combining the naturalistic with the grotesque, Malvern had high relief red flower buds and green leaves on a textured, multi-colored background. The factory offered baskets with leaf and branch handles, vases, candleholders, bowls, wallpockets, and flower inserts, in shades of green, magenta, yellow, and brown (Fig. 212). The long stemmed flowers wound around the vases and bowls in serpentine fashion.

Between 1930 and 1932, Harry Weller hired two Italians from Sicily, Sam Celli and Frank Dedonatis. He asked them to create a new line for the Pottery. They designed a number of glossy white pots with underglaze decoration, sometimes called "Dedonatis Wares," since Frank often signed them F. DDTIS. This never did become a line. Ruth Axline helped Frank decorate the new wares. Glossy white vases, flower pots, and ashtrays appeared with freehand decoration in pink, blue, red, or brown (Fig. 213). In January 1980, Ruth described the process of decoration: "One stroke petals were applied rapidly with dexterity. Usually blue or pink was the predominating color. The designs were the typical freehand Italian floral designs in underglaze decoration with a white glossy glaze . . . The ware was all hand dipped . . . mostly one fire." As more orders for these pots came in, Carl Weigelt and Ruth decorated and lined them.

Darsie, Glazed Hudson vases with dogs and cats, Paragon, modern black and white vases, and a beer mug labeled Ein Stein, all appeared in *C & G* in August 1934. A late Deco line, Paragon came in bowls with flower

Fig. 213: *Marked Weller:* Two Dedonatis Ware vases, 6¾" high. Each vase is artist signed by Frank Dedonatis: F.D.D. Collection: Esther and Martin Myers.

Fig. 212: *Marked Weller:* Malvern vase 5½" high. Collection: Dorothy Daniel.

inserts, vases, and candlesticks, pictured in the catalogs with stylized flowers framed by angular leaves, in magenta, gold, blue, and white semigloss. The rope and tassel motif distinguished Darsie (Fig. 214). The molded embossed cord was looped around the top of the vase, tied, and the tassels fell down the front of the vase. Made in matt cream, blue, and green vases, wallpockets, and a console set, Darsie had a colonial design, according to C & G. The black and white vases were "simple modern vases of trim and squared lines in black and white that may be used to give a harlequin effect," wrote C & G of this unnamed line.

The Ein Stein beer mugs, with Einstein's face on each one, sold well. In fact, after the repeal of prohibition in 1933, the beer mugs kept the factory alive. "The beer mugs were hot. In fact they were packed straight from the kiln, so hot we sometimes had to wear gloves," Ruth Axline wrote, May 12, 1980. Ruth described how everyone, artists, modelers, supervisors, all joined together to pack the mugs for shipment. The factory made hundreds of beer mugs and still could not meet the demand for them.

On July 12, 1934, *PGB* described Manhattan as a line with a soft two-tone glaze with an embossed decoration in a deeper tone. On one pitcher, brown stylized daisies stood out against a rust colored background. Often,

Fig. 214: *Marked Weller:* Darsie vase 5½" high, Patricia vase 5" high, Novelty Line Monkey with Peanut ashtray 5" high, and Manhattan vase 6" high. Collection: Dorothy Daniel. Photo by Leach.

Fig. 215: *Marked Weller:* Classic vase 7½" high. Photo by D.L. Hill.

raised deep green leaves or flowers emerged from a medium green background on a vase or a pitcher. The line had a rugged, carved look, with ornamentation in relief.

Classic displayed flowing arches that swept from the top to the bottom of each vase (Fig. 215). *C & G* described it in July 1934, as "simply modeled with lacy open work in a twisted type of latticing." The reticulated rim, the glossy white, tan, green, or blue glaze, the dainty stylized flowers made Classic a graceful and elegant line, in vases, wallpockets, bowls, and planters.

Patricia appeared in January 1934, with a solid white, tan, or green glaze, or a mottled one. Ducks, pelicans, and swans were molded into vases, bowls, ashtrays, and planters. Some bowls had long-necked swans or ducks' heads around the rim. Swan-shaped handles ornamented the vases. Patricia was whimsical and imaginative.

In spite of the Depression, Weller continued to develop and to sell new lines. While artist decoration was sporadic, it was competent and colorful. The hand painted flowers on Bonito looked as fresh as real daisies, roses, or columbine. With expert modelers Dorothy Laughead and Rudolph Lorber, the molded wares also achieved recognition and respect.

Chapter XVI
The Thirties at Weller: 1934-1940

While the early thirties marked the near demise of Weller Pottery, the mid thirties saw a resurrection, a new elan. The year 1934 was the apogee. The Weller artists emerged victorious with Cretone, Geode, Glazed Hudson dog vases, Raceme, and Stellar. By 1935 the Pottery again curtailed freehand decoration and instructed the modelers to devise new lines. Dorothy Laughead modeled several new lines: Arcadia, Bouquet, Chase, Floral, and Pastel.

The Weller catalogs pictured Cretone, Geode, the Novelty Line, Raceme, and Stellar together on one page, reproduced here (Fig. 216). Examine it carefully. On the first line of the catalog page stood the Novelty Line Dog Barking Ashtray, Kangaroo Ashtray, Three Pigs Ashtray, Frog Cigarette Stand, Frog Cigarette Tray, Dog with Bone, and Monkey with Peanut Ashtrays, all noted on the 1936 Price List, but offered earlier in a red, white, or blue glaze. The catalogs also showed the Novelty Line dachshund, fox, turtle and seal ashtrays. In July 1934, *C & G* described a menagerie of ashtrays with monkeys, pigs, kangaroos, and dogs (Figs. 217, 218).

In the Novelty Line, the Pottery also created several face masks shown here on the catalog page, row 2, numbers 409, 410, 411. These bizarre masks came in small vases and in wallpockets. The Man and Woman vases, numbers 411, 410, measured 2½ and 6 inches, respectively, and had faces with raised features in an off white gloss or a dark brown glaze. They sold in pairs for $2.50. The Egyptian wallpocket, number 409, showed classic inspiration, according to *PGBS*, August 30, 1934. It came in glossy gray, white, or brown (Fig. 219). Other Novelty wallpockets included the teapot, pitcher, cup and saucer, numbers 408, 407, and 406, in white, blue, or orange semi-gloss. Two vases and a decanter completed the line, numbers 412-414.

The Novelty Line catalog page also pictured four matt finish, artist decorated lines: Cretone, Geode, Raceme, and Stellar. Witness numbers 1, 4, and 6 which are Geode, while 3 and 8 are Stellar. Stellar had hand painted blue stars on a white background, or white stars on a black, or a blue background (Fig. 220). Geode had blue stars and comets with sweeping tails on a white background, or white stars and comets on a medium blue background (Fig. 221). Mae Timberlake often decorated and signed these vases. "The decorative treatment consists of comets and stars—a motif that has already found considerable success as applied to glassware, either by cutting or in gold decoration," wrote *PGBS*, May 17, 1934. In these four lines, the Weller decorators used Art Deco designs: stylized flowers, comets, stars, and gazelles.

Fig. 217: *Marked Weller:* Novelty Line Dog with Bone Ashtray 4½" high, with white gloss glaze.

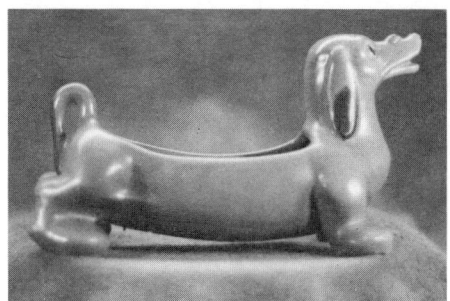

Fig. 218: *Marked Weller:* Novelty Line Dachshund ashtray 6" long.

Fig. 219: *Marked Weller:* Novelty Line brown Egyptian wallpocket 10" high. Collection: Robert Miller and Glen Vogt.

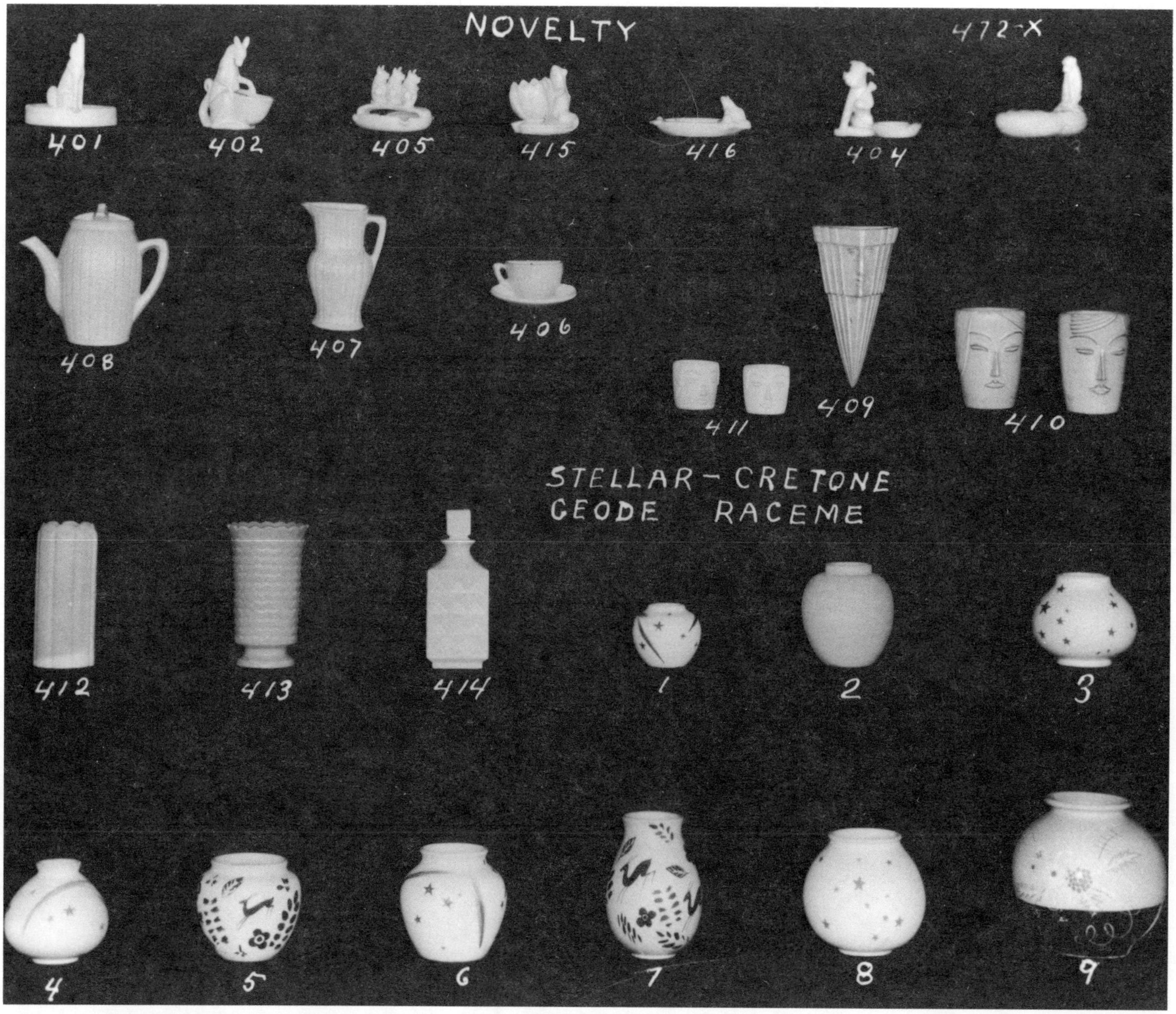

Fig. 216: Weller catalog page of Cretone, Geode, Raceme, and Stellar, with the Novelty Line. Courtesy of Ohio Historical Society.

Fig. 220: *Marked Weller:* Stellar black vase 5" high. Collection: Esther and Martin Myers.

Fig. 221: *Marked Weller:* Geode white vase 3½" high, with blue stars, artist signed M.T.

Fig. 222: *Marked Weller:* Cretone white vase 6½" high, artist signed M.T. Courtesy of Robin Crawford, Dave Rago. Photo by Leach.

The artists drew leaping gazelles surrounded by locust leaves and flowers on Cretone, numbers 5 and 7 on this catalog page. The company offered three color treatments in Cretone: white with black decorations, black with white, and yellow with brown. Pictured here is a white Cretone vase with four black gazelles slip decorated by Mae Timberlake (Fig. 222). The company incised the mark Weller Pottery in script on the base of each Cretone, Geode, Raceme, and Stellar vase.

Raceme was number 9 on this catalog page. A raceme is a cluster of flowers on a stalk, an apt description of the decoration on Weller Raceme. "In this line the lower portion is in a black and the upper in a blue-gray, the line of demarkation between them being very sharply drawn. Both are in a particularly soft and velvety glaze. Superimposed on the vases, with the center just above the color change line, is a slip decoration featuring a cluster in blue and white. This is most unusual and eye-catching," wrote *PGBS*, May 17, 1934. Hester Pillsbury decorated the Raceme vase shown here with stylized blue and white flowers and leaves (Fig. 223). She used dark blue and white slip for the flowers on the light blue background and white slip for the flowers on the black background at the bottom of the vase. The January 1, 1935 Price List offered the four lines: Cretone, Geode, Raceme, and Stellar, noting that each was hand decorated. Vase sizes for the four lines ranged from 3½ inches to 9 inches high.

Raceme Glossy appeared as number 2, row 3 on this catalog page. I named the line Raceme Glossy, since it resembled Raceme with the bi-color decoration. Its high gloss and lack of slip decoration, however, differentiated it from Raceme. The Raceme Glossy vase pictured here shades from pale green to pale orange (Fig. 224). Some vases shaded from blue to green. All had one color on the top half of the vase, and a contrasting color on the bottom half.

The Novelty Line grew and branched out into the Decorated Novelty Utility Line. It included the famous Mammy group with the teapot, cooky jar, and syrup pitcher, all crowned by a black mammy. The sugar and creamer set had two little black boys as handles on the sugar bowl, and

Fig. 223: *Marked Weller:* Raceme vase 9" high, artist signed H.P. Photo by D.L. Hill.

Fig. 224: *Marked Weller:* Raceme Glossy vase, shading from pale green to pale orange, 5¾" high. Collection: Dorothy Daniel. Photo by Leach.

Fig. 225: *Marked Weller:* Decorated Novelty Utility Line sugar bowl 3¾" high and creamer 4" high. Collection: The James S. Morgans. Photo by Ginny Graves.

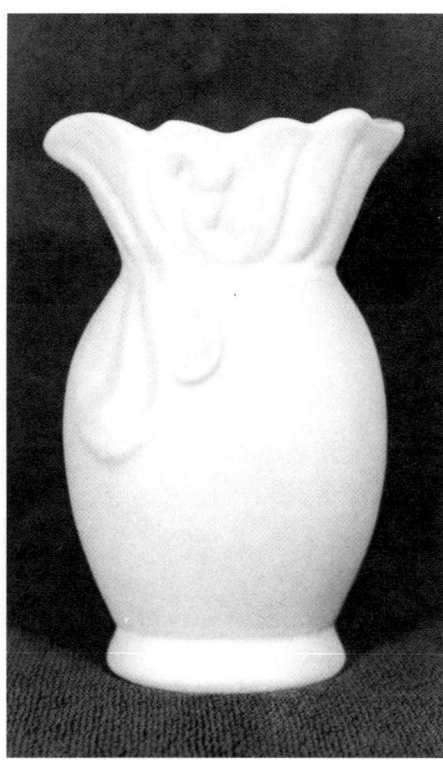

Fig. 226: *Marked Weller:* White Pastel vase 6½" high. Collection: Dick and Nancy Sigafoose.

one little fellow as the handle on the creamer (Fig. 225). A batter bowl with a pouring spout and a black-boy handle finished the set. While collectors call it the Mammy line, the company named it the Decorated Novelty Utility Line in the Weller catalogs. Collectors in search of Black Memorabilia find this line irresistible.

Dorothy Laughead created Arcadia, Bouquet, Floral, and Pastel, all noted in C & G in August 1935. Arcadia had a glossy green, ivory, or rosy beige background, with a built up leaf motif. Some bowls displayed rounded peaches under the leaves. The company offered vases, bowls, console sets, and covered dishes. On the Bouquet line, Dorothy molded daffodils, dogwood, or lilies of the valley on a tan, green, or blue matt background.

With wide, barely perceptible vertical ribs and tiny raised white flowers, Floral came in vases, double vases, and console sets in green, blue, or tan colors. Embossed wild roses, dogwood, or lilies of the valley enhanced each piece. The catalogs pictured console sets with oblong bowls and matching candleholders. Pastel appeared in vases, planters, candleholders, and bowls with raised swirls, on a peach, green, maize, white, or blue background (Fig. 226). In matt blue, the embossed curves on the vases suggested the undulating waves of the sea.

Roba had a shaded and textured green, orange, blue, or white background with tree branch handles. Crisply molded apple blossoms, gladiolas, wild roses, or oak leaves decorated each piece. An enchanting line, Roba came in console sets, vases, hanging planters, wallpockets, pitchers, and cornucopia vases, pictured in the catalogs.

Weller introduced Atlas, Dorland, and Ting in 1936. Noted for its star shapes, Atlas comprised vases, candleholders, bowls, and covered boxes with creamy interiors, in semi-gloss ivory, beige, or blue (Fig. 227). The geometric shapes of Atlas were derived from Art Deco. Like Atlas, Dorland appeared in C & G in 1936, with a blue, tan, or green matt finish and with sweeping, graceful curves recessed into each piece. The company offered candleholders, vases, and bowls in Dorland.

Created by Rudolph Lorber, Ting reflected a Chinese influence with its oriental shapes and leaf and snake handles. Witness the page of Ting from

Fig. 227: *Marked Weller:* Bouquet vase 5" high, Atlas star vase 7" high, and Roba pitcher 6" high. Collection: Kathryn Powell. Photo by Leach.

Fig. 228: Weller catalog page of Ting Ware. Courtesy of Ohio Historical Society.

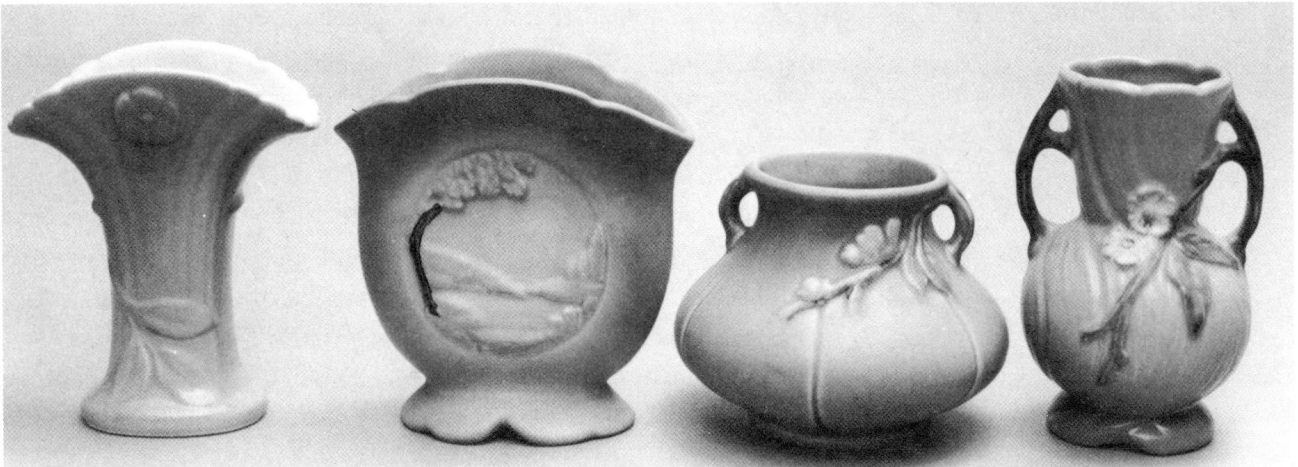

Fig. 229: *Marked Weller:* Raydence fan vase 6½" high, Senic vase 6½" high, Floral vase 4½" high, and Roba vase 6½" high. Collection: Kathryn Powell. Photo by Leach.

Fig. 230: *Marked Weller:* Mi-Flo vase 10" high, Rudlor vase 7" high, Panella ginger jar 6½" high, Arcadia vase 5½" high, and Blossom cornucopia 6" high. Collection: Dorothy Daniel. Photo by Leach.

the catalogs (Fig. 228). Each vase stood on an imitation teak, black pottery base. Ting had an ivory semi-gloss glaze and curved handles shaped like serpents, scrolls, or acanthus leaves. Lorber named Ting for the Sung Dynasty Ting Ware, which also had an ivory glaze, with carved molded designs of lotus, peonies, dragons, and fish. The elegant work of the Sung Dynasty in China, 960 to 1279 A.D., often inspired the Weller artists and modelers.

C & G introduced Raydence and Senic in February 1937 (Fig. 229). Raydence included several classic shape vases in glossy green, yellow, or white, with white interiors. Embossed leaves or flowers stood out at the base of each vase. The Pottery offered Senic vases with a soft matt finish in azure blue or green, with scenes of mountains, lakes, and gardens. The modelers also embossed sailboats and seascapes on the vases and console sets. Impressionistic, visually enchanting, Senic delights collectors today.

PGBS pictured a Mi-Flo vase in November 1938. The line came in white, yellow, and green with flowers and fruit in relief: tulips, daisies, lilies, apples, or pears, in bright contrasting colors. Some Mi-Flo vases resembled a beehive with concentric bands mounting the vase. The handles on the vases looked like large commas standing on end (Fig. 230).

Lucille Cox described the Weller plant and its products in PGBS in November 1938. Cox wrote, "To walk through the warehouse of the S. A. Weller Company is like seeing a large palette of colors. Every piece is a work of beauty.... The originality and uniqueness of their products is so striking it compels instant attention." She described the display room: "In their big display room east of Zanesville is a large hand painted vase that won first prize at the St. Louis Exhibition. Also there is a picture of the first pottery built in the woods of southern Ohio sixty-six years ago and a portrait of S. A. Weller." The Weller show rooms stood on Route 40, east of Zanesville, with the mammoth seven foot Aurelian vase on permanent display.

Rudlor resembled Mi-Flo, but it had wide, concentric bands which slanted diagonally instead of horizontally. White or pink flowers emerged in relief on the Rudlor vases, candlesticks, and bowls. Background colors of green, white, and yellow duplicated those on Mi-Flo.

Gloria, Lido, and Softone came out between 1935 and 1940. With raised colored decorations of dogwood, blackberries, iris, or daisies, Gloria had a dark rust or a green background, on console sets, vases, and pitchers (Fig. 231). The company made Lido in shaded colors, ivory to tan, pink to maroon, blue green to lavender blue, in vases, pitchers, hanging baskets, console sets, double candleholders, baskets, and planters. The pieces had raised or indented swirls, or leaves in relief. The swirled shapes united Dorland, Lido, Pastel, and Softone (Fig. 232).

Softone featured a pink, tan, or blue semi-gloss glaze. Each piece displayed three to four raised swirls which converged with another set of swirls in the center. Pictured in Figure 232 are the comport number 17 and the cornucopia vase number 7 from the catalog. Shapes included vases, baskets, bowls, hanging planters, candleholders, and pitchers. Classic and simple, this was a restful line.

Fig. 231: *Marked Weller*: Gloria vase 5" high. Collection: Dora Betts.

Fig. 232: *Marked Weller:* Loru vase 7¾" high, Softone cornucopia 3" high and comport 5" high, Dorland vase 6" high, and Lido vase 6½" high. Collection: Bob Bettinger and Dorothy Daniel. Photo by Leach.

Fig. 235: *Marked Weller:* Wild Rose cornucopia 5½" high. Collection: Dorothy Daniel.

Fig. 233: *Marked Weller:* Two blue Cameo rectangular vases 8½" high, on the right and the left, and in the center a blue Cameo handled vase 13" high. Collection: Robert Miller and Glen Vogt.

Fig. 236: *Marked Weller:* Oak Leaf vase 9" high. Collection: Lee Dietrich.

Fig. 234: *Marked Weller:* Blue Cameo footed bowl 4" high, Lido blue candleholder 2½" high, and Delsa blue pitcher 6" high. Photo by Leach.

Fig. 237: *Marked Weller:* Regal cornucopia vase 7" high.

Dorothy Laughead developed Cameo in the late thirties, with raised white flowers on a blue, brown, or green background (Fig. 233). The factory offered Cameo baskets, pitchers, bowls, planters, and vases, with curved handles and wide vertical ribs. Cameo had graceful lines, good modeling, and delicate pastel backgrounds.

Another product of the late thirties, Delsa had a background of tiny indented circles with pink, white or yellow flowers in relief. Background colors were green, blue, or white. Note the blue pitcher here with raised white dogwood flowers (Fig. 234).

Panella appeared in the late thirties with embossed pansies on a shaded background. Colors verged from light green, blue, or amber, to dark green, blue, or amber. The company made vases, bowls, wallpockets, covered jars, and baskets. Dorothy Laughead designed Wild Rose with a muted green or a rust background with one or two large, embossed white roses like those on wide brimmed picture hats (Fig. 235). The line came in vases, baskets, candleholders, and bowls.

Oak Leaf featured a green oak leaf, and sometimes one or two acorns, embossed on a brown, green, or blue background. Wallpockets, baskets, bowls, planters, vases, and pitchers comprised the line (Fig. 236). Loru sported vertical panels and stylized leaves. Vases, bowls, planters, and cornucopias shaded from light to dark blue, from maroon to dark gray, and from green to brown. Loru had strong symmetry and colors.

Blossom featured a robin's egg blue or a green background, with two embossed white wild roses clustered close together. Production included vases, planters, ewers, and double vases.

Mistakenly called Candis, Regal had a glossy white or a green background with stylized daisies and roses embossed and recessed.

Fig. 238: *Marked Weller:* Blue Chase vase 6½" high. Photo by Leach.

Sometimes, the raised white flowers were tinted light green, as on the cornucopia vase pictured here (Fig. 237). The company produced Regal candleholders with matching bowls, hanging planters, vases, and ewers.

Chase was the most appealing line of the late thirties. Designed by Dorothy Laughead, with a white horse, rider, and hounds in high relief on a deep blue, black, or brown background, Chase imitated Wedgwood and evoked the British sport of fox hunting. Sometimes, Chase came with a silver overlay decor, or in light blue or lavender, with the rider and hounds painted in bright colors. The vases often portrayed the horse and the rider jumping a fence (Fig. 238).

In the late thirties, diminishing profits led Weller executives to develop and to promote cheaper lines, such as Arcadia, Darsie, Dorland, and Pastel, which were monochromatic and dull. Other lines, such as Blossom, Bouquet, or Floral, had only a few, raised white flowers as decoration. Lack of bright colors and prosaic modeling characterized much of the production. The Chase line was a welcome change with its white horses, hounds, and riders silhouetted against a black or a navy blue background. (Fig. 239).

The thirties were the years of transition at Weller. The decade began exuberantly with Cretone, Geode, Raceme, Stellar, and the Novelty animals. By 1935, the company abandoned freehand decoration and decided to produce only molded wares. Some of these lines, Cameo, Chase, Roba, and Senic, showed flair and beauty, while other lines had a lackluster quality, portending the demise of Weller Pottery.

Fig. 239: *Marked Weller:* Blue Chase vase 9″ high.

Chapter XVII
Garden Ware, Planters, Wallpockets, and Cookware

From 1904 to 1948, Weller Pottery produced a variety of garden items and cookware. In the twenties and thirties, the company offered birdbaths, sprinklers, urns, jars, and figurines for the garden. Weller Graystone urns stood on patios and low brick walls. "An urn or birdbath of beautiful Graystone will add a fresh element of beauty to your garden, yet seem to have lived years there. Its mellow gray blends at once with sky and leaves. Graystone is the garden pottery of Weller Ware," read the ad in *Better Homes and Gardens,* May 1928.

In 1931 the catalog *Garden Decorations by Weller* promoted Graystone and Coppertone garden ware in birdbaths, sundials, garden figurines, sprinklers, fountains, jardinieres, gazing balls, toadstool seats, and oil jars. The catalog enumerated several garden figurines decorated in underglaze colors, the Coppertone, or the Graystone finish: the Rabbit in Matt Glaze, the Cat in White Gloss Glaze, the Pelican in White Matt, the Angry Duck, the Happy Ducks, the Scottie Pup, the Dancing Frog, the Banjo Frog, Pan with Rabbit, Tree Squirrel, Sitting Squirrel, Gnomes on Toad Stool, Chicken, Rooster, and Bulge-Eyed Dog (Figs. 240-244). Coppertone frogs came in two sizes, 11½ by 15 inches and 8 by 11½ inches. The Pottery made several dogs: the popular Bulge-Eyed Dog, the Scottie Dog and Pup, and the Spaniel. Three cats appeared, two white cats about 15 inches long, and a black Cat on Roof. Note the animals in the color section (C-25).

Fig. 240: *Marked Weller:* Scottie Dog 12" high. Collection: George and Judy Alig. Photo by Alig.

Fig. 242: *Marked Weller:* Rooster 12½" high, behind two Chicken Hens 7½" high. Collection: George and Judy Alig. Photo by Alig.

Fig. 241: Weller Gnome on Tree Trunk 19" high, and *marked Weller* Gnome on Boulder 18" high. Collection: George and Judy Alig. Photo by Alig.

Dorothy Laughead modeled the cats, dogs, rabbits, squirrels, and frogs, while Rudolph Lorber modeled the ducks and swans. A black crow emerged in several different sizes, set on a peg to stick into the ground. The Greek god Pan came in two variations: Pan with Rabbit, or Pan with Fife.

The Weller catalogs illustrated the Coppertone frog sprinkler, the Scottie Dog, the Swans, the Double Ducks with sprinkler heads, the Goose, the Pelican, the Rabbit, and also the Graystone Garden wares: hanging planters, jars and peds, low bowls, the Goose Boy, and the Fish on Tail Birdbath. The 1928 Price List compared Graystone to Barrie Granite, in its color and texture. Designed by Rudolph Lorber before 1912, Graystone was made of waterproof clay with a rough, gray cement-like finish.

Urns, columns, benches, fountains with classical figures attracted the gardeners of the twenties and reflected their fascination with Hellenistic art. Weller responded to this obsession with antiquity, with the Graystone line. "Graystone is like the ancient art of Greece and Rome," boasted the Weller ad in *House and Garden* in April 1929, picturing a Graystone sundial. The cupid-like figure of the Graystone Goose Boy in the birdbath appeared in an ad in *House and Garden* in April 1928 (Fig. 245). The Graystone urn

Fig. 243: *Marked Weller:* Sitting Squirrel 12" high. Collection: George and Judy Alig. Photo by Alig.

Fig. 244: *Marked Weller:* Spaniel 10½" high. Collection: George and Judy Alig. Photo by Alig.

Fig. 245: Weller ad from *House and Garden*, April 1928, showing the Graystone Goose Boy in a Graystone bird bath.

Fig. 246: Weller Coppertone Frog Sprinkler with propeller, 13" high, on the right. From left to right: Three Coppertone frogs, 8" high, 4" high, and 2" high. Collection: George and Judy Alig. Photo by Alig.

advertised in *Better Homes and Gardens* in May 1928, with its swags of fruit and flowers and its molded columns was "pure Greek in effect." With the ads in *House and Garden* and *Better Homes and Gardens*, Weller reached out to the affluent customer, who could well afford the ingenious Graystone and Coppertone garden wares.

The 1941 Price List noted the Graystone Birdbath and Pedestal with these inserts: the Boy with Fish, the Goose Boy, and the Fisher Boy, as well as fountains, gazing globes, and sundials, at prices from $3.00 to $13.00. Garden ware was very profitable for the company.

The trade journals also promoted Weller garden ware. On May 29, 1930, *PGBS* remarked that the Coppertone frog sprinkler could throw out a stream of water within a radius of 16 feet (Fig. 246). In April 1930, *C & G* pictured the Coppertone frogs, the Pelican, and the Rabbit around a birdbath with a 21 inch high Muskota Fisher Boy (Fig. 247). They also showed a garden table with toadstool seats, a large spaniel, strawberry jars, and urns. In April 1932, *C & G* described the Weller Swans, which could float on ponds or lakes. One Swan held his head up high, while the other bent his head down to preen his feathers. The Swans were 14½ to 18½ inches high (Fig. 248).

Potenza garden ware came in jars, peds, fern dishes, and bowls, in a rough green finish, decorated with raised red vines, according to *PGB*, April 21, 1921. The factory also made birdhouses and hanging planters in a sandstone finish called Terra Cotta, pictured in the catalogs, and Anco flower pots with saucers. *Pottery for the Florist* described Anco and its "unglazed buff clay with a dark brown filling in the recesses of the design."

With more leisure time for home activities, the growth of garden clubs and gardening as a sport, the popularity of outdoor living rooms, garden ware was de rigueur in the thirties. The Denver Dry Goods Store sold seventy-five birdbaths in two days, after mounting a realistic window display of Weller birdbaths and animals inside a picket fence.

In addition to the garden animals, the Pottery made several glossy, colored figurines. Measuring from 7 to 12½ inches high, these included:

Fig. 247: *Marked Weller*: Coppertone Bird Bath with Muskota Fisher Boy, 54" high overall. This comes in four sections: the Fisher Boy stands on a molded fishes base, which sits in a bowl or basin, set on a pedestal. Collection: Robert Miller and Glen Vogt.

Fig. 248: Two Weller Swans, 18½" high and 14½" high. Collection: George and Judy Alig.

Chanticleer Rooster, Pesca the Old Man with Fish, Silva the Dancer, and the Gloucester Woman. The Chanticleer Rooster came in a royal blue or a red glaze, Silva the Dancer in a bright yellow, Pesca in a reddish brown, the Gloucester Woman with the basket on her shoulder, in a glossy white or a turquoise glaze (Figs. 249, 250).

Designed by Dorothy Laughead, the Cactus planters resembled the figurines discussed above, but were much smaller. These fourteen 3½ to 5½ inch high figurines included a camel, cat, duck, horse, snail, frog, fish, monkey, elephant, kangaroo, Pan with Lily, Boy with Bag, Boy with Basin, and Boy with Basket. Ruth Axline recalled that the factory made Cactus in the thirties, that it was dipped in glaze and given one firing. Devised as a bread and butter item, rapidly produced and quick selling, Cactus was one of the lines which "kept the plant going," Ruth wrote on January 31, 1980. Cactus came in glossy yellow, blue, rust red, red, and brown (Figs. 251, 252).

Recently, pottery collectors in Nebraska discovered two new animal planters in factory boxes labeled: The Weller Pottery, Zanesville, Ohio. In the boxes carefully packed for shipment, they found several Duck-Rabbit-Penguin and Three Face Dog planters, in a white, a yellow, or a green gloss glaze. The Duck-Rabbit-Penguin measured 6½ inches high, while the Three Face Dog measured 7½ inches (Fig. 253). Both animals carried diamond shaped cardboard tags labeled: The Ruby Company, 225 Fifth Avenue, NYC. There was no Weller mark on these planters.

The Three Face Dog had three heads in one. I researched the design patent number on the base of the dog, #123,112, and discovered that the Patent Office issued it to Arthur W. Lindwall of Hollis, New York, on October 15, 1940, as a "Design for a Toy or Similar Article." The patent drawing pictured a three headed dog similar to the Three Face Dog planter. Perhaps, the Ruby Company contracted with Weller Pottery to make the planter, using the design patented by Arthur W. Lindwall. The tag on the dog read:

Fig. 249: *Marked Weller:* Pesca, Old Man with Fish 12½" high, with brown gloss glaze. Artist signed on the base C.B.M. Collection: Robert Miller and Glen Vogt.

Fig. 250: *Marked Weller:* Silva the Dancer 8" high, in yellow gloss glaze. Collection: Betty Blair.

Fig. 251: *Marked Weller:* Cactus Line: Blue Frog 4" high, rust-red Elephant 4" high, yellow Elephant 4" high, and blue Snail 4" high. Collection: Robert Miller and Glen Vogt.

Fig. 252: *Marked Weller:* Cactus Line Pan with Lily, with rust-red glaze, 5½" high.

Fig. 253: White Three Face Dog planter 7½" high and yellow Duck-Rabbit-Penguin planter 6½" high.

Fig. 254: *Marked Weller:* Woodcraft Squirrel wallpocket 9" high.

Fig. 255: Woodcraft wallpocket 9½" high.

>LOOK AT ME
>With all Three Faces
>BUY ME—
>Get in my good graces.
>I'll follow you around
>The room, and chase
>Away that
>"Old Man Gloom"

Purviance and Schneider pictured the Duck-Rabbit-Penguin in *Weller Art Pottery in Color*, plate 24d. The planter had two bases. If tilted on one base, it resembled a duck, if set on the other base, it resembled a rabbit. From the front it looked like a penguin. Its tag read, "The Believe It or Not Pets," with this descriptive poem:

>I'm a little
>PENGUIN
>BUNNY or DUCK
>Depending upon
>>how you set me up.

It is hard to prove conclusively that these two planters came from Weller Pottery. In the forties, in search of extra income, however, the Pottery may have agreed to produce them for the Ruby Company.

Weller offered wallpockets in all glazes and lines from Arcola to Woodcraft. Note the two Woodcraft wallpockets pictured here, one with a full figure squirrel at the base, the other shaped like a cross with molded red flowers nestled against the simulated tree bark (Figs. 254, 255). The company offered dozens of wall vases in some of the best lines: Ardsley, Cloudburst, Glendale, Hudson, Klyro, Pearl, Roma, Sabrinian, and Selma. The Weller wallpockets were colorful, with rich glazes and detailed modeling. Witness the lady in colonial dress on the glossy wallpocket pictured here (Fig. 256).

From 1916 to 1936, wall vases decorated living and dining room walls and held cut flowers or spring bulbs. "The Useful Wallpockets," by Clarence Weed in *House and Garden* in January 1916, described their uses. He wrote, "It is significant that one of the most interesting lines of progress in recent pottery manufacture has been the production of a great variety of designs of . . . wallpockets intended for use on walls or other vertical surfaces. . . . A living, growing plant upon the wall of living-room or dining-room may have the value of a beautiful picture with the added interest that comes from watching buds grow into blossoms." He advised the gardener to plant German or English Ivy, Japanese morning glories, daffodils, hyacinths, or paperwhite narcissus in the wallpocket and to hang it next to a Japanese print in a place of honor in the living room.

Today we regard Weller wallpockets as colorful curiosities to gather and to display in groups. But from 1916 to 1936, they held flowers and plants and hung prominently on the living room wall. That is why Weller produced so many wallpockets in various glazes, shapes, and designs, truly beautiful creations!

The Pottery made cooking ware from about 1904, until it closed in 1948. C & G mentioned Brown and White Cookware on April 7, 1904. This glossy, nut brown, green, or dark pink line came in custard cups and a matching serving bowl, covered casseroles, beanpots, pitcher and mug sets, teapots; tumblers, and mixing bowls, all shown in the catalogs (Fig. 257). An ad in C & G on December 18, 1919, called Weller the largest manufacturer of brown and white cooking ware.

Cream Light Blue Banded Ware had a glossy white background with blue bands around the mid section (Fig. 258). The factory made bowls, casseroles, canisters, mugs, and pitchers of various sizes. As a youngster, I watched my mother stir cake batter in the Reno bowl, a tan mixing bowl with brown bands around the middle. Reno bowls came in all sizes, from large batter bowls to small custard cups.

The Kitchengem Egg Beating Pitcher appeared in the catalogs. With raised horizontal ribs and a glossy green or pink glaze, the pitchers were used to beat eggs and to pour them into bowls (Fig. 259).

Color Banded Beverage Sets had a glossy white or a pastel background. Used for iced tea or lemonade, the sets included a tall pitcher, six mugs,

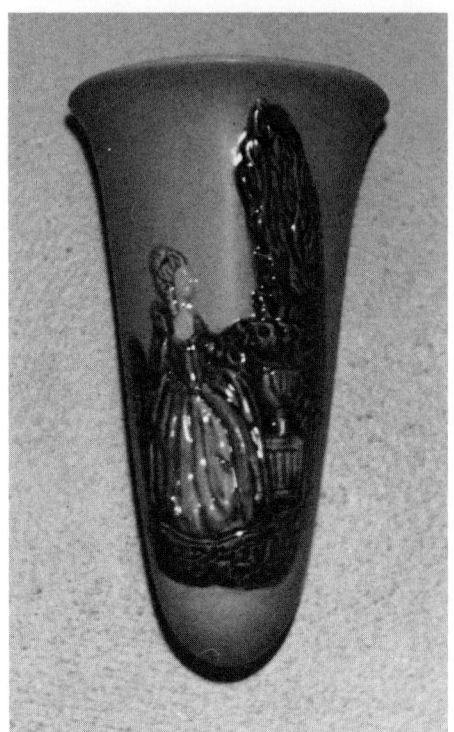

Fig. 256: *Marked Weller:* Wallpocket 8½" high, with lady in colonial dress. Collection: Lee Dietrich.

Fig. 257: *Marked Weller:* Brown and White Cookware custard set, with green glaze. Covered dish 5" high with four custard cups 2" high. Collection: Robert Miller and Glen Vogt.

Fig. 259: *Marked Weller:* Pink Kitchengem Egg Beating Pitcher 5½" high. Collection: Lee Dietrich.

Fig. 258: *Marked Weller:* Cream Light Blue Banded bowls: 6", 7", 9" diameter, and bowl on the top row 5" diameter. Collection: Robert Miller and Glen Vogt.

Fig. 260: Ollas Water Bottle 11½" high, with red trim and red underplate. Photo by D.L. Hill.

Fig. 261: *Marked Weller:* Blue Pierre teapot 8½" high. Photo by Leach.

Fig. 262: *Marked Weller:* Gold Decorated brown teapot 5½" high. Collection: Dick and Nancy Sigafoose.

Fig. 263: Terose teapot 7" high, with green rabbit finial on the pot lid.

and a cooky jar. Green stripes formed an X on a pink glazed cooky jar. Blue stripes adorned a white cooky jar.

Dorothy Laughead designed the Ollas Water Bottle in the late thirties. Gourd shaped, orange, red, or green at the top, and white at the bottom, it rested on a matching plate (Fig. 260). Designed to keep drinking water cool, the Ollas Water Bottle was a best seller.

The catalogs pictured the Pierre line with a semi-gloss finish and a basketweave, embossed effect. Note the blue teapot here (Fig. 261). The company offered Pierre blue, tan, or lavender dinner sets with plates, a teapot, a creamer, a sugar, a custard set with a casserole and six matching cups, a cooky jar, a mixing bowl set, and a milk pitcher.

Weller produced several teapots, from the Gold Decorated to the Terose and the Pineapple pots. The Gold Decorated teapots had a glossy golden brown, jade green, salmon pink, royal blue, or Alice blue background, with a transfer decoration of gold bands of flowers and gold trim, and a white interior. The teapots held from 7 to 48 ounces (Fig. 262).

Terose emerged in January 1933. It came in glossy white, tan, or brown dinnerware and cookware: mugs, tumblers, teapots, bowls, creamers, sugars, pitchers, canisters, casseroles, pudding pans, mixing bowls, cooky jars, and a child's tea set. Dorothy Laughead designed the cream colored, matt Terose teapot in a pumpkin shape, with a lid with a green stem or a green rabbit finial (Fig. 263). The factory also produced a handsome yellow Pineapple teapot with a green lid.

In August 1933, C & G advertised Chelsea Kitchenware. Chelsea had a cream ivory glaze, with narrow, fluted vertical ribs, banded at the rim or the base in red, green, yellow, or black. Bowls, pitchers, teapots, covered custard bowls with underplates, and tiny canisters appeared in the Chelsea line.

From 1904 to 1948, Weller garden ware, planters, wallpockets, and cookware provided decorative accessories and everyday tableware to thousands of homes in America and abroad. Low priced, well modeled, serviceable, these wares kept the factory vital and prosperous.

Chapter XVIII

The Weller Artists

Only a few of the Weller artists received formal training in art. Most had on the job training. Ruth Axline learned her craft from decorator Sarah McLaughlin at the factory. Charles Chilcote took lessons from Karl Kappes. Norris Schneider wrote and visited several Weller artists and their descendants. His collection of letters, notes, and documents from the artists, as well as his articles on them in *The Times Recorder* and *The Times Signal* of Zanesville provided fertile ground for research, and much of the substance of this chapter. Interviews with Ruth Axline and Dorothy Laughead augmented and enriched the field.

Ruth Axline worked at Weller from 1929 to 1936. After she had finished college, Ruth joined the decorating department under director Ed Pickens. Her co-workers included: Frank Dedonatis, Rudolph Lorber, Margaret McGinnis, Sarah Reid McLaughlin, Hester Pillsbury, the Timberlake sisters, Naomi Walch, and Carl Weigelt. Sarah McLaughlin taught Ruth how to decorate Hudson vases with berries, leaves, and flowers, a process described in detail in Chapter XI. Shown here is a sketch of irises which Sarah made for Ruth to copy (Fig. 264). Sarah had worked for William Long at Lonhuda Pottery before she came to Weller. A skilled artist, she decorated a four foot high Aurelian vase with roses for the St. Louis World's Fair in 1904, and several large Hudson Pictorial vases around 1920.

During the thirties, Ruth decorated Bonito and Coppertone and painted stripes on cookware. The work day at the Pottery lasted nearly ten hours. Ruth worked during the week from 6:30 a.m. to 4:00 p.m., and five hours on Saturday, for $10.50 per week, paid in cash. She carried her lunch and took thirty minutes to eat. "I can still remember how long a day seemed and how tired I was. I walked to work then, too," Ruth confided, July 25, 1980. Ruth explained that each line had a quota for the day's work, for example, twenty-five pieces of Bonito to decorate per artist. Supervisors made sure that each decorator met her quota.

While Ruth was there, the Pottery employed several relatives of Sam Weller, from sons-in-law to nephews. Nephew Harry Weller became president of the company in 1925. He was a short, stout, dressy man, who always smoked a big cigar. Harry and his brother Frank Weller ran the company. Frank took charge of mixing the glazes. "He was extremely well liked and seemed to enjoy life to the fullest," Ruth wrote, March 1, 1980.

Ruth remembered Zanesville as a Saturday night town. Saturday night was the time to shop, to visit friends, and to go out on the town. There was no time during the week for these activities. After she left Weller in March

Fig. 265: Ruth Axline, Weller decorator from 1929 to 1936.

1936, Ruth worked for the Mosaic Tile Company for twenty years and then for LePere Pottery as art director for over seven years. Today she is retired and lives in Zanesville (Fig. 265).

A Rookwood artist, Edward Abel also worked for Weller from about 1897 to 1900. He was listed in the 1897 Zanesville City Directory as an employee of S. A. Weller. At the Pottery, Abel decorated Aurelian, Lonhuda, and Louwelsa vases and signed them E. A., E. Abel, or simply Abel. He was adept at bird, fish, and animal portraits (Fig. 266).

Samuel Weller's nephew Levi J. Burgess worked at the Pottery from about 1899 to 1907. On Louwelsa wares he painted Indian heads, for which he was paid $1.00 per head. His portraits exhibited skill and competence. Witness the Rembrandtesque portrait of artist Jean Francois Millet in Chapter IV. Burgess also decorated Dickensware II, Dresden, Eocean, and Perfecto (C-1, 2, 3, 8).

Burgess married Katharine Stanbery, daughter of George Stanbery of the American Encaustic Tiling Company. They are shown here in their wedding photo (Fig. 267). He and his wife built the beautiful large house at 1245 Blue Avenue in Zanesville, which had a theater. Dorothy Laughead

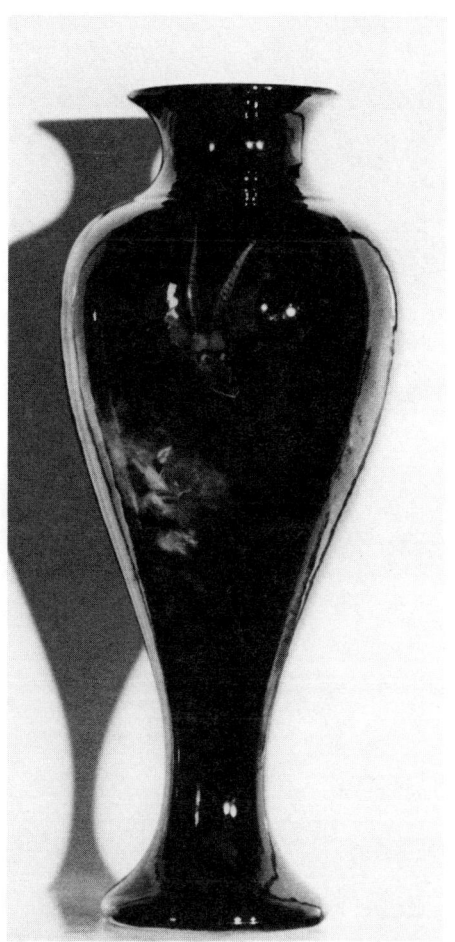

Fig. 266: *Incised* Aurelian: Vase 13" high, decorated with a dragon and signed by artist Edward Abel.

Fig. 264: A sketch of irises made by Sarah McLaughlin for Ruth Axline to copy, when Ruth began to decorate Weller ware. Courtesy of Ruth Axline.

recalled that her brother and Burgess put on shows there. In December 1909, Burgess opened the Blue Lion Art Emporium. Five years later, he started the Blue Lion Tea Room on the West Pike with decorator C. Minnie Terry. He left Zanesville for Cincinnati, where he was a commercial illustrator for several years. After the death of his wife and his daughter, he moved to California. At age 61, he died of a heart attack in Hollywood, on January 22, 1943. Irvin Smith, husband of Louise Weller and president of Weller Pottery, acquired the Burgess home on Blue Avenue. Later, the house became Mary's Rest Home.

Charles Chilcote was born May 27, 1888. After his father's death, young Charles lived with his grandfather Curtis Williams at White Cottage, ten miles from Zanesville. Williams was a potter and taught his grandson how to throw a pot. When Chilcote exhibited some skill in pottery making, Williams introduced him to his friend Sam Weller. In 1978 Chilcote wrote

Fig. 267: Mr. and Mrs. Levi J. Burgess on their wedding day. Courtesy of Norris Schneider.

to Norris Schneider, "My grandfather took me to Mr. Weller and he said to send me down and he would make a pottery man of me." Chilcote was 16 years old. He received no pay the first year, except for train fare from White Cottage to Zanesville and tuition for drawing lessons twice a week with Karl Kappes. The second year he earned $3.00 a week, which was raised soon to $5.00 per week.

Weller Pottery was at its zenith in 1904, the year Chilcote was hired. More than thirty artists, including Burgess, Haubrich, Kappes, Rhead, Sicard, and Upjohn, worked with him in the studio at Putnam. In an interview with Norris Schneider in December 1968, Chilcote described the studio: "The windows were draped, the walls hung with paintings and plaques made by the various artists. There were fresh flowers brought in every day." The head of the art department Charles Upjohn instructed Chilcote how to paint with slip on a vase and how to incise designs on Dickensware. He began to decorate Louwelsa first, then Eocean, and finally Dickensware II. He would choose a design from a table of drawings in the workroom, put the drawing upright in front of him, and proceed to copy it on to a vase. Witness the Eocean vases by Chilcote in the color section (C-1).

Chilcote watched both Rhead and Sicard at work. He saw Frederick Rhead make Jap Birdimal with a small bag full of slip, with a tube protruding from the bag. He became friends with Jacques Sicard. Chilcote claimed that Sicard and Gellée came from France on a five year contract. He told Norris Schneider, "They were very secretive and had a room which they kept locked, and the only one permitted to enter was Mr. Weller. Fortunately, they were very friendly to me, and I was permitted to go in and to watch them decorate, perhaps because I was a boy."

Sometime before 1906, Chilcote and Frank Ferrell left Weller to work for a year at J.B. Owens Pottery, where Chilcote said they duplicated the lines they were making at Weller and received higher wages. Chilcote moved on to Peters and Reed Pottery and remained there for fourteen years. He returned to Weller for a year to experiment with the formula for Sicard. In 1936 he moved to Detroit. He came back to Zanesville in 1968 and died there on April 5, 1979.

Anthony Dunlavy was born in Athens, Ohio in 1874 to native Irish parents. Without formal training in art, he began to work for the American Encaustic Tiling Company in 1897. After serving in the Spanish American War in 1898, he joined the staff at Weller, where he decorated Louwelsa and Dickensware II. He drew realistic portraits of monks and Indians, with skillful delineation of facial features. Witness the monk vase in Chapter V.

By 1905 Dunlavy had moved to Roseville Pottery to decorate Rozane. In 1907 he worked for the Zanesville Tile Company. In the early 1920s, he returned to Weller. Art Wagner recalled that he and Dunlavy decorated Lamar. Dunlavy painted the black trees on the red background. In 1922 he gave a Lamar vase to his wife for Christmas. He worked for J.B. Owens in the twenties also, designing tile catalogs. After a short period at Hull Pottery in 1930, he moved to Linden, New Jersey. He returned to Ohio before the decade ended. In 1941 he went to California, where he died in

1943. He changed jobs often. He decorated pottery, trimmed windows, designed catalogs, and drew cartoons. He did his most creative work at Weller Pottery, the splendid portraits in Dickensware II and Louwelsa, signed A.D. (C-2).

Frank Ferrell was born in Zanesville, May 22, 1878. He lived and worked there, as a pottery designer, until his death at age 83 in 1961. As an artist and designer at Weller Pottery until 1905, he decorated Aurelian, Dickensware II, Etched Floral, Jap Birdimal, and Louwelsa (Fig. 268). He gave directions for slip painting on vases in "Painting in Underglaze," in *Keramic Studio* in November 1908: "Apply color in the same manner as in oil painting. Apply the colors heavily and lay them on smoothly because of burning off in the fire. The grounding and decorating must all be done in the green state while the vase is yet wet." Pictured in this book are several pieces decorated by Ferrell: the Etched Floral vase in Chapter V, the prize winning seven foot high Aurelian vase in Chapter VI, and the Louwelsa oil lamp in Chapter VII.

Ferrell left Weller in 1905 to work for J.B. Owens, and then for Peters and Reed Pottery, where he devised the Moss Aztec line in 1912. From 1918 to 1954, he was art director at Roseville. Here he designed at least one new molded line a year, from Ferrella to Pinecone.

Albert Haubrich was born July 8, 1875, in Biersdorf, Germany. He came to America at age 5 in 1880 and settled in Steubenville, Ohio. He worked at Weller Pottery from 1897 to 1903, slip painting Eocean and Louwelsa. He decorated Louwelsa vases, pitchers, and steins with leaves, flowers, monks, and cavaliers. No one painted leaves as beautifully as Haubrich, from gold and red maple leaves to green tropical palms (Fig. 269).

Between 1903 and 1904, Haubrich worked for J.B. Owens Pottery. When Albert Radford established Radford Pottery in Clarksburg, West Virginia in July 1904, he asked Haubrich to join him as head of the decorating department. Radford died a month later in August 1904. Haubrich probably left Radford Pottery shortly thereafter. Sometime between 1905 and 1908, he worked for William Long at Clifton Pottery, where he decorated several Tirrube vases, including a stork vase. He ran an art school in Clarksburg, called the Haubrich Decorating Company, from about 1909 to 1920. In the early twenties, Haubrich moved to Columbus and started his own business as a fresco painter and an interior decorator. He died in Columbus on April 9, 1931.

John J. Herold was born in Carlsbad, Austria in 1871, where he attended art schools and worked in china, glass, and pottery factories. In 1891, at age 20, he came to the United States. He began to work for Weller in 1898. He skillfully decorated several Aurelian, Dickensware, and Louwelsa vases. His signature appeared on a three sided Dickensware fish vase, a Bleak House vase, and an Aurelian vase with yellow ducklings on a nest, shown in the color section (C-7).

Herold moved to J.B. Owens Pottery in 1899 and remained there thirteen months. At Roseville Pottery by 1901, he advanced quickly from technical supervisor to plant superintendent. Here, he created the Roseville imitation of Sicard called Mara and the dramatic new line Mongol with its rouge

Fig. 268: Matt Louwelsa pitcher 12½" high, artist signed Ferrell in white slip, and decorated with grapes and leaves. Photo by D.L. Hill.

Fig. 269: *Incised* Aurelian: Oil Banquet Lamp 27" high, dated March 1898, artist signed A. Haubrich in slip, and decorated with tropical leaves. Collection: Tommy and Norma Smith. Photo by Sigafoose.

flambé glaze, which won first prize at the St. Louis Exposition in 1904. The fumes from the Chinese Red or flambé glaze affected his lungs, and for his health he moved to Golden, Colorado in 1908, where he built an experimental pottery. With funding from Adolf Coors, he established the Herold China and Pottery Company in 1910, with Coors as president, and his son as vice president. When Coors insisted that his son replace Herold as manager of the pottery, he returned to Ohio to work for the Guernsey Earthenware Company in 1914, and the Ohio Pottery in 1915. He died April 18, 1923. Frederick Rhead wrote a eulogy for Herold, which appeared in the Zanesville papers and in *PGBS*. He called Herold one of the greatest practical potters of the day.

Weller hired Josephine Imlay to decorate Louwelsa in 1899. Her co-workers included: Elizabeth Ayers, Lizabeth Blake, Levi Burgess, Mary Gellie, Albert Haubrich, Karl Kappes, Claude Leffler, Sarah McLaughlin, the Mitchell sisters, Eugene Roberts, Hattie Ross, Minnie Terry, and Helen Windle. They all worked together on the popular Louwelsa line. Miss Imlay recalled that Sam Weller rarely came to the decorating studio at Putnam, where she worked. On September 6, 1901, however, he did appear, to announce dramatically, "McKinley was shot!" Miss Imlay worked at Roseville Pottery after she left Weller in 1902.

Karl Kappes was born in Zanesville, May 28, 1861. His parents operated a hotel called Mechanics Hall. After graduating from Zanesville High School, Kappes enrolled in an art school in Cincinnati. He went to New York to study with the American Impressionist artist William Merritt Chase. Homesick, he hiked from New York back to Zanesville, carrying a knapsack filled with paintings and art supplies. He sold pictures along the way to subsidize his trip. After studying art in Munich, Kappes opened a studio at Third and Main Streets in Zanesville, where he gave art lessons and painted portraits (Fig. 270). He taught several local artists including Charles Chilcote, Andrew Loomis, and William Stemm. Around 1898-99, he came to work at Weller. In 1901 he was foreman at the Pottery, and in 1904 head of the art department. In this position, Kappes decorated Louwelsa vases and directed the work of artists he had taught in his studio. After he left Weller in 1909, he painted and sold landscapes and portraits of nudes. He continued to paint and to teach art students, until his death on November 16, 1943. Collectors today seek not only the Louwelsa vases he signed, but also his oil paintings. Hanging in the Zanesville Art Center, Kappes' painting "Back Streets" reflects the influence of the Impressionists and the Ash Can School in Germany.

Born in Mettlach, Germany, John Lessell emigrated to America and worked in several pottery and china factories: Arc-En-Ciel, Ford City China, J.B. Owens, and Weller Pottery. He founded his own company, Lessell Art Ware, in Parkersburg, West Virginia in 1911, where he made pottery which resembled copper and bronze. The firm failed in 1912.

From 1920 to 1924, John Lessell was head of the decorating department at the Ceramic Avenue plant at Weller Pottery. Sam Weller had hired him, hoping that he would duplicate the Sicard line. Instead, Lessell developed Chengtu, Lamar, LaSa, and Marengo. These lines sold poorly, because they

Fig. 270: Karl Kappes in his studio at Third and Main Streets in Zanesville. Courtesy of Mose Mesre.

were overpriced, reflecting the high cost of production. Lessell's overglaze luster lines won high praise, however, from the cognoscenti (Fig. 271).

Lessell left Weller for a sojourn at Camark Pottery. He joined the Art China Company in Zanesville in 1924, as its head pottery expert, and went with the company when it moved to Newark, Ohio in 1925. At age 59, he died of chloroform poisoning in Newark on December 22, 1926. He took the chloroform by mistake, thinking that it was prescribed medicine, according to his obituary in *Ceramic Industry* in February 1927. The obituary stated that Lessell had been in the United States forty years, and that he had learned the pottery trade in Europe. At the time of his death, Lessell was vice president of the Art China Company, Newark, Ohio, and was the sole owner of several patented glaze formulas.

Edwin L. Pickens, the brother of Mrs. Samuel Weller, worked at the Pottery for several years and became supervisor of the Putnam plant around

Fig. 271: *Marked Weller:* Marengo vase 8½″ high, with a light blue background and dark blue trees, designed by John Lessell. Collection: Paul and Rosemary Enoch. Photo by Ralph Crowell Associates.

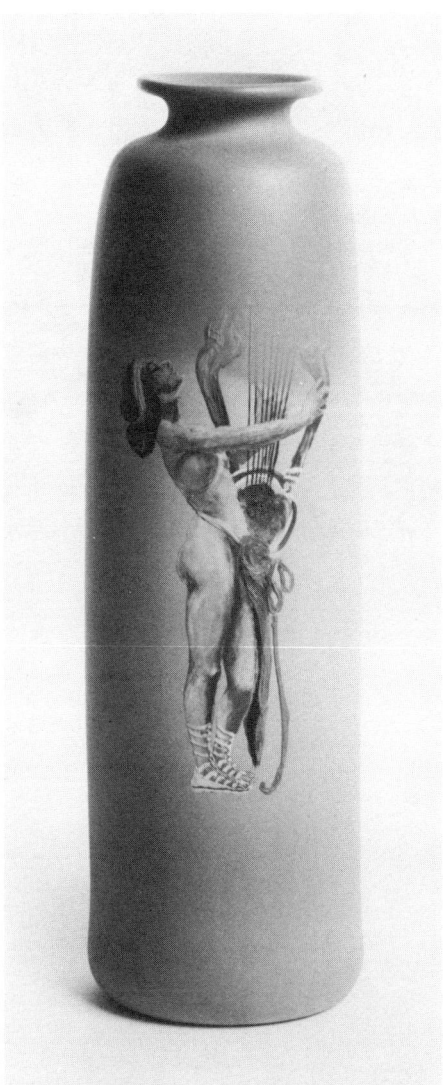

Fig. 272: Slip decorated vase 17½" high, signed E.L. Pickens, with an Amazon woman and her harp. Collection: Cort and Chris Michener. Photo by West and West.

1909. He headed the decorating department in 1929, when Ruth Axline worked there. His fine sgraffito work enhanced Dickensware II and Etched Matt. He may have created the flowing haired maiden on Etched Matt, since a plaque in that line bore his signature. He incised dragons, nudes, fish, ducks, hunting dogs, and Don Quixote on large Dickensware II vases. He often worked with Upjohn. Sometimes, they both signed vases, i.e. "Washington Crossing the Delaware," (C-7), and "The Winemaker," (C-14). Pickens was one of the best sgraffito artists at Weller. Collectors today cherish his work (Fig. 272).

Hester Pillsbury worked at Weller from about 1897 to 1936. She was listed in the 1897 Zanesville City Directory as an artist at S. A. Weller, boarding at 284 Putnam. Undoubtedly, she could walk to work at the Putnam plant. In January 1902 *House Furnisher* pictured the diminutive Hester, standing with two huge, five feet high Louwelsa vases which towered over her. Fellow decorator Ruth Axline observed that Hester was friendly and considerate of others. She had a quick temper, however, and when she was mad, she jumped up and down. She excelled at slip decoration and worked very fast on each vase. Protective of her work, she kept it behind a screen so that no one could copy it. Her artist monogram appeared on Bonito, Cretone, Hudson, Louwelsa, Perfecto, Raceme, Rochelle, and Stellar (Fig. 273). Note the beautiful Hudson Pictorial vases by Hester in the color section (C-9). She was a superb artist.

Albert Radford came to the United States from the Wedgwood factory in England in 1882. He developed a cameo decorated ware at the Radford Art Pottery in Tiffin, Ohio in 1896. Between 1898 and 1900, he worked at Weller Pottery, where he may have devised the matt blue vase with white cameos of mermaids and seahorses, pictured in Chapter VIII. He became General Manager of the Zanesville Art Pottery and then, a designer at J.B. Owens. He established The A. Radford Pottery Company in 1903 in Zanesville. Here he continued to make the Wedgwood-type wares. By July 1903, he had to sell Radford Pottery to Arc-En-Ciel. He moved to Clarksburg, West Virginia, with Albert Haubrich, to set up his third company, Radford

Fig. 273: *Marked Weller*: Cretone vase 8" high, Hudson vase 10½" high, and Hudson vase 9" high, all decorated and signed by Hester Pillsbury.

Pottery. He started to operate the plant in July 1904, and died one month later of a heart attack.

William H. Stemm worked for Weller from about 1898 to 1918, with a one year interval in 1902 at J.B. Owens. He took drawing lessons from Karl Kappes, who also taught him to decorate Eocean and Louwelsa. He painted birds and butterflies on jars, peds, and umbrella stands. Weller paid him $25 to $30 per week. Stemm worked under Karl Kappes until around 1909, when Ed Pickens became the head of the decorating department.

C. Minnie Terry was born May 18, 1866 (Fig. 274). She attended the Putnam Seminary in Zanesville, where she studied art. From 1894 to 1910, she listed herself as an artist, decorator, and designer in the Zanesville City Directories. Sometime between 1899 and 1910, she decorated Louwelsa at Weller Pottery. Edwin AtLee Barber identified her as a Weller artist in his *Marks of American Potters* in 1904. She also worked for J.B. Owens and Roseville Potteries. In 1912 Levi J. Burgess hired her as a clerk at the Blue Lion Art Emporium, an interior decorating shop on North Fourth Street in Zanesville. She opened the Blue Lion Tea Room on the West Pike in 1914 and worked there until her death on December 29, 1917.

Fig. 274: C. Minnie Terry, Weller decorator. Courtesy of Norris Schneider.

Mae and Sarah Timberlake worked for Weller and also for Owens and Roseville Potteries. As a condition of her employment, Mae insisted that each Pottery hire her sister Sarah, who was a less skilled decorator. The two sisters were very close and worked at adjoining benches in the factory. Mae depended upon Sarah to set up her brushes and paints for her. Ruth Axline worked with the Timberlake sisters after 1929, when both were quite old, having worked for years at Weller. Mae was extremely shy and timid, according to Ruth. "She could go all day without talking to anyone," Ruth said. "When someone spoke to her, she drew back, frightened. But she was very sweet and never cross." Sarah laughed and talked with the other decorators, while Mae withdrew from everyone to concentrate on her art.

The Weller supervisors gave Mae the largest and most difficult Hudson vases to decorate. She also painted Aurelian, Cretone, Eocean, Geode, Louwelsa, and Stellar. Her Hudson Pictorial vases won praise from everyone. Note the Hudson peacock vase on the cover of this book. Mae could paint seven large vases, 12 to 18 inches high, per day, covering each vase with marvelous color and detail. She was an exceptional artist.

The Weller artists were a talented group of men and women. Some were in their teens when they came to work at the Pottery. Most of them had no artistic training, yet they were able to paint scenes, portraits of men, animals, houses, castles, and flowers on wet clay vases! Seeking higher wages, they migrated back and forth from Weller to Owens to Roseville, and often decorated identical lines in all three places. At Weller they usually had a quota, a set number of vases to decorate per day. After they finished with a vase, they never saw it again, since it was fired and glazed in another department. Despite the long hours, low wages, and arduous work, they appeared cheerful, even playful. One photo showed them all in costume for a Halloween party (Fig. 275). The artists provided a vital spirit and a creative ingenuity that allowed Weller Pottery to flourish.

Fig. 275: The Weller decorators dressed for a costume party. Courtesy of Norris Schneider.

Chapter XIX
Artists of Distinction:
Laughead, Lorber, Rhead, and Upjohn

Among the talented artists at Weller Pottery, five stood out: Dorothy Laughead, Rudolph Lorber, Frederick Hurten Rhead, Jacques Sicard (discussed in Chapter IX), and Charles Babcock Upjohn. These artists designed new lines and created works of art for the company.

Frederick H. Rhead was born in Hanley, Staffordshire, England on August 29, 1880, the son of Frederick Alfred Rhead, a distinguished potter. Frederick H. Rhead attended the Wedgwood Institute, Burslem, and the Stoke-on-Trent, Hanley, and the Fenton Government Art Schools. He received diplomas in modeling, perspective, and painting. He taught design at the Longton Government Art School. From 1899 to 1902, he was art director of Wardle and Company, Hanley, and at the same time, he helped his father to organize the art pottery for Wileman and Company (Figs. 276, 277).

On June 6, 1902, Rhead emigrated to America. "I came to the United States on the old Cunard liner Umbria, sailing from Liverpool on June 6th 1902, to manage a little six kiln pottery in Tiltonville, Ohio, a branch of the Wheeling Potteries Company. Here I made some of the first matte glazes made in the United States. In those days I did a lot of experimental work in bodies and glazes and when the possibilities for development seemed to be complete for a particular factory, I changed to another pottery. After two years I went to Zanesville, Ohio, to be art director for the Roseville Pottery," Rhead wrote in an unpublished note, from the files of the Museum of Ceramics at East Liverpool, England.

From this narrative we learn that Rhead arrived in America in 1902 and went to work at a pottery in Tiltonville, Ohio, a branch of the Wheeling Potteries Company. In September 1902, the Tiltonville Pottery became the Avon Faience Company, managed by William P. Jervis, an Englishman. Jervis may have invited Rhead to join him at Tiltonville, to help manage the new company. Here Rhead and Jervis developed an artware decorated in underglaze Art Nouveau designs, some of which were tube lined in white slip, a technique Rhead employed at Wardle and Company in England, and later in Jap Birdimal at Weller. Both Rhead and Jervis left the Avon Faience Company by mid 1903. Rhead joined Weller Pottery in 1904, while Jervis went to the Corona Pottery.

The duration of Rhead's employment at Weller remains a mystery. On February 11, 1904, C & G wrote, "Frederick Rhead, late art director of the

Fig. 276: Frederick Hurten Rhead. Courtesy of Norris Schneider.

Fig. 277: Ewer 9¼" high, signed on the base: "F.H. Rhead, Art Nouveau," decorated by Frederick H. Rhead, c. 1898, at art school. Courtesy of Bernard Bumpus.

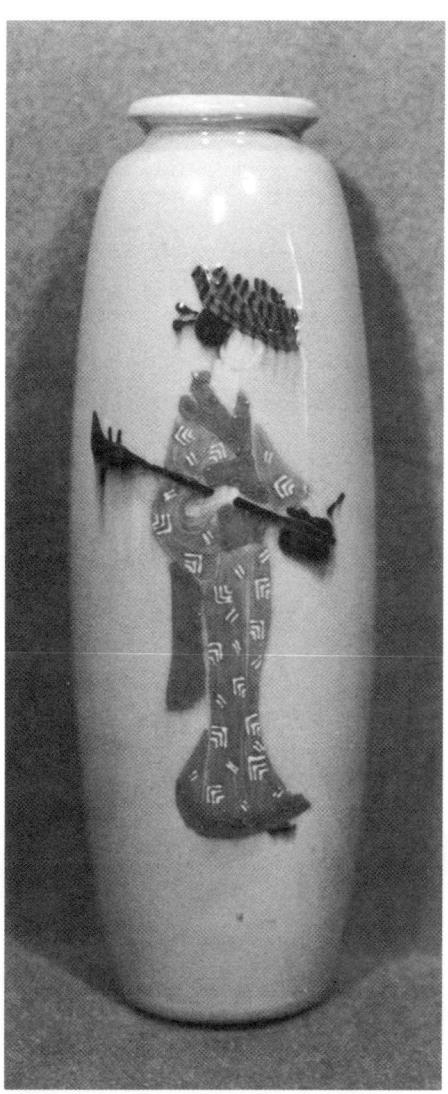

Fig. 278: Weller Jap Birdimal geisha vase 10" high, artist signed V.M.H. Collection: Dick and Nancy Sigafoose.

Avon plant of the Wheeling Potteries Co., went last week with the S.A. Weller Pottery Co., Zanesville." Rhead omitted all references to his time at Weller in his biography in *The National Cyclopaedia of American Biography*, and in the personal note quoted above. The Zanesville City Directories showed Rhead in Zanesville from 1904 to 1908. Probably, Rhead came to work for Weller Pottery the first week in February 1904 and remained there several months. Sometime in 1904, he moved to Roseville Pottery as art director.

Lines attributed to Rhead at Weller Pottery included: Art Nouveau, Dickensware III, Jap Birdimal, and Rhead Faience. The Art Nouveau line, however, appeared a month before he came to work at Weller. While he could not have devised Art Nouveau, Rhead did create Dickensware III and Jap Birdimal.

Rhead introduced raised line decoration or tube lining on Jap Birdimal and Rhead Faience. Several pieces bear his signature, including the three piece tea set pictured in Chapter VIII. The geese, the leafy trees, the windmills found on these lines resembled the work Rhead did at the Wardle and the Wileman Potteries in England. Rhead drew the designs of fish, birds, and geishas and gave them to the Weller artists to copy on to individual pieces of Jap Birdimal or Rhead Faience (Fig. 278).

Tube lining also appeared on Third Line Dickensware, a line attributed to Rhead by Gordon Mull. The first references to Dickensware III in the trade journals occurred in July and August 1905, months after Rhead's departure from Weller. Rhead probably designed the new line and supervised its production, before he left the Pottery. Working under Rhead, Gordon Mull tube lined in white slip the inscriptions from Dickens' novels on the discs on the back of each piece of Dickensware III. The presence of tube lining and the use of illustrations from Frederick Barnard marked Dickensware III as a Rhead design. Rhead was a friend of Frederick Barnard, the illustrator of Dickens, discussed in Chapter V.

In a series of articles called "Pottery Class," for *Keramic Studio* in October and November 1909, Rhead discussed sgraffito and raised line decoration. He wrote of the latter in October 1909: "Like Sgraffito, it (raised line) is decoration in relief, but this relief is applied, instead of being formed by cutting away the background as is done in sgraffito. A small flexible rubber bag is filled with slip and a glass tube is inserted in the bag which is made to fit quite tightly around the tube." Rhead described how to hold the tube, as one holds a pencil, and how to force the slip through the glass tube. He continued his discussion of tube lining in November 1909: "The ware must be in the most perfect condition, not harder than green; the design must have a strong outline which is tubed in black or some other dark color. It is important that the outline should be quite high in relief rather than wide, and that the lines which are supposed to meet should quite touch." Rhead used tube lining at Avon Faience, Roseville, and Weller Potteries.

After only a brief stay at Weller, Rhead left to become art director of Roseville Pottery, from late 1904 to 1908, where he created the tube lined Aztec as well as Della Robbia, and Olympic. Thereafter, he worked again with William Jervis at Jervis Pottery in Oyster Bay, New York, and at University City Pottery in Missouri, as a pottery instructor. In October 1911, Rhead joined Arequipa Pottery and remained there until July 1913. He moved next to Santa Barbara to establish the Pottery of the Camarata, later incorporated as Rhead Pottery (Fig. 279). He became director of research at the American Encaustic Tiling Company in Zanesville in 1917 and stayed there until 1927. From 1927 to 1942, he was art director of the Homer Laughlin China Company in Newell, West Virginia, where he created the famous Fiesta dinnerware.

Frederick Rhead was not only a potter, but also a writer. He wrote *Studio Pottery* in 1910 and edited *The Potter* in 1916-1917. He was associate editor of the *Journal of the American Ceramic Society* in the twenties and wrote a weekly column, "Chats on Pottery," for *The Potters Herald* in the thirties.

Rhead died of cancer on November 2, 1942, at age 61. His obituary in *The New York Times,* November 4, 1942, revealed that he had become a U.S. citizen in 1918, and that he had done architectural faience work in theaters, hotels, and public buildings in collaboration with Leon V. Solon.

Rhead's articles provided a scholarly commentary on the art of making pottery. He evaluated modern potters with a keen eye. "The Paris Exposition of 1900 brought together the ceramic works of the various countries, and in the decorated types, a fair proportion were executed in underglaze colors. The English wares were of the Morris-Crane school, decorated on a white body, or buff and terra cotta bodies using white as an opacifier. The French were at this time running wild with their abominable L'Art Nouveau decorations. . . .," Rhead observed in "Some Notes on Historical and Modern Decorative Processes," in the *Journal of the American Ceramic Society,* in February 1923. His disdain for Art Nouveau and Matt Green wares permeated his articles.

Rhead attacked Matt Green pottery in *The Potters Herald* on July 11, 1935:

> When she (Adelaide Robineau) commenced making porcelains around 1903 the influence of the Paris Exposition of 1900 was still dominating the craftworkers of this and other countries. This country was saturated with Grueby, Van Briggle, Teco and Rookwood. The commercial art potteries were hitting it high with their miserable matt glaze imitations, the schools were teaching that 'shiney' glazes were 'in bad taste' and that if a glaze were dull in texture, if the shape was heavy and clumsily made, if the piece had a dull wooden ring when struck, and if the color was green at any price, such a concoction was infinitely preferable to the finest Sung monochrome.

Rhead admired the work of Newcomb College, Robineau Pottery, and Rookwood. In May 1922 in the *Bulletin of the American Ceramic Society,* he reviewed an exhibition of American pottery and concluded, "The American potter is surely and definitely becoming master of his craft."

Charles Babcock Upjohn was born in Brooklyn on June 26, 1866 (Fig. 280). His grandfather was the renowned architect Richard Upjohn, designer

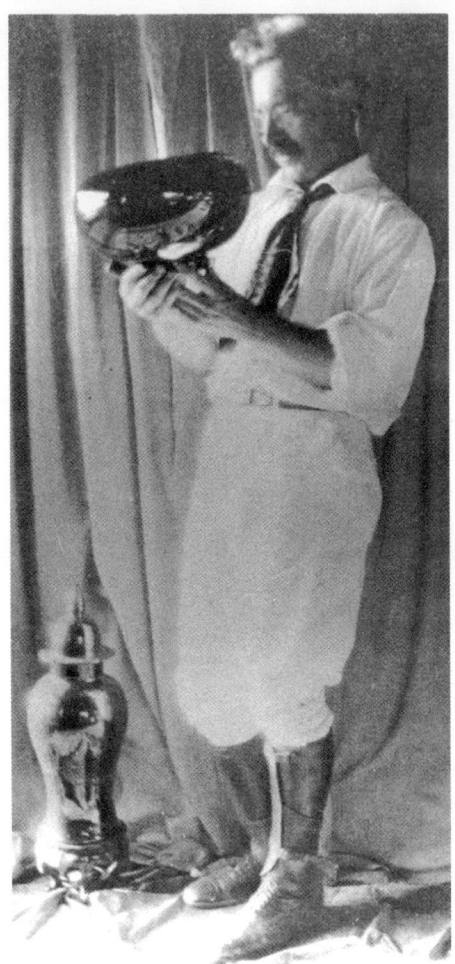

Fig. 279: Frederick H. Rhead at Santa Barbara, California, studying a mirror black bowl, c. 1916. Photo courtesy of Paul Evans.

Fig. 280: Charles Babcock Upjohn. Courtesy of Norris Schneider.

Fig. 281: *Impressed* Dickensware Weller Second Line vase 10½" high, with a monk singing and playing the mandolin, artist signed with the Upjohn monogram.

Fig. 282: Weller Dickensware Second Line Circus Vase, 20" high, artist signed by Charles Upjohn, Gordon Mull, and L. Knaus, and dated 1902. Courtesy of the National Road/Zane Grey Museum. Photo by Mose Mesre.

of the gateway to the Boston Commons and Trinity Church in New York. After graduating from Peekskill Military Academy, Charles attended the Metropolitan Art School. Then he joined the firm of architects headed by his grandfather and his father. In 1890 he went to Africa to assist missionaries in building missions in the interior and on the west coast of Africa. In Liberia he contracted malaria and left to get treatment in London. After he recovered, he studied art in England, France, and Italy. Upon his return to New York, Upjohn was apprenticed to the Viennese sculptor Karl Bitter.

In 1895 Sam Weller hired Charles Upjohn as head designer at the Pottery. Here he created Second Line Dickensware and trained a bevy of artists to slip paint Eocean and Louwelsa wares and to incise Dickensware II. As noted in Chapter V, Upjohn himself designed and decorated some admirable pieces, from the tobacco jars to the Circus vase (Fig. 281).

Upjohn married Louisa Van Horne in 1897. In 1900 he took a year leave of absence from Weller Pottery to serve as a designer and a modeler for the Cambridge Art Pottery, when it was first organized. He returned to Weller and remained there until 1904. That year he started his own pottery, the C. B. Upjohn Company, in Zanesville. Lack of sufficient capital caused the pottery to close in 1906. Upjohn, however, left in June 1905, relinquishing his interest in it. He moved to Trenton, New Jersey, to work for the Trent Tile Company.

Ten years later in 1915, Upjohn joined the faculty at Teacher's College, Columbia University, as a teacher of clay modeling, pottery, and ceramics. In 1940 he retired from Columbia after twenty-five years of teaching and moved into the studio of sculptor George Grey Barnard. Upjohn died in 1953 at age 87.

Charles T. Upjohn informed Norris Schneider on November 15, 1970, that his grandfather Charles B. Upjohn was color blind: "Only his immediate family were aware that he was color blind, unable to distinguish between green and red. This handicap could explain his continuing urge toward sculpture and even wood carving in his early years." He continued, "I think a critical eye could discern this weakness for in some early works, I think even in some Dickensware, the greens have a greenish brown cast and reds are on the brownish grey side."

Upjohn's finest achievement at Weller was the Circus Vase, dated 1902, pictured here (Fig. 282). The vase stands twenty inches high and has fifteen characters, including seven spectators, deeply carved in sgraffito. A drama ensues all around the vase. Seven spectators watch a tightrope walker, while a magician, a young blond performer, and three dogs wait to perform. A black attendant pulls back a sheet, which serves as a privacy curtain, to reveal a clown giving a baby his bottle and two children huddled around a stove. With Gordon Mull and L. Knaus, Upjohn realistically portrayed the hardship and the poignancy in the life of the itinerant circus performer. They signed the vase with Latin abbreviations: C.B. Upjohn, Sc. (Sculptor); G. Mull, del. (Designer), and L. Knaus, Pinxt (Painter).

Rudolph Lorber was born in Vienna, Austria and educated in Bohemia. He moved to England and from there emigrated to America in 1903. Lorber's son William R. Lorber wrote to Norris Schneider on December 20, 1969, that Lorber came to Weller Pottery around 1905 and remained there until his retirement in 1940. Sam Weller asked Lorber to design new molded lines for the company. The hiring of Lorber marked the transition from art wares to molded wares. Lorber created several lines: Blue Drapery, Blue Ware, Coppertone, Dechiwo, Elberta, Flemish, Forest, Graystone, the Happy Ducks, Hobart, Ivory, Knifewood, Lavonia, Muskota, Neiska, Pearl, Pumila, Roma, Selma, Seneca, Sydonia, Ting, Wood Rose, and Zona (Figs. 283, 284). To model a design for a new line, Lorber added decorations in clay to a plaster of Paris model, using his tools of ebony wood, according to his son. In 1933, he became the head of the art department.

Lorber found ideas for new lines in scenery, in nature, even in *Vogue* magazine! Some of his best work occurred in the naturalistic lines, Knifewood and Selma. He designed the horned owl, the squirrel sitting upright on a branch to eat an acorn, the swans peacefully gliding down the stream. Lorber also devised the marvelous figurines in the Lavonia and Hobart lines, the Hobart Woman vase, Leda and the Swan, and the Graystone Goose Boy. Dorothy Laughead assisted him. Together they created the Elberta and Sydonia lines.

Dorothy England Laughead was born July 19, 1895. In an interview I had with her in November 1978, we discussed her association with Weller. Her father James England was a traveling salesman for the Pottery and later became manager of the Weller Theater. As a youngster, Dorothy visited the plant and gazed in awe at the seven foot high Aurelian vase. "If you can carry that home, you can have it," Sam Weller told her. She tried and tried to lift it.

After she attended business college and decided against a career in business, Dorothy joined the art department at the Pottery. She worked for Weller sporadically from 1913 to 1925. In 1925 she came to work full time at the Putnam plant. She was a decorator, a modeler, and a designer. Her initials, D. E. for Dorothy England, marked some of the finest Hudson vases. She designed these lines: Arcadia, Bonito, Bouquet, Cactus, Cameo, Chase, Floral, Pastel, Silvertone (with Leffler), Terose, Wild Rose, and the Ollas Water Bottle.

Dorothy preferred to model rather than to decorate. She was surprised her first year at Weller to find that some of the decorators hid their work

Fig. 283: *Marked Weller*: Ivory vase 10" high, designed by Rudolph Lorber. Collection: Dora Betts.

Fig. 284: *Marked Weller*: Ting Console Set, designed by Rudolph Lorber. Collection: Barbara Watson.

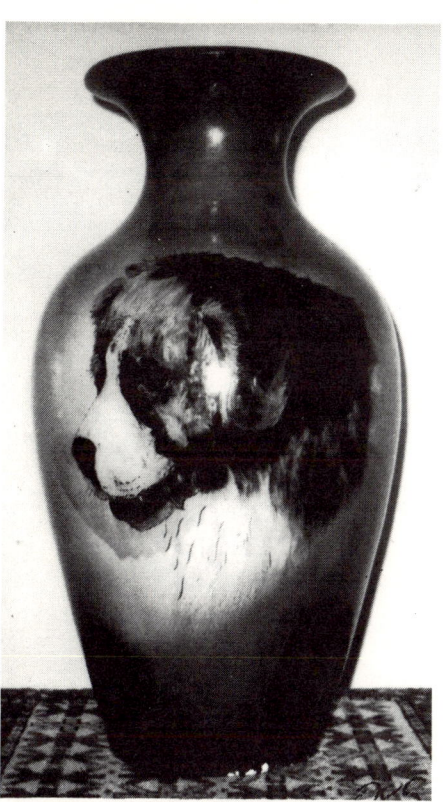

Fig. 285: *Marked Weller:* Decorative Etched Ware floor vase 27½" high, artist signed "A. Wilson after Landseer," with a portrait of a St. Bernard dog. Collection: Carl and Amy Schaefer.

behind cardboard partitions, so that no one could copy it. Artist Claude Leffler taught Dorothy how to decorate Hudson vases. She began by painting irises or lilies of the valley on the pottery, discovering that certain flowers went on certain shapes. Soon she became quite proficient at slip decoration.

Dorothy began to model in 1924, when her supervisors saw that she could do it. She worked with Rudolph Lorber. "I like to model best," Dorothy told me in 1978. She described how she drew a shape to scale for a vase and gave it to the mold maker, who made a plaster model for her. After she had the plaster vase back, she would model flowers and cut the markings on it. From this shape, a mold was made of the vase.

When Rudolph Lorber retired as head designer in 1940, Dorothy took his place. Her best work included these lines: Bonito, Cactus, Cameo, Chase, Silvertone, Terose, and the animal figurines. She designed dogs, cats, rabbits, squirrels, and frogs. The near life-size Weller animals were Dorothy's finest achievement. The wide-eyed Scottie Pup, the Spaniel, the Cat with its tail straight up in the air, the Squirrel, all seemed drawn from nature itself.

During the interview I had with Dorothy in 1978, she admitted that her pay was low the years she worked at the Pottery. She recalled anecdotes about Sam Weller and the artists at the Putnam plant. She remarked, "Mr. Weller didn't want reptiles on any vases!" She remembered that William Stemm painted thousands of nasturtiums very quickly, and that Albert Wilson did so many dog portraits that he was called "Doghead Wilson" (Fig. 285). She recalled that Hester Pillsbury, nicknamed "Pilly," fell asleep one day while painting blackberries on a vase. Confused when she awoke, she painted a bird on the other side.

Dorothy worked thirty-five years at the Pottery. In the thirties, her supervisors instructed her to devise new lines which would be inexpensive to produce and require little hand labor. In response, she created Arcadia, Bouquet, Cameo, Floral, Pastel, and Wild Rose. Her swan song was the wonderful Chase line with the raised white horses, hounds, and riders, set

Fig. 286: *Marked Weller:* Rabbit 8" high by 12" long, designed by Dorothy Laughead. Collection: Nick Pedotto. Photo by Tom Turnquist.

against a dark, matt background. Dorothy was a skilled artist, decorator, and designer. Collectors today cherish her Hudson and Chase vases, as well as her lifelike dogs, cats, squirrels, and rabbits (Fig. 286).

The American Art Pottery Association honored Ruth Axline and Dorothy Laughead in Zanesville in 1980 and in 1981 (Fig. 287). At the annual convention banquet in July 1980, they received a standing ovation. A special table with the art work they decorated was on display at the convention. Dorothy enjoyed the praise she received from pottery collectors. She died December 21, 1982, at the age of 87.

Dorothy Laughead, Rudolph Lorber, Frederick H. Rhead, and Charles B. Upjohn ranked first among the Weller artists. With Jacques Sicard, they brought artistic competence, recognition, and renown to Weller Pottery.

Fig. 287: Weller decorators Ruth Axline and Dorothy Laughead in 1980. Photo by Duke Coleman.

Chapter XX

Conclusion

Forty years ago, a large bonfire devoured the invoices, the catalogs, the correspondence, and the glaze formulas of Weller Pottery. After the fire, Norris F. Schneider obtained the surviving records and catalog pages and donated them to the Ohio Historical Society, where pottery scholars can study them today. With these records, the information and ads from the trade journals, and the reminiscences of the Weller artists, I have written a history of the Pottery. It is time now to evaluate the company and its products.

On the sixtieth anniversary of the Pottery, December 1931, *Crockery and Glass Journal* devoted an entire article to Weller, "Three Score Years of Achievement," comparing Sam Weller to Henry Ford. "Long before Henry Ford inaugurated his mass production methods Weller was using plaster of Paris molds to speed up production, at all times insisting upon high quality in his ware," they wrote. "His business increased. Always experimenting with new glazes Weller gave increasing attention to decoration. Costly experiment followed costly experiment. Many of the colors would not survive firing. Eventually persistence won out and a long

Fig. 289: *Incised* Eocean Rose Weller: Vase 6" high, artist signed F. Collection: Dick and Nancy Sigafoose.

Fig. 290: *Marked Weller:* Hudson Pictorial vase 6¼" high, with swans. Collection: Sally Hautmann.

Fig. 291: *Marked* Weller Sicard vase with handles, 9" high. Collection: H.M. Dietrich.

Fig. 288: *Impressed* Dickensware Weller: First Line blue vase 6" high, artist signed L.M.C., and Glazed Dickensware vase 12" high, with the title incised on the back of the vase: "Grandfather Smallweed astonishes George. *Bleak House.*" Collection: Robert Miller and Glen Vogt.

line of exceptional pottery developed.... Homes all over the country came to possess Weller flower pots, jardinieres, kitchen pottery, bowls, candlesticks and the endless variety of art objects."

Sam Weller endeavored to bring high quality, mass produced pottery to the American public at affordable prices. He succeeded in his aim and became wealthy and distinguished in the business world. His motto seemed to be, "Turn it out fast and price it low." This permitted the production of thousands of pieces of pottery, a great boon to Weller collectors today!

It was a monumental achievement. The Pottery introduced a vast array of lines from 1895 to 1940, from the subtle Louwelsa to the striking Sicard, from the Hobart nudes to the Brighton birds, from the Graystone garden wares to the Terose teapots. Aesthetically, some lines stood out: the Dickensware vases with scenes from Dickens, the early Eocean vases, the Hudson Pictorial and floral wares, Jap Birdimal, Louwelsa, and Sicard (Figs. 288-291).

While emulating Rookwood's Iris and Standard Glazes, with Eocean and Louwelsa, Weller began some innovations. After 1897, the Pottery introduced Aurelian, Dickensware, Etna, Jap Birdimal, and Sicard, lines without an American prototype. Hiring some of the best designers in Europe and the United States, Sam Weller transformed the production of American pottery. From France came Jacques Sicard on a five year contract, from England came Frederick H. Rhead, and from Austria, Rudolph Lorber. While Rhead, Sicard, and Upjohn dominated the early period at Weller, Lorber enlivened the middle period with his imaginative lines, from Blue Ware and Coppertone to Wood Rose and Zona. Frank Ferrell, John Herold, Hugo Herb, Karl Kappes, Dorothy Laughead, John Lessell, Ed Pickens, and Charles Upjohn, all contributed skillful designs which made Weller a leader in American pottery (Figs. 292-295).

Weller manufactured millions of pots from 1895 to 1948. With the large volume of production, flaws in the pottery were inevitable. With the emphasis on quality today, the imperfections in Weller ware stand out. It is true that certain vases and jars were misshapen or carelessly molded. On some wares, the decoration ran under the glaze. At times, fingerprints or streaks marred the finished product. The standard glaze on Louwelsa and Aurelian was subject to crazing. The Weller booklet "A Definition of Art Pottery" admitted candidly, "Many of these highest priced art pieces will craze."

By 1936 there was a noticeable decline in the quality of the molded wares. After decades of work at the factory, the designers had lost energy and inspiration. As a result, the late wares often lacked sharp detail or pleasing coloration. Certain lines were monochromatic, while other lines possessed minimal decoration, as noted in Chapter XVI. In an effort to boost sales, the Pottery hired a new female designer, but sales continued to drop off.

The haste with which the decorators worked, the quotas they had to fill, so many items to decorate per day, all worked against perfect quality. Today knowledgeable collectors expect and tolerate some imperfections in their Weller wares.

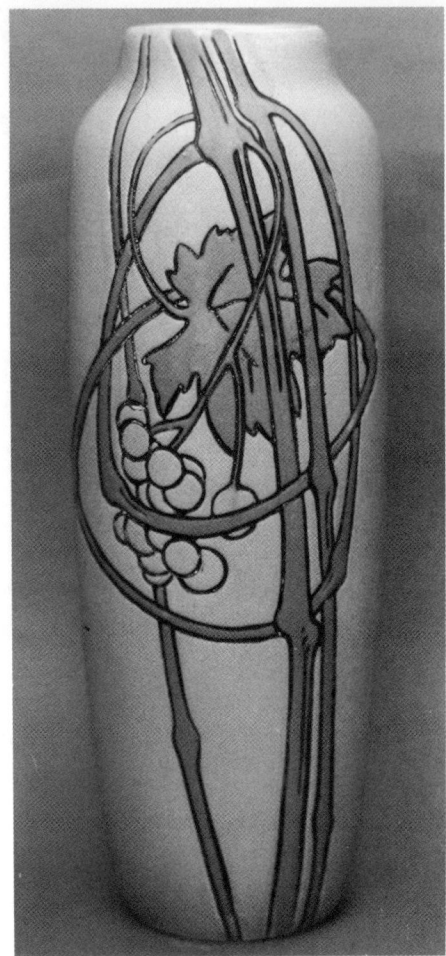

Fig. 292: *Marked Weller:* Etched Floral vase 13½" high, decorated with grapes and leaves. Photo by D.L. Hill.

Fig. 293: *Marked Weller:* Yellow vase 4½" high, and green vase 6" high, with red flowers. Both are unnamed lines. Collection: Dorothy Daniel.

Fig. 294: *Incised* Aurelian: Oil Banquet Lamp 36" high, artist signed by John Herold. Collection: Tommy and Norma Smith. Photo by Sigafoose.

Fig. 295: *Impressed* Dickensware Weller: First Line jardiniere 11" high, with fluted top, artist signed L.M., and First Line jardiniere 9" high, signed by Hugo Herb on the bottom, inside the jar. Collection: Robert Miller and Glen Vogt.

This criticism is not meant to denigrate the achievements of Sam Weller and his Pottery. His status as the Paul Bunyon of American pottery remains unchallenged. The true test of Weller pottery is its popularity today.

Numerous collectors throughout the United States avidly pursue and buy Weller pottery, to decorate their homes and offices. Artist signed Dickensware, Eocean, Hudson, Louwelsa, Rhead Faience, and Sicard vases have brought prices from $200 to $7000. Collectors in Zanesville paid $6000 for the Dickensware Circus Vase by Upjohn. Large Hudson Pictorial and Sicard floor vases sell for over $5000. From Alvin to Zona, however, most lines cost much less than $100, leaving the Weller market viable and competitive with the other potteries. Indeed, it is possible to find an artist signed Bonito or Louwelsa vase for under $100. Today few of us can afford a Tiffany lamp or a Rookwood Indian portrait, but we can all afford one or several pieces of Weller pottery.

The success of Weller Pottery derived from the acumen, the drive, and the ambition of its founder, Sam Weller. It was Weller who often arose in the middle of the night to draw a sketch for a new line, who had the wit to hire Jacques Sicard and Charles Upjohn, who nourished young, talented workers like Charles Chilcote and Hester Pillsbury, and who employed the best artists, modelers, designers, decorators, jigger men, and kiln bosses he could find. Sam Weller gave them all a place to experiment, create, and produce the infinite variety of Weller pottery.

Appendix A

Chronology of Weller Pottery

1872: Samuel A. Weller establishes Weller Pottery in a log cabin in Fultonham, Ohio.

1882: Weller leases a frame building on South Second Street in Zanesville to use as a warehouse.

1890: Weller erects a plant at Putnam between Pierce Street and Cemetery Drive to manufacture jars, peds, umbrella stands, hanging baskets, and vases.

1893: Weller sees Lonhuda pottery at the Chicago Exposition.

1894: Weller buys Lonhuda Pottery from William Long and hires him to supervise its production.

1895: Fire destroys the Lonhuda Department in the Putnam plant. Weller hires Charles Upjohn as head of the decorating department.

1899: Weller purchases the old American Encaustic Tiling Company plant on Marietta Street.

1902: D. C. Applegate supervises 300 workers at Putnam and 150 workers at the Marietta Street plant.

1903: The Weller Theater opens on April 27.

1904: Weller sets up a working pottery exhibit at the St. Louis Exposition. Karl Kappes heads the decorating department.

1905: Weller Pottery becomes the world's largest pottery, with four acres, 300,000 feet of floor space, 500-600 employees, and 22 lines.

1907: The Pottery sets an export record with shipments to England, Germany, and Russia.

1908: Weller considers establishing a plant in Colorado.

1920: Weller buys the Zanesville Art Pottery which becomes plant #3, the Ceramic Avenue plant. John Lessell heads the decorating department.

1922: Weller Pottery is incorporated with Samuel Weller as president, and Harry Weller as vice president.

1925: Samuel Weller dies. Harry Weller becomes president of the company.

1931: All the plants, #1, 2, 3 are consolidated into one, plant #3, the Ceramic Avenue plant.

1932: Frederic Grant becomes president of Weller Pottery, after Harry Weller dies in an auto accident.

1933: Irvin Smith becomes president of the company. Rudolph Lorber heads the art department.

1937: Walter Hughes becomes the last president of the company.

1947: Essex Wire purchases the controlling stock in the Pottery.

1948: Weller Pottery ceases to operate.

Appendix B

Officers of Weller Pottery

1922

Board of Directors, S. A. Weller Inc.

    Samuel A. Weller, president
    Harry A. Weller, vice president
    Frederic J. Grant, treasurer
    Joseph T. Bagley, secretary

1925

Board of Directors

    Harry A. Weller, president
    Frederic J. Grant, vice president and treasurer
    Edgar E. Bagley, assistant secretary
    Joseph T. Bagley, secretary
    Walter J. Gitter, sales manager
    Members of the board: Fred Gitter, William C. Hughes, Paul M. Phillips, C. H. Taylor (the New York sales representative), Frank E. Weller, Mrs. Samuel Weller.

Appendix C
Signatures of the Weller Artists

Edward Abel

E. A
ABEL

Virginia Adams

VA
V. ADAMS

W. Allsop

M. Ansel

M. AnsEL

Ruth Axline

RA   AX
REA

Elizabeth Ayers

EA   EA

Anna Fulton Best

AB   AB
A
BEST

Elizabeth Blake

EB   EB
E. BLAKE

Lisabeth Blake

L·B·   LB   LB

Florence Bowers

Oscar Bronkar

OB

E. Brown

E. Brown

Levi J. Burgess

L·J B·

L·J·Burgess

Jennie Burgoon

John Butterworth

JB

Sam Celli

Charles Chilcote

C·C·

Chilcote

M. Cipich

M·C·

M. CIPICH

Laura Cline

Lc

Nell Corbin

NC   nc

K. Coyleone

Coyleone

Anna Dautherty

A·D·

A. Davis

A. DAVIS

Frank Dedonatis

F.D.D.

FOOTIS

Charles J. Dibowski

C·J·D·

C·J·D

Anthony Dunlavy

AD

C. A. Dusenbery

C.A. DUSENBERY

C.D.

Frank Ferrell

F.F.

Ferrell

Charles Fouts

F

E. Fox

Fox, E.

Henry Fuchs

H. FucHS

Gazo Fudji

Henri Gellée

H. Gellée

Mary Gellie

M G

M. Gibson

MG

m Gibson

Arthur Goetting

A G

Katherine de Golter

K. G.

K G

Charles Gray

C. G.

G

William F. Hall

W. H.   WH

W. F. Hall

Delores Harvey

D. H.

H.

Albert Haubrich

A. H.

A Haubrich

Hugo Herb

H. H.

John J. Herold

J. H.   J. H.

Edith Hood

Hood

Roy Hook

RH   RH   RI

Jean Hunter

J. HUNTER

Madge Hurst

MH   MH

Josephine Imlay

J. I.

JI

Anna Jewett

J.

Karl Kappes

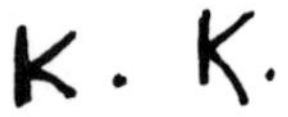

K. K.

Kennedy

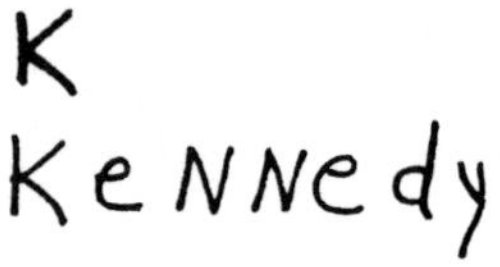

K

KeNNedy

L. Knaus

K

LK LK

Joe Knott

Rose Langstaff

Dorothy England Laughead

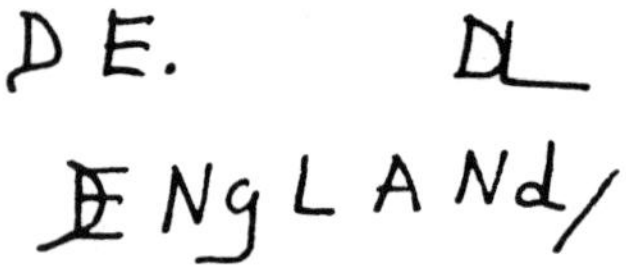

D E.   D

ENgLANd/

Claude L. Leffler

C·L·   &

CL LEFF/ER

John Lessell

JL

Lessell

A. V. Lewis

AL

William A. Long

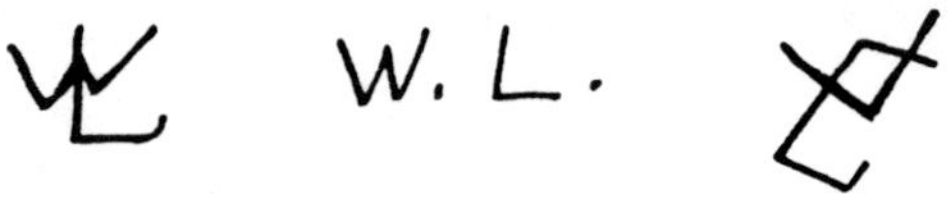

W   W. L.

Rudolph Lorber

R Lo

M. Lybarger

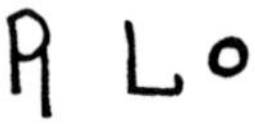

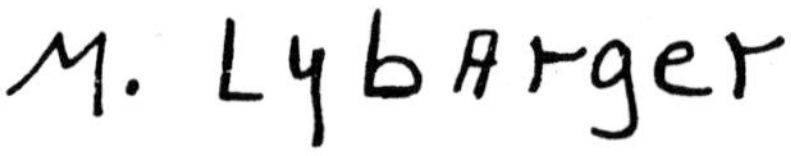

M. LybArger

Cora McCandless

McE

Margaret McGinnis

L. McGrath

L. McLain

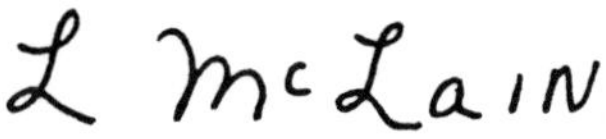

L McLain

Sarah Reid McLaughlin

Lelia Meloy

Hattie Mitchell

Lillie B. Mitchell

Minnie Mitchell

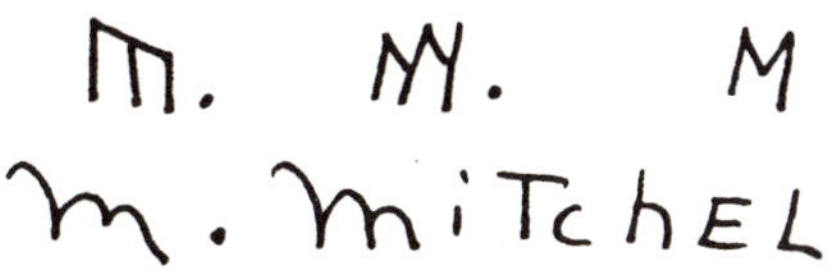

L. Morris

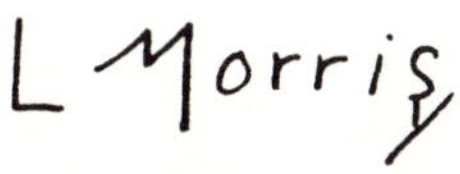

Gordon Mull

M. Myers

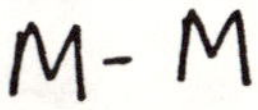

Lizzie Perone

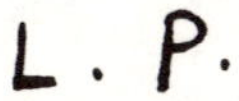

Edwin L. Pickens

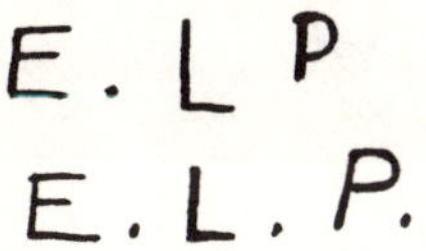

Mary L. Pierce

Hester W. Pillsbury

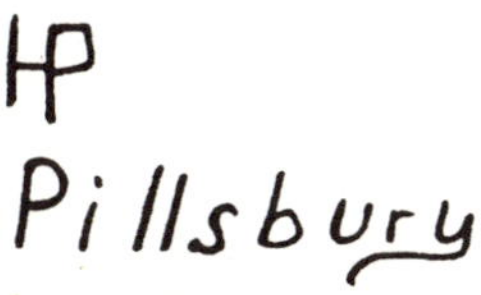

Albert Radford

Marie Rauchfuss

Frederick H. Rhead

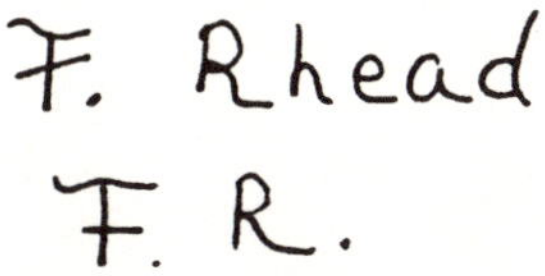

Eugene Roberts

Harry Robinson

Hattie M. Ross

Henry Schmidt

Norman Scothorn

N. S.

Tot Steele

William H. Stemm

WHS   WS

R. Lillian Shoemaker

R̶S̶

Jacques Sicard

SICARD

E. Sulcer

E. SuLcER

Skoin

SKOIN

C. Minnie Terry

Helen Smith

HS   SH   JH

Madeline Thompson

M.T.

Irvin Smith

IS

Mae Timberlake

M. T.
Mae Timberlake

Jessie R. Spaulding

Sarah Timberlake

S.T.   S/T

Amelia Browne Sprague

SB   A.B.S.

R. G. Turner

R. G TuRNer

Fred Steel

F/S

Charles B. Upjohn

Arthur Wagner

Edna Wilbur

E W

Naomi Walch

N
WAlch

Albert Wilson

AL WILSON

Carl Weigelt

C W

Helen B. Windle

H. W.

T. J. Wheatley

T. J. W.

Louise Wood

L W

W

Carrie Wilbur

N. B. There are no signatures available for some Weller artists. The *Collector's Guide to American Pottery Artists, Potters and Designers and Their Marks*, by Foster and Gladys Hall, provided some of these signatures. This booklet was privately printed and is now out of print and unavailable.

Signatures of Unknown Artists

Cill

C~

WEe

NE

K. V. H.

J. J. H.

V. M. H.

J. J.

E. L.

S. L.

XL

J. B. L.

CBM

Cmm

MBP

FNR

C. a. R.

S

4.

LT

H. U.

K. W.

KAW

MFW

X

Appendix D
Artists at Weller Pottery before 1904

Listed in Edwin AtLee Barber, *Marks of American Potters*

Virginia Adams
Elizabeth Ayers
Lizabeth Blake
Levi J. Burgess
Anna Dautherty
Anthony Dunlavy
Frank Ferrell
Mary Gellie
Albert Haubrich
Madge Hurst
Josephine Imlay
Karl Kappes

Sarah Reid McLaughlin
Hattie Mitchell
Lillie B. Mitchell
Minnie Mitchell
Gordon Mull
Edwin L. Pickens
Hester W. Pillsbury
Eugene Roberts
Tot Steele
C. Minnie Terry
Helen B. Windle

Appendix E

Marks on Weller Pottery

Lonhuda 1895-1896
Impressed

Louwelsa
Impressed

Perfecto
Impressed

Etna
Impressed

Floretta
Impressed

Art Nouveau
Impressed

Turada
Impressed

Dickensware I, II
Impressed

Dickensware III
Embossed on the base

WELLER

Dickensware Tobacco Jars
Hand incised under the lid, and found on some Dickensware II vases

DicKENS
WELLER

Sicard
Impressed on the base

SICARDO
WELLER

Written on the side

WELLER SICARD

Weller Sicardo

Eocean and Eocean Rose
Incised

Eosian
WELLER

Eocean
Weller

Eocean Rose
Weller

Weller Matt Ware
Incised

WELLER MATT
WARE

Aurelian
Incised

Aurelian
WELLER

Hunter
Incised

Hunter

Etched Floral
Incised

Weller

WELLER

Etched Matt
Incised

WELLER
ETCHED
MAT

Auroro
Incised

Weller

Auroro Weller

Fudzi
Incised

Weller

Weller Rhead Faience
Incised

Weller Rhead Faience   *Weller Faience*

Weller Art Tiles
Incised

```
┌─────────────┐
│   WELLER    │
│     ART     │
│    TILES    │
└─────────────┘
```

LaSa
Written on the side

WELLER LASA

Greenaways
Incised

S A Weller

Barcelona
In colored slip

Weller

Three Sizes of Impressed Block Weller Marks

Before 1910

WELLER

After 1910

WELLER

WELLER

Ink Stamp Marks

Hand Incised Weller Marks

Weller Pottery

Weller

Pottery

Script Signatures in the Mold

Weller Pottery

Weller Pottery Since 1872

Weller Ware Hand Made

Weller

Paper Label

Resource Centers

The Rakow Library, Corning Museum of Glass, Corning, New York
Library of Congress, Washington, D.C.
Ohio Historical Society, Columbus, Ohio
Ohio State University Library, Columbus, Ohio

Sources Available at the Ohio Historical Society

The Weller Catalogs
Weller Pottery
Garden Decorations by Weller
Pottery for the Florist
Weller Pottery Price Lists 1928-1941
Notebooks of Norris F. Schneider

Bibliography

Barber, Edwin AtLee. *Marks of American Potters*. Philadelphia: Patterson and White Company, 1904.

Battersby, Martin. *Art Nouveau*. London: Hamlyn Publishing Group, 1971.

Benjamin, Marcus. "American Art Pottery." *Glass and Pottery World*, 15(March 1907), pp. 13-18.

Buchanan-Brown, John. *Phiz*. New York: Charles Scribners Sons, 1978.

Charleston, Robert J. *World Ceramics*. Secaucus, N.J.: Chartwell Books, 1968.

Clark, Edna. *Ohio Art and Artists*. Detroit: Richmond, Garrett and Massie, 1975.

Cobb, Lura Milburn. "A Visit to Some Zanesville Potteries." *The Southwesterner's Book*, 2(Dec. 1905), pp. 6-10.

Coleman, Duke. "The Art of Albert Haubrich." *American Art Pottery*, May 1980, pp. 1, 4, 5.

Cook, Mary Elizabeth. "Our American Potteries—Weller Ware." *Sketchbook*, 5(May 1906), pp. 340-346.

Cox, Lucille. "Successful Potters for Sixty-Six Years." *Pottery, Glass and Brass Salesman*, 54(Nov. 1938), pp. 24-25.

Dale, Sharon. *Frederick Hurten Rhead: An English Potter in America*. Erie Art Museum. Erie, Pennsylvania, 1986.

Eidelberg, Martin. "Art Pottery." *The Arts and Crafts Movement in America 1876-1916*. Robert J. Clark, ed. Princeton: Princeton University Press, 1972, pp. 119-186.

_____. "The Ceramic Art of William H. Grueby." *The Connoisseur*, 184(Sept. 1973), pp. 47-54.

Evans, Paul. *Art Pottery of the United States*. New York: Charles Scribners Sons, 1974.

_____. "The Confusing McCoy Potteries." *Spinning Wheel*, 29(Jan. Feb. 1973), pp. 8-9.

_____. "Rhead Reflections—Part I." *Pottery Collectors Newsletter*, 9(Sept. Oct. 1980), pp. 45-48.

Fanale, James. "Weller Louwelsa." *Pottery Collectors Newsletter*, 6(June 1977), pp. 51-52.

Ferrell, Frank. "Painting in Underglaze." *Keramic Studio*, 10(Nov. 1908), p. 160.

Gitter, Josephine. "Pottery Industry in Muskingum County, Ohio." *Bulletin of the American Ceramic Society*, 15(Oct. 1936), p. 372.

Godden, Geoffrey A. *British Pottery*. New York: Clarkson N. Potter, 1975.

Hall, Foster E. and Gladys C. *Collector's Guide to American Pottery Artists, Potters and Designers and Their Marks*. Privately printed, Punta Gorda, Fla., 1978. (Out of print).

Hamlin, A. D. F. "L'Art Nouveau, Its Origins and Development." *The Craftsman*, 3(Dec. 1902), pp. 129-143.

Henzke, Lucile. *American Art Pottery*. Camden, N.J.: Thomas Nelson and Sons, 1970.

_____. "A Visit with Naomi Walch, A Weller Artist." *Pottery Collectors Newsletter*, 2(June 1973), pp. 103-107.

Hughes, Robert. *Heaven and Hell in Western Art*. New York: Stein and Day, 1968.

Huxford, Sharon and Bob. *The Collectors Encyclopedia of Weller Pottery*. Paducah, Ky.: Collector Books, 1979.

Jervis, William P. *A Pottery Primer*. New York: O'Gorman Publishing, 1911.

_____. *The Encyclopedia of Ceramics*. New York: Blanchard, 1902.

_____. *Rough Notes on Pottery*. Privately printed, Newark, N.J., 1896.

Kitton, Frederick, ed. *Complete Works of Charles Dickens*. London: George D. Sproul, 1903-.

——————————. *Dickens and His Illustrators*. London: George Redway, 1899.

Klein, Dan. *All Colour Book of Art Deco*. London: Octopus Books, 1974.

Kovel, Ralph and Terry. *The Kovels' Collector's Guide to American Art Pottery*. New York: Crown Publishers, 1974.

Leonard, Anna B. "Pottery and Porcelain at the Paris Exposition." *Keramic Studio*, 2(Aug. 1900), pp. 73-75.

——————————. "A Visit to the Pottery of Auguste Delaherche." *Keramic Studio*, 2(Sept. 1900), pp. 96-98.

Lewis, Thomas W. *Zanesville and Muskingum County, Ohio*. 3 vols. Chicago: S. J. Clark Publishing Co., 1927.

Locke, Josephine C. "Some Impressions of Art Nouveau." *The Craftsman*, 2(July 1902), pp. 201-204.

London, Rena. "Out of the Mould: Camark Pottery." *National Glass, Pottery and Collectables Journal*, 1(June 1979), pp. 26-27.

McClinton, Katharine Morrison. *Art Deco, a guide for collectors*. New York: Clarkson N. Potter, 1972.

McLaughlin, Mary Louise. *Pottery Decoration under the Glaze*. Cincinnati, Ohio: Robert Clark and Co., 1880.

Mebane, John. *The Complete Book of Collecting Art Nouveau*. New York: Coward-McCann, Inc., 1970.

Moses, John. "American Potteries." *One Hundred Years of American Commerce*. Chauncey M. Depew, ed. New York: D. O. Haynes and Co., 1895.

Nelson, Marion John. "Art Nouveau in American Ceramics." *Art Quarterly*, 26(1963), pp. 441-459.

——————————. *Art Pottery of the Midwest*. Minneapolis: University Art Museum, University of Minnesota, 1988.

——————————. "Indigenous Characteristics in American Art Pottery." *Antiques*, 89(June 1966), pp. 846-850.

Purviance, Louise and Evan, and Norris F. Schneider. *Zanesville Art Pottery in Color*. Leon, Iowa: Mid America Book Co., 1968.

——————————. *Weller Art Pottery in Color*. Des Moines: Wallace Homestead Book Co., 1971.

Rhead, Frederick H. "American Ceramic Society Exhibition." *Bulletin of the American Ceramic Society*, 1(May 1922), pp. 10-17.

——————————. "Chats on Pottery." *The Potters Herald*, July 11, 1935, p. 6.

——————————. *The Potter*, 1(Dec. 1916).

——————————. "Pottery Class." *Keramic Studio*, 11(Sept. 1909), pp. 104-110.

——————————. "Pottery Class." *Keramic Studio*, 11(Oct. 1909), pp. 137-138.

——————————. "Pottery Class." *Keramic Studio*, 11(Nov. 1909), pp. 159-161.

——————————. "Some Notes on Historical and Modern Decorative Processes." *Journal of the American Ceramic Society*, 6(Feb. 1923), pp. 356-397.

Ries, Heinrich and Henry Leighton. *History of the Clay-Working Industry in the United States*. New York: John Wiley and Sons, 1909.

Rose, Arthur V. "Sicardo Ware." *House Furnisher*, 13(Oct. 5, 1903), p. 19.

——————————. "Weller's Art Pottery Factory at St. Louis." *House Furnisher*, 15(Oct. 1904), p. 11.

Ruge, Clara. "American Ceramics—A Brief Review of Progress." *International Studio*, 28(Mar. 1906), pp. 21-28.

——————————. "Development of American Ceramics." *Pottery and Glass*, 1(Aug. 1908), pp. 3-8.

Sargent, Irene. "Some Potters and Their Products." *The Craftsman*, 9(Aug. 1903), pp. 328-337.

Schneider, Norris F. "Albert Haubrich, Weller Pottery Decorator." *Pottery Collectors Newsletter*, 1(May 1972), pp. 107-108. (First published in *The Times Recorder*, Zanesville, Feb. 27, 1972.).

_____. "Charles Chilcote Recalls His Experiences at the Weller Pottery Art Studio." *Pottery Collectors Newsletter*, 2(May 1973), pp. 97-98. (First published in *The Times Recorder*, Zanesville, Dec. 8, 1968.).

_____. "Dunlavy and Purdy Created Art Pottery." *The Times Recorder*, Sept. 28, 1969, p. 9b.

_____. "Frenchman Left Mark on Famous Pottery." *Pottery Collectors Newsletter*, 1(Apr. 1972), pp. 89-91. (First published in *The Times Recorder*, Zanesville, Jan. 1, 1969.

_____. "Herold Honored for Roseville Glaze." *The Times Recorder*, November 4, 1979, p. 8c.

_____. "Lawton Gonder Ceramics." *Pottery Collectors Newsletter*, 6(May 1977), pp. 41-42.

_____. "Razing of Mansion One More Step in Changing Face of Market Street." *Sunday Times Signal*, June 12, 1955, p. 12.

_____. "Rhead Brothers Created Local Art Pottery Line." *The Times Recorder*, Feb. 22, 1976, p. 7c.

_____. "Sam Weller Built Theater as Symbol of His Status." *The Times Recorder*, Jan. 19, 1964, p. 8b.

_____. "Some of the Nation's Top Entertainers Appeared at Weller in Half-Century." *The Times Signal*, Jan. 3, 1954, p. 1.

_____. "World-Famous Dickens Line Created in Zanesville." *The Times Recorder*, Apr. 4, 1976, p. 5c.

_____. "World-Famous Artist Karl Kappes Kept Studio in Masonic Temple." *The Times Recorder*, Oct. 5, 1975, p. 10a.

Selz, Peter and Mildred Constantine. *Art Nouveau*. New York: The Plantin Press, 1972.

Schafer, Thomas. *Pottery Decoration*. London: Watson-Guptill, 1976.

Smith, Kenneth. "Laura Ann Fry, Originator of Atomizing Process For Application of Underglaze Color." *Bulletin of the American Ceramic Society*, 17(Sept. 1938), pp. 368-372.

Stoddard, W. B. "Some Beautiful Holiday Offerings." *Pottery, Glass and Brass Salesman*, 18 (Dec. 12, 1918), pp. 93-94.

Weed, Clarence Moores. "The Useful Wall-Pockets." *House and Garden*, 39(January 1916), pp. xvi-xvii.

"Among the Potteries." *China, Glass and Lamps*, 26(Sept. 8, 1906), p. 16.

"Another Art Pottery Now Planned for Colorado." *Clay Record*, 33(Nov. 16, 1908), p. 31.

"China and Earthenware." *China, Glass and Lamps*, 7(Feb. 14, 1894), p. 17.

_____. *China, Glass and Lamps*, 7(Mar. 14, 1894), p. 18.

_____. *China, Glass and Lamps*, 7(Nov. 7, 1894), p. 15.

"The Clay Working Industrial Exhibit, Mines and Metallurgy Building, World's Fair, St. Louis, Mo." *Brick*, 20(June 1904), pp. 291-304.

"The Closing of the World's Fair." *Brick*, 21(Dec. 1904), p. 253.

"Cultivating Eskimo Trade." *Brick and Clay Record*, 60(Feb. 21, 1922), p. 295.

"Death Claims Sam Weller." *Pottery, Glass and Brass Salesman*, 32(Oct. 9, 1925), p. 10.

"Glances in Gotham." *Glass and Pottery World*, 14(Feb. 1906), p. 20.

"In the Zanesville Area." *Glass and Pottery World*, 17(Mar. 20, 1909), p. 30.

"Lonhuda Art Ware." *Glass and Pottery World*, May 1905, p. 33.

"Lonhuda Pottery." *Pottery and Glassware Reporter*, 28(Dec. 15, 1892), p. 15.

"Lonhuda Pottery." *Brick*, 6(Mar. 1897), p. 154.

"The Louisiana Purchase Exposition." *Brick*, 20(June 1, 1904), pp. 281-286.

"New Jardinieres, Flower Pots, Etc." *Pottery and Glass*, 3(August 1909), pp. 65-66.

"New Pottery Plant for Zanesville, Ohio." *Clay Record*, 5(Nov. 14, 1894), p. 25.

"A New Pottery Ware." *Clay Record*, 9(Sept. 28, 1896), p. 15.

"Obituary." *Crockery and Glass Journal*, 101(Oct. 8, 1925), p. 15.

"Obituary Samuel A. Weller." *Bulletin of the American Ceramic Society,* 4(Oct. 1925), pp. 625-627.

"Personal." *Brick,* 11(Aug. 1899), p. 50.

"Pottery News." *Brick,* 21(Dec. 1904), pp. 258-259.

"Pottery Notes." *Brick and Clay Record,* 52(Mar. 12, 1918), p. 36.

"Pottery Party Line." *Pottery Collectors Newsletter,* 2(Nov. 1972), p. 24.

"Pottery Trust Points." *China, Glass and Lamps,* 17(Dec. 15, 1898), p. 11.

"The Potteries of Zanesville, Ohio." *The Clay Worker,* 37(June 1902), pp. 650-651.

"Rhead, Frederick Hurten." *National Cyclopaedia of American Biography.* New York: James T. White Co., 1956, XLI, p. 204.

"Rhead Goes to Laughlins." *Pottery, Glass and Brass Salesman,* 36(Aug. 4, 1927), pp. 11, 23.

"A Rival of Rookwood." *China, Glass and Lamps,* 13(Feb. 10, 1897), p. 20.

"S.A. Weller's New Matt Glazes." *American Pottery Gazette,* 1(April 1905), p. 41.

"Steubenville, O." *China, Glass and Lamps,* 7(Dec. 20, 1893), pp. 17-18.

"Three Score Years of Achievement." *Crockery and Glass Journal,* 109(Dec. 1931), pp. 78, 101.

"Weller, a Household Word." *House Furnisher,* 15(Jan. 1905), p. 34.

"Weller Will Build a Pottery at St. Louis Exposition." *Clay Record,* 23(July 14, 1903), p. 30.

"What the Other Fellow is Doing." *Ceramic Industry,* 5(Nov. 1925), p. 454.

"Zanesville Art Pottery." *Crockery and Glass Journal,* 62(Dec. 14, 1905), pp. 77-89.

"Zanesville, Ohio." *Illustrated Glass and Pottery World,* 6(Jan. 1898), p. 22.

Biography

Ann Gilbert McDonald is a writer and an antiques dealer. Her first book, *Evolution of the Night Lamp*, appeared in 1979. She has written over sixty articles, including cover stories for *Antiques and Collecting Hobbies* and *The Antique Trader Weekly*, and articles for *Antique Review, Glass Collector's Digest, Pottery Collectors Newsletter*, and *Spinning Wheel*.

Ann received a B.A. in English and French Literature from Nazareth College of Rochester, an M.A. from Cornell University, and a Ph.D. from George Washington University. She taught literature at Marymount College of Virginia, and at Georgetown University.

Listed in *Who's Who in the South and Southwest* and the *International Who's Who of Women*, Ann is a member of the National League of American Penwomen, the Northern Virginia Antique Arts Association, and the Opera Theater of Northern Virginia. She is married to Washington attorney Bradley G. McDonald, and they have a son Perry.

Fig. 296: The author Ann Gilbert McDonald with the Louwelsa oil lamp, artist signed by Frank Ferrell. Photo by Roger B. Smith.

207

Index of Weller Lines

Page numbers in *italic* type indicate pictures or illustrations. Color pictures are preceded by the word *color*.

Alpha, *137, 138*
Alvin, 8, *132*
Anco, 159
Animal planters: Duck-Rabbit-Penguin, *160-161*; Three Face Dog, *160-161*
Animals, *color 125-26*; 157-161, 179-180. *See also* Garden Ware Figurines
Ansonia, *134-35*
Arcadia, 150, *152*, 156
Arcola, 95, *96*
Ardsley, 8, *color 123*; 135, *137*
Art Nouveau, 4, *60, 61, 63*, 175, mark, *196*
Atlas, *color 120*; *151*
Aurelian, 4, *color 111, 118*; *165*, history and technique, 52-53, *182*;
   lamps, 48, 50, *169*; *183*; mark *197*; World's Fair 1904, 44-46
Auroro, Aurora, Auroral, 52, *54-56*, *color 115-116*; mark, *197*
Baldin, *86*
Barcelona, *color 119*, 130, mark, *198*
Bedford Matt Green, 64
Bells of San Juan, *75*, *color 120*
Besline, 101, *102*, *color 123*
Blo Red, 51, 139, *140*
Blossom, *color 123*, 152, 155, *156*
Blue Drapery, 95
Blue Ware, 9, 51, *86-88*
Bo Marblo, 51, *87*
Bonito, *142-143*, 145, *183*
Bouquet, 10, *151*, 156
Breton, *color 123*, *137*
Brighton, *50-51*, *color 126*, 135, *136*
Bronze Ware, 51, *100*
Brown and White Cookware, 8, *162*
Burnt Wood, 70, *71-73*, 75
   Decorated Burnt Wood, *71*, 73
Cactus, *160*
Cameo, 10, *154*, 155, 156
Cameo Jewel, 56, *57*
Candis. *See* Regal
Chanticleer Rooster, *160*
Chase, *155-156*, 179-180
Chelsea Kitchenware, 163
Chengtu, 100-102, *color 123*
Clarmont, *color 122*, 130, *135*
Classic, *147*
Claywood, 70, *73*, 75
Cloudburst, 99, 101, *102*
Color Banded, 162
Colored Glaze, *98*, *color 123*
Coppertone, 99, *100*, *157-159*
Copra, 50, *80*
Cornish, *144*, 145

Cream Light Blue Banded, *162*
Cretone, 148, *149*, 150, *171*
Crystalline, 81
Darsie, 145, *146*, 156
Dechiwo, 70, *71*, 72
Decorative Etched Ware, *179*
Dedonatis Ware, 145, *146*
Delsa, *154*, 155
Delta, 30, *31*, 80, *color 113*
Denton, *87*
Dickensware I, 40-41, *color 106*; *181*, *183*, lamps 48, 50; mark, 196
Dickensware II, 2, *3*, *4*, 33-42, *color 107-111*, *113*, *114*, *118*, *119*, *123*; artists who decorated, 165, 167-168, 171, *177*; circus vase, 177, *color 108-109*; created by Upjohn, 33-39, *177*; history and technique, 33-39, *34-38*, 52, *182*; Weller Theater souvenirs, *17*, 42; mark, 196
Dickensware II variations
    Glazed Dickensware, 36, 40, *181*, *color 110*, *116*
    Tobacco Jars, *34-35*, mark, 197
Dickensware III, *38*, *color 110*, *116*, *119*; created by Rhead, 40-41, *175*; history of, 40-41; mark, 197
Dorland, 151, *154*, 156
Dresden, 68, *69*
Eclair, 83, *84*, *color 120*
Ein Stein Beer Mugs, *146*
Elberta, 141, *142*
Eldora-Chelsea, 81, *82*, *color 121*
Eocean, *4*, *6*, 52, *54*, *color 105*, *110*, *120*, history of, 55, 182-83; mark, 197
Eocean
    Eocean Rose, *color 105*, *120*; *181*; mark, 197
    Late Eocean, *54*, 55
Etched Floral, *39*, *182*, mark, 197
Etched Matt, *39-40*, 171, mark, 197
Ethel, 83, *color 121*
Etna, *56*, 57, *color 124*; mark, 196
Euclid, 137
Evergreen, *color 123*, 140, *142*
Fairfield, *6*, *88*
Flemish, 8, 91, *92*, *93*
Fleron, *134*, 135
Floral, 151, *152*, 156
Florala, 82, *84*, 85, *color 121*
Florenzo, 8, *color 121*, 137
Floretta, *4*, *57*, 58, *color 123*, mark, 196
Forest, 8, *87*, *90*, 91, *color 123*
Foxy Grandpa Incense Burner, *color 124*
Fra Bel Ita, 94
Frosted Matt, 51, *99*
Fruitone, 94, *color 123*
Fru Russet, 68, *69*
Fudzi, *7*, *68*, *color 115*, mark, 198
Garden Ware, 157-59
    Coppertone, 157-*159*
    Graystone, 157, *158*, 159
Garden Ware Figurines: Bulge-Eyed Dog and Pup, *color 126*; 157; Cats, *color 126*; 157, *158*; Chicken Hens, *157*; Coppertone Bird Bath with Muskota Fisherboy, *159*; Coppertone Frog Sprinkler, 158, *159*; Crow, *158*; Ducks, *color 125*; 157, *158*; Elephants, 90, *color 126*; Frogs, 157-*159*; Graystone Goose Boy, 158, *159*; Gnomes, *color 124*; *157*; Goose, *158*; Pan with Fife, *158*; Pan with Rabbit, 157, *158*; Pelican, *color 125*; 157-59; Rabbit, 157-59, *179*; Rooster, *color 125*; *157*; Scottie

Dog and Pup, *157*, 158; Spaniel, 157, *158*; Squirrels, 157, *158*; Swans, 158, *159*
Geode, *color 122*, 148, *149*, 150
Glendale, 8, 96, *97*, 98
Gloria, *153*
Gloucester Woman, 160
Golbrogreen, 4, 59
Gold Decorated Teapots, *163*
Golden Glow, *142*
Graystone, 8, 157, *158*, *159*
Greenaways, *69*, mark, *198*
Greenbriar, *color 123*; *145*
Greora, 100, *color 123*
Hobart, 8, *color 122*; *129*, *130*, *135*, *178*
Hudson, *76-79*, *color 113*, *114*, *120*, *122*, *123*; artists who decorated, 76-80, 164, 171, 172; history and technique, 76-80, 182-83; lamps, 51
Hudson variations
    Blue and Decorated, 76, *77*, *78*
    Glazed Hudson, 78, *79*, *color 120*, *122*; *145*
    Hudson Pictorial, 4, *76*, *181*, *color 113*, *114*
    Rochelle, *79*, 80
    White and Decorated, 76, *77*, *78*, *color 122*
Hunter, 4, 41, mark, *197*
Ivoris, *142*
Ivory, 8, *80*, *83*, *178*
Jap Birdimal, 4, 7, *58*, *59*; created by Frederick Rhead, 58, *175*, *182*
Juneau, *145*, *color 123*
Kenova, *130*
Kitchengem, *162*
Klyro, *color 123*; *132*
Knifewood, 96, *97*, *178*
Lamar, 100, 101, *102*
LaSa, 51, 100, *101*, *102*, *color 116*, mark, *198*
Lavonia, 8, *color 122*; *128-130*, *178*
Lido, *color 122*, *153-154*
Lonhuda, Denver, 24
Lonhuda Faience, Weller, 1, *23*, 21-26, *color 105*, *106*, *history and technique*, 21-24; mark, *196*
Lorbeek, *128*, *130*, *135*
Loru, *color 123*; *154*, 155
Louella, 95
Louwelsa, 2-4, 26-32, *26-28*, 52; artists who decorated, 165-172; history and technique, 26-29, 182-83; lamps, 48-51; marks, 196; portraits, *26-28*; portraits in *color*, *106*, *110-112*, *118*; silver overlay, 26
Louwelsa variations
    Blue Louwelsa, 28, 30, *color 119*
    Matt Louwelsa, 28-29, *168*
Luster, *101*, *102*
Malta, 8, *135*, *136*
Malvern, *color 123*; *145*, *146*
Mammy Line. *See* Novelty Line
Manhattan, *146*, 147
Marbleized. *See* Bo Marblo
Marengo, 100, *101*, *102*, *170*
Marvo, 8, *color 123*, *137*
Matt Floretta, 40, *color 107*
Matt Green, 7, 50, 61-64, *63*, *color 115*
Matt Ware, 50, 62, *63*, mark, *197*
Melrose, 95, *96*, *color 119*
Mi-Flo, *152*, 153

Mirror Black, 100, *color 123*
Monochrome, 4, 59
Morocco, 86, *87*
Mottled Ware, 98, *99, color 120*
Muskota, 8, *88-90, color 121, 122*
Narona, *74, 75, color 116*
Neiska, 10, *143, 144*
Nile, 100, *color 118, 123*
Norwood, 70, *73, 74*
Noval, *83, 84*
Novelty Line, 148-151, *146, 148, 149*
    Decorated Novelty Utility Line (Mammy Line), *150*
Oak Leaf, *154, 155*
Ollas Water Bottle, *163*
Oriental, 4, 59
Orris, *color 119, 130-132*
Panella, *152, 155*
Paragon, *144, 145*
Parian, 104
Pastel, *151, 156*
Patra, *143*
Patricia, *146, 147*
Pearl, 85
Perfecto, 4, *29-30, color 119*, mark, *196*
Pesca, the Old Man with Fish, *160*
Pierre, *163*
Potenza, 159
Pumila, 8, *133, 134*
Raceme, 148, *149, 150*
    Raceme Glossy, *150*
Ragenda, *145*
Raydence, *152, 153*
Regal, *154-156*
Reno, 162
Rhead Faience, 7, *58, 59, color, 113, 115*; created by Frederick Rhead, 58, *175, 182*; mark, *198*
Roba, *151, 152*
Rochelle, *79, 80*
Roma, 10, 49-50, *80, 81, color 121*
Rosemont, *87, 88*
Rosemont II, *14, color 118, 145*
Rubina, 58
Rudlor, *152, 153*
Sabrinian, *139, 140*
Selma, 51, *96, 97, color 123*
Seneca, 10, *143, 144*
Senic, *152, 153*
Sicard, Sicardo, 3, 4, 7, 52, 61, *66, 67, color 117, 119*; created by Jacques Sicard, 64-67; found in Weller home and Weller Theater, 14-17; history and technique, 64-67, *181-183*; marks, *197*
Silva the Dancer, *160*
Silvertone, *color 123, 132, 134*
Softone, *153, 154*
Souevo, 25, 69, *70, color 120*
Stellar, 148, *149, 150*
Sydonia, *color 122, 141, 142*
Teakwood, 70, *73*
Terose, *144, 163*
Terra Cotta, 159
Ting, 10, 15, *151, 152, 153, 178*

Tivoli, *84, 85*
Tupelo, *84, 85*
Turada, 3, 48, 50, *52, color 119,* mark, *196*
Turkis, *color 123,* 145
Tutone, *color 122,* 140, 141
Underglaze Blue Ware, 100
Velva, 144
Velvetone, 10, *color 120; 135*
Voile, 10, 51, *86,* 91, *color 122*
Wallpockets, *88, 97, 104, 128, 148, 149;* history and use, *161-162*
Warwick, *98*
Wayne Ware, 10, 137
Weller Art Tiles, 140, *141;* mark, *198*
Wild Rose, *154, 155*
Woodcraft, 10, 90-91, *color 107, 122, 124;* lamps, 49-50; wallpockets, *161, color 124*
Wood Rose, *98*
World's Fair St. Louis 1904, 44-47, *color 119;* presidential plaques, 46-47; souvenirs, *46-47*
Zona, 10, 102, *103,* 104
    Zona Baby Ware, *103*
    Zona Utility Ware (apple dinnerware) 10, 102, *103,* 104

General Index

Page numbers in *italic* type indicate pictures or illustrations. Color pictures are preceded by the word *color*. The Weller lines, from Alpha to Zona, are in the preceding index, "Index of Weller Lines."

A

Abel, Edward, decorator, 165, mark, 187
Adams, Bill, 17
Adams, Virginia, decorator, 7, 195, mark, 187
Allsop, W., decorator, 187
American Art Pottery Association, 180
American Encaustic Tiling Company, 3, 10, 25, 43, 165, 167
Animals. *See* "Index of Weller Lines"
Animal planters, *160-161*
Ansel, M., decorator, mark, 187
Arc-En-Ciel Pottery, 169, 171
Art China Company, 170
Artists at Weller Pottery before 1904, 195
Artists' signatures, 187-194; signatures of unknown artists, 194
Arts and Crafts movement, 50, 62
Art Deco at Weller, 127, *128-130*, 141, *148-149*, 151
Art Nouveau movement, 60-61, 67, 127, 176
Atomizer technique on pottery, 6, 23, 26, 55
Author biography, 206
Axline, Ruth, decorator, 2, *164-165*, *180*, mark, 187; biography, 164-65, *180*; decorated Bonito, *142-143*; decorated Hudson, 78; described decoration on Chengtu, 100, Coppertone, 99, Dedonatis Ware, 145; packed beer mugs, 146; discussed other decorators, 171-72; salary, 2, 164
Ayers, Elizabeth, decorator, *color 105*, 169, 195, mark, 187

B

Barber, Edwin AtLee, *Marks of American Potters*, 52, 172, 195
Barlow, Hannah B., *38*, 39
Barnard, Frederick, *35-36*, 37, 41, 175
Beer mug production, 146
Beethoven on Cameo Jewel, *56-57*
Best, Anna Fulton, decorator, mark, 187
Birdbaths, 157, *158-159*
Bird figurines, *89,90, 130, 135, 136, 137, color 122-126;* 157, *159*
Blake, Elizabeth, decorator, *color 110*, 195, mark 187
Blake, Lizabeth, decorator, *26, color 118,* 169, 195, mark, 187
Blue Lion Art Emporium, 166, 172
Blue Lion Tea Room, 166, 172
Bowers, Florence, decorator, 187
Bronkar, Oscar, decorator, mark, 187
Brown, E., decorator, mark, 187
Browne, Hablot Knight (Phiz), 35, 37-38, 41
Brush McCoy Pottery, 7, 89, 91, 127
Burgess, Katharine Stanbery, 165-166
Burgess, Levi J., decorator, *4, 26,* 54-55, 65, 69, *color 105-107, 110, 112,* 195, mark, 188; biography, 165-*166*

Burgoon, Jennie, decorator, 188
Butterworth, John, decorator, mark, 188

C

California mission churches on Bells of San Juan, *75, 120*
Camark Pottery, 102, 170
Celli, Sam, decorator, 145, 188
Chaplet, Ernest, 60
Chase, William Merritt, 169
Chilcote, Charles, decorator, 2, 4, 65, *color 105,* 166-67, 183, mark, 188
Chinese influence on Weller pottery, 101, 102, *133-34,* 142-43, 151, *152, 153*
Cipich, M., decorator, mark, 188
Clifton Art Pottery, 24-25, 168
Cline, Laura, decorator, mark, 188
Console sets, *82, 84, 85*
Cookware, 10, 11, *162-163*
Coors, Adolf, 169
Corbin, Nell, decorator, *143,* mark, 188
Costume party for decorators, *172-173*
Cowan Pottery, 127
Coyleone, K., modeler, *color 118,* mark, 188
Curphey, William, Jr., Weller grandson, 16-17
Curphey, William, Sr., Weller vice president, 10

D

Dautherty, Anna, decorator, 195, mark, 188
Davis, A., decorator, mark, 188
Day, Alfred, 22
Dedonatis, Frank, decorator, *145-146,* 164, mark, 188
de Feure, George, 60
de Golter, Katherine, decorator, mark, 189
Delaherche, Auguste, 60-62
Denver China and Pottery Company, 24
Devils on Dechiwo, 72
Dibowski, Charles, decorator, mark, 188
Dickens, Charles, and Weller Dickensware, 33, 35-39, 41;' *Bleak House,* 181; *David Copperfield, 36, 37, 38, color 110; Dombey and Son, 35, 36, 37, color 119; Nickolas Nickleby, color 119; Pickwick Papers, 38, color 107, 116*
Dickens illustrators and Weller Dickensware, 33-39, *36,* 41; Frederick Barnard, 35-*36,* 37, 41; Hablot Knight Browne, 35, 37-38, 41
Dinnerware, 10, 102-104, 163
Dogs. *See* Garden Ware Figurines in "Index of Weller Lines"
Doulton Ware and Weller Dickensware, *38,* 39
Duck-Rabbit-Penguin and Three Face Dog planters, *160-161*
Duncan, Isadora, 87
Dunlavy, Anthony, decorator, 7, *34, color 106,* 195, mark, 188; biography, 167-68
Dusenbery, C.A., decorator, mark, 188
Dutch painters and Louwelsa, 28

E

Egg beating pitcher, *162*
England, Dorothy. *See* Laughead, Dorothy England
England, James, manager of Weller Theater, 17, 178
Essex Wire Corporation, 10, 11, 46

F

Face masks in pottery, *148-149*
Fanale, James, collector of Louwelsa, 26-27
Fauley, Sumner, 1
Ferrell, Frank, decorator, 7, 27, *39*, 44, 45, *48*, 65, 182, 195, mark, 188; biography, 167-*168*
Floor vases, *179*, 183
Flower inserts or flower frogs, *88, 89, 90, 98, 121, 122*
Fouts, Charles, decorator, mark, 188
Fox, E., decorator, mark, 188
Frogs and frog sprinkler, *99*, 157-*159*
Fry, Laura A., Lonhuda decorator, 22-23
Fuchs, Henry, decorator, mark, 189
Fudji, Gazo, decorator, 7, 68, 189
Fultonham, Ohio, 1

G

Garden ware, 10, *157-159*
Gellée, Henri, decorator, 2, 64, *65*, 67, *color 117*, mark, 189
Gellie, Mary, decorator, 169, 195, mark, 189
Gibson, M., decorator, mark, 189
Gladding, McBean and Company, 10, 103
Glaze as decoration, 98, 100, 145
Goetting, Arthur, decorator, mark, 189
Grant, Frederic, Weller president, 10, 67, 139
Grant, Frederic, Weller grandson, 16
Gray, Charles, decorator, mark, 189
Grueby Pottery, 62, 176
Grueby, William, 62

H

Hall, William, decorator, mark, 189
Hand turned wares, 5-6, *134-135*
Harper, Helen, Lonhuda decorator, 22
Harvey, Delores, decorator, mark, 189
Haubrich, Albert, decorator, 4, *28*, 171, 195, mark, 189; biography 168-*169*
Herb, Hugo, modeler, 4, 17, 47, 182, *183*, mark, 189
Herold China and Pottery Company, 169
Herold, John J., decorator, 7, 45, 53, *color 111*, 182-*183*, mark, 189; biography, 168-69
Hood, Edith, decorator, *77*, mark, 189
Hook, Roy, decorator, mark, 189
House and Garden ads, 99, 101, *158*, 159
Hughes, Walter, Weller president, 10, 139
Hunter, Jean, decorator, mark, 189
Hunter, W.H., 22
Hurst, Madge, decorator, 7, 195, mark, 189

I

Imlay, Josephine, decorator, 7, 26, 27, 169, 195, mark, 189

J

Japanese subjects on Weller pottery, 58, *color 113; 175*
Jardinieres and pedestals, 3, 4, *28*, 52, 53, 93, 96, 137
Jervis, William P., 52, 64, 174-76
Jewett, Anna, decorator, 142, mark, 190

K

Kappes, Karl, decorator, 41, *color 110*, *111*, 167, 182, 195, mark, 190; biography, 169-*170*; head of art department, 4, 169-170, 172; painter, 169; taught Weller artists, 167, 172

Kennedy, decorator, mark, 190

Keramic Studio, 58, 61, 168, 175

Knaus, L., decorator, *color 108*, *109*, mark, 190

Knott, Joe, decorator, 190

L

Lamps made at Weller, *48-51*, *169*, *183*; candelabra lamps, *49-50*; chandeliers, *49-50*; electric lamps, *49-51*; floor lamps, *50-51*; Matt Green Mission style lamps, 50, 64; oil banquet lamps, *169*, *183*; oil lamps, *48-50*. See also "Index of Weller Lines"

Langstaff, Rose, decorator, 142, 190

Laughead, Dorothy England, decorator, modeler, designer, 19, 78, 141, 178-*180*, 182, mark, 190; biography, 178-180; decorated Hudson, 78, 178-79; designer of: animals, 158, 179-180; Arcadia, 151, 178; Bonito, 142, 178-79; Bouquet, 151, 178; Cactus, 160, 178-79; Cameo, 155, 178-79; Chase, *156-157*, 178-80; Floral, 151, 178; Ollas Water Bottle, *163*, 178; Pastel, 151, 178; Silvertone, 178; Terose, *163*, 178-79; Wild Rose, 155, 178; head designer, 179; honored by American Art Pottery Association, 180; modeled with Lorber, 179

Leffler, Claude, decorator, 7, 78, 169, 178-79, mark, 190

Lessell Art Ware, 169

Lessell, Jennie, decorator, 100

Lessell, John, 100-102, 182, mark, 190; biography, 169-170; designer of Chengtu, Lamar, LaSa, Marengo, 100, 169; designed Le-Camark at Camark Pottery, 102, 170; head of decorating department, 169

Lewis, A.V., decorator, mark, 190

Lindwall, Arthur W., 160

Long, William, 1, *21-25*, mark, 190; art director J.B. Owens, 24; association with Weller, 1, 2, 23-25; biography, 21-25; Clifton Art Pottery founder, 24-25; creator of Crystal Patina and Clifton Indian Ware, 24-25; creator of Lonhuda, 21-24; Denver China and Pottery Company founder, 24; painter 22, 25

Lonhuda Faience pottery, *23-24*, 26; made at Denver, 24; made at Weller, 23-24, 26

Lonhuda Pottery, 1, 20, 21-24, *color 120*; history 21-23; sold to Weller Pottery, 23

Lorber, Rudolph, artist, designer, modeler, 8, *56*, *57*, 177-178, 182, mark, 190; biography, 177-178; designer of Blue Drapery, 99, Blue Ware 86, Coppertone 99, Dechiwo 71-72, Elberta 141, Flemish 93, Forest 91, Graystone 158, Happy Ducks 158, Hobart 129, Ivory 80, Knifewood 96, Lavonia 129, Muskota 88, Neiska 143, Pearl 85, Pumila 133-34, Roma 80, Selma 96, Seneca 143, Sydonia 141, Ting 151, Wood Rose 98, Zona 102; head of art department, 178

Louisiana Purchase Exposition 1904. See World's Fair St. Louis 1904

Lybarger, M., decorator, mark, 190

M

McCandless, Cora, decorator, mark, 190

McGinnis, Margaret, decorator, 142, 164, 190

McGrath, L., decorator, 190

McKinley, William, 46, 169

McLain, L., decorator, mark, 190

McLaughlin, Sarah R., decorator, 22, *76*, 78, 164, 169, 195, mark, 190

Mammy Line, *150-151*

Marks on Weller Pottery, 196-199

Martin, Edwin and R.W., 39

Massier, Achille, 66-67
Massier, Clement, 60, 61, 64, 66-67
Matt Green, 61-64, *63*, 127, 176. *See also* "Index of Weller Lines"
Meloy, Lelia, decorator, 191
Mitchell, Lillie B., decorator, 7, 49-50, 76, *77-78*, 195, mark 191
Mitchell sisters: Hattie, Lillie B., Minnie, decorators, 169, 195, marks, 191
Morris, L., decorator, mark, 191
Mull, Gordon, decorator, 40, *color 108*, 109, 175, 195, mark, 191
Myers, M., decorator, mark, 191

N

Naturalistic designs on Weller pottery, 86-93, 96-99, *color 124*
Newcomb Pottery, 43, 176
Nichols, Maria Longworth, 23
Nudes and flappers, *90 color 121*, 127, *128, 129*

O

Overglaze luster at Weller, 100-102
Owens, J.B., Pottery, 6-7, 24, 52, 62, 167-69, 171-72

P

Paris Expositions, of 1893, 60; of 1889, 61, 64; of 1900, 62; of 1925, 127
Perone, Lizzie, decorator, *color 110*, 119, mark, 191
Peters and Reed Pottery, 43, 132, 167, 168
Pickens, Edwin L., decorator, 8, 39-40, *color 111*, 118, 164, 170-171, 182, 195, mark, 191; head of decorating department, 171, 172; sgraffito artist, 171, *111, 118*; worked with Upjohn, 171
Pierce, Mary L., decorator, mark, 191
Pillsbury, Hester, decorator, 7, 76-80, *color 113*, 140, 150, 164, 179, 183, 195; biography, *171*; decorated Hudson, 76, *78-80, 113*; mark, 191
Pittsburgh Glass and Pottery Exhibition, 7, 40, 80, 99, 142, 144
Plaques, 141
Pope Leo XIII on Cameo Jewel, 56-57
Price List of 1928, 90, 93, 96, 103, 129, 137
Price Lists of 1933, 145; of 1935, 150; of 1936, 148; and of 1941, 159

R

Radford, Albert, decorator, 52, 168, 171-72, mark, 191
Radford Pottery, 168
Rauchfuss, Marie, decorator, mark, 191
Reflets Métalliques; made by Massier, 64; pursued by Sam Weller, 66-67
Rhead, Frederick Alfred, 174
Rhead, Frederick Hurten, designer, 7, 58-59, 102, *color 115*, 167, 169, *174-76*, 182, mark, 191; art director of Homer Laughlin China Company, 176; art director of Roseville Pottery, 7, 174-75; art director of Wardle and Company, 174; biography, 174-76; creator of Dickensware III, 41, 175; creator of Jap Birdimal and Rhead Faience, 4, 7, *58-59*, 175; designer for Weller, 174-75; established Rhead Pottery, 176; introduced tube lining, 174-75; worked at Arequipa Pottery and Santa Barbara, *176*; worked at Avon Faience Company, 174; worked with William Jervis, 174, 176; wrote about pottery, 102, 169, 175-76
Roberts, Eugene, decorator, 80 *color 118*, 169, 195, mark, 191
Robinson, Harry, decorator, mark, 191
Rookwood Pottery, 6-7, 28, 102, 176; compared to Lonhuda, 21-22; competitor to Weller, 2, 6, *7*, 55, 182; imitated Grueby, 62; St. Louis Fair, 43-45
Roosevelt, Theodore, 18, *46, 47*
Roseville Pottery, 6-7, 127, 168-69; competitor to Weller, 6, *7*, 88; hired Weller artists, 167-69, 172; St. Louis Fair, 43-45

Ross, Hattie, decorator, 169, mark, 191
Ruby Company, 160-161

S

Schmid, David, 8, 138
Schmidt, Henry, decorator, 52, 191
Schneider, Norris F., 10, 17, 67-68, 161, 164, 167, 178, 181
Schultz Theater, Zanesville, 17
Schwerber, Aloysius J., mold maker, 6
Scothorn, Norman, decorator, mark, 192
Sgraffito technique at Weller, 2, 33-42, 175
Shoemaker, R. Lillian, decorator, mark, 192
Sicard, Jacques, decorator, 2, 3, 46, 64-67, *color 117, 119; 181-183*, mark, 192; employed by Massier, 64; employed by Weller, 64, *65-67*, 174; leaves Weller, 67; making Sicard, 64-65, 167; "Memo of a Conversation with Sicard," 66
Skoin, decorator, mark, 192
Smith, Helen, decorator, *36, 37, 40*, mark, 192
Smith, Irvin, Weller president, 10, 139, 166, mark, 192
Solon, Leon V., 176
Spaulding, Jessie R., Lonhuda decorator, 22, *color 120*, mark, 192
Sprague, Amelia Browne, decorator, mark, 192
Squeeze bag decoration. *See* Tube Lining.
Steel, Fred, decorator, mark, 192
Steele, Tot, decorator, *7, 195*, mark, 192
Stemm, William H., decorator, *color 119*, 169, 172, mark, 192
Stickley, Gustav, 62
Sulcer, E., decorator, mark, 192

T

Taft, William Howard, 18, 23
Taylor, C.H., Weller's New York sales representative, 3, 28, 48, 52, 96
Teapots, *59, color 115; 144, 163*
Terry, C. Minnie, decorator, 166, 169, *172, 195*, mark, 192
Thompson, Madeline, decorator, mark, 192
Tiles, 140-141, mark, 198
Timberlake, Mae, decorator, *7, 27*, 76, 80, 140, 148-50, 164, mark, 192; biography, 172; decorated Cretone, 148-149; decorated Hudson, 76, 80, *color 113, 114*
Timberlake, Sarah, *7, 80, 172, mark, 192*
Toothbrush holder and towel bar, *93*
Tube Lining, 41, 52, 58, 174-75
Turner, R.G., decorator, *color 106*, mark, 192

U

Umbrella stands, *53, 56, 87*
United Commercial Travellers, UCT, 132
Upjohn, Charles B., 2, 4, 33-42, *color 108-111, 113, 118*, 167, 176-77, 182-83, mark, 192; apprenticed to Karl Bitter, 33, 177; biography, 176-77; creator of Circus vase, 177, *color 108-109*, 183; creator of Dickensware, 33-39, 177; head of C.B. Upjohn Company, 177; head of Weller decorating department, 2, 4, 33-42, 177; married Louisa Van Horne, 177; taught ceramics at Columbia University, 177; worked at Cambridge Art Pottery, 177; worked at Trent Tile Company, 177

W

Wagner, Art, decorator, 100, 167, 193
Walch, Naomi, decorator, 76-77, 80, 142-143, 164, mark, 193
Wallpockets, *161-162*. *See also* "Index of Weller Lines"

Weigelt, Carl, decorator, 100, 145, 164, mark, 193
Weller Art Pottery in Color, 161
Weller, Frank, 8, 19, 164
Weller, Harry, 8, 10, 19, 139, 164
Weller mansion in Zanesville, 12-17, 13-16, 19-20; Gold Room, 14, 15, 16, 20
Weller Pottery Catalogs: *Definition of Art Pottery,* 6, 182; *Garden Decorations by Weller,* 8, 157; *Weller Pottery* (c. 1905). 4, 59, 137; *Pottery for the Florist,* 8, 91, 98, 99, 134
Weller Pottery Catalog illustrations: Breton *137,* Delta *31,* Eldora-Chelsea *82,* Flemish *92,* Florala *82,* Lavonia *128,* Lorbeek *128,* Malta *136,* Novelty Line *149,* Orris *131,* Pumila *133,* Rochelle *79,* Souevo *70,* Stellar-Cretone-Geode-Raceme *149,* Ting *152*
Weller Pottery chronology, 184-85
Weller Pottery competitors: Grueby, 62; Owens, 6, 7, 24, 52; Rookwood, 2, 6, 7, 43-45, 55, 182; Roseville, 6, 7, 43-45, 88
Weller Pottery corporate officers 1922 and 1925, 186
Weller Pottery history, 1-11; demise of the Pottery, 10, 11, 156; domestic competition, 2, 6, 7; effects of the Depression, 10, 139, 143; exports, 7; factory in Colorado, 7, 8; family involved, 8, 10, 17, 164; florists use Weller, 8, 104; foreign competition, 8, 10; incorporation, 8, 186; imperfections in Weller wares, 6, 182; loss of sales, 7, 10, 11, 156; response to Arts and Crafts movement, 50, 62; sixtieth anniversary, 141, 181; World's Fair St. Louis, 43-47; World War I, II, 10, 94; workday, 164
Weller pottery manufacture: blending, 5-6, firing and glazing, 5-6; jiggering, 5-6; kilns, 3, 5, 8, 10; molding, 5-6; slip decoration, 6, 26
Weller Pottery plants: Ceramic Avenue, 8, 9, 10, 139, 169; Marietta Street, 3, 8; Putnam plant, 1, 3, 8, 24, 167, 171
Weller, Samuel A.: birth and childhood, 12; building Weller Theater, 17; businessman, 18-19, 182; children Louise and Ethel, 10, 12, 13, 19, 26, 83; citizen of Zanesville, 12, 19; correspondence with Massier, 66-67; death, 8, 19; founder Weller Pottery, 1; genealogy of Weller family, 12; owner of *Times Recorder,* 12, 17; place in history, 183; relationship to employees, 19, 179; relatives, 8, 10, 17; Republican convention delegate 1908, 18; wealth, 4, 12, 14; wife Hermine, 12, 19; Woodlawn Cemetery burial, 19
Weller Theater, 17-18, 42
Wheatley, Thomas J., decorator, mark, 193
Wilbur, Carrie, decorator, 193
Wilbur, Edna, decorator, mark, 193
Williams, Curtis, 166
Wilson, Albert, decorator, 179, mark, 193
Windle, Helen, decorator, 169, 195, mark, 193
Wood, Louise, decorator, mark, 193
World's Fair, Buffalo 1901, 44, 46
World's Fair, Chicago 1893: introduction of Lonhuda pottery, 1, 22, 44
World's Fair, St. Louis 1904: Aurelian vases on display, 44, 45, 46, 164; map plaques, 46-47; participating pottery companies, 43-45; presidential plaques, 46-47; Weller's Gold Medal, 45-46, 153; Weller's model pottery, 43, 45; Weller Pottery at St. Louis, 43-47, 44-47; World's tallest vase, 44-45, 53

Z

Zanesville Art Pottery Company, 8, 138, 171
Zanesville, Ohio: home of Weller Pottery, 1-11; home of Sam Weller, 12-20; home of Weller artists, 164-173